# SEA SENSE

*(Hans C. Engels)*

# SEA SENSE

Safety Afloat in Terms of Sail,
Power, and Multihull Boat Design, Construction
Rig, Equipment, Coping with Emergencies,
and Boat Management in Heavy Weather

Written and Illustrated by
RICHARD HENDERSON

International Marine Publishing Company
Camden, Maine

Richard Henderson also wrote *Hand, Reef and Steer* and *The Racing Cruiser*, and co-authored *Sail and Power*.

Copyright © 1972
by International Marine Publishing Company
Library of Congress Catalog Card No. 70-187102
International Standard Book No. 0-87742-022-X
Second printing, 1973
Printed in the U.S.A.

*To My Mother*
*VERA P. HENDERSON*
*Who has always been*
*a cautious sailor*

# Contents

# Preface

Over twenty-three hundred years ago, a Greek historian wrote the following description of his meeting with a Phoenician seaman: "I found the mate of the steersman, who is called the prow's man, so well acquainted with the location of each article that even when absent he could tell where everything lay and what their number was, just as a person who has learnt to read could tell the number and order of the letters in the name Socrates. I saw this man examining, at an unoccupied time, everything that is of use on board a ship; and on my asking him the reason, he replied, 'Stranger, I am looking to see whether anything is lacking or out of order; for it will be no time to look for what is missing or out of place when a storm comes up at sea.' "

Those exact words could be used today to indicate a high degree of nautical competence. Sailors with that kind of careful proficiency possess a quality that might be called "sea sense," which essentially is a blending of common sense with seamanship. Sea sense has been a requirement aboard ships since before the time of the above mentioned Phoenician sailor, but this quality was never so badly needed as it is today, because never have there been so many landsmen taking to the sea. Not only are there numerous greenhorns afloat, but there are a surprising number of non-seamen involved in nearly all phases of the boating industry.

The primary and essential ingredient of sea sense is a thorough awareness of safety afloat. Every skipper has the responsibility of seeing that he is well informed in matters relating to: safety in the selection and equipping of his vessel; preparedness for emergencies or accidents; and proper, seamanlike management of his vessel under adverse as well as favorable conditions. He owes this not only to himself and his crew, but to those aboard other vessels in his vicinity.

This book is a dissertation on safety in small craft, both sail and power, monohull and multihull, with emphasis on some points that are seldom found in the average seamanship manual. Of course some of the points discussed are controversial, particularly some in the area of boat management in heavy weather offshore; but in those cases I have collected and collated the opinions of dozens of experienced seamen and established authorities through not only their published writings, but through personal letters and conversations.

I sincerely hope this book will be helpful to boatmen, especially novices, but seasoned seamen as well, in avoiding serious trouble afloat. It will attempt to point out potential problems and suggest means of avoiding or overcoming them. In addition, it will mention many actual experiences to show how some of the problems have been handled, whether successfully or not, in the past. If *Sea Sense* helps prevent just one serious accident at sea, then, of course, it will have been well worth the effort.

RICHARD HENDERSON
GIBSON ISLAND, MARYLAND

# Acknowledgements

This book could not have been written without considerable advice from experienced seamen and experts in subjects related to boating safety. Most helpful of all has been my good friend Harold R. White, marine engineer and yacht yard manager, who not only supplied me with much information, but looked over those parts of the manuscript that dealt with mechanical matters. Also, I am especially grateful to Roderick Stephens Jr., authority on seamanship and yacht design, for his thoughts on boat management in heavy weather. The late naval architect-design critic Robert G. Henry was most generous in expressing his opinions on what constitutes a seaworthy boat. I am indebted to William T. Stone for advice in certain matters related to boating legislation and rules of the road. Victor Jorgensen, publisher of *The Telltale Compass*, has been most helpful in supplying me with safety-related information, and also I appreciate the suggestions made by Captain Sven T. Simonsen, director of the Coast Navigation School. William W. Robinson, editor of *Yachting* magazine, was very helpful in the area of research suggestions, and David Q. Scott of the U. S. Naval Institute also made some valuable suggestions. Once again, Dr. Roger P. Batchelor was most encouraging and helpful, and Roger C. Taylor, president of International Marine Publishing Company, did a splendid job of helping with the planning and editing of the manuscript. In addition, I am grateful for information through letters or conversations from: John Guzzwell, Frank Casper, Eric C. Hiscock, Richard Page, Frik Pottgieter, Peter Spronk, Spaulding F. Dunbar, Scott Allen, Francis C. Stokes, Frederick B. Thurber, Harry C. Primrose, James L. Potter, Richard F. Jablin, Robert Peterman, and John Hedden. Finally, I want to thank my typist, Patty M. Maddocks, not only for her competence, but also for her speed and dependability.

# 1 / SAFETY IN HULL DESIGN AND CONSTRUCTION

Sea sense begins with the careful selection of a safe, seaworthy, and soundly constructed vessel. Of course, the design concept and scantlings will depend largely on the purpose for which the craft is intended. Obviously, there are great differences in the design and construction of a day sailer or cruising houseboat intended for protected waters and an offshore powerboat or sailing ocean racer. Nevertheless, in every type of vessel there should be an ample margin of safety, because there will be times when boats will be caught in heavy weather or will be subjected to stresses beyond those which the builder, designer, or owner might normally expect. Even very experienced boatmen are bound to make occasional mistakes in seamanship or weather forecasting that may put tremendous strains on a boat or her equipment, while an enthusiastic racing skipper may drive his craft beyond the limits of normal safe operation.

In my opinion there are a good number of boats being produced today that have glaring safety deficiencies in design, construction, and equipment. These deficiencies may not be as dangerous for a boat intended for navigating protected waters close to shore as for a boat intended for offshore use, but the former type of craft is the one most often manned by the boating novice, who knows little of design, construction, or what to expect in the way of potential dangers.

Several years ago I helped deliver a brand new boat, produced by a well-known builder, to her home port, and after being underway for a few hours, we noticed that the boat seemed sluggish. Peering down below, I noticed that water was over the cabin sole. Some minutes later we discovered that the bilge pump was back-syphoning water into the bilge. The pump was neither looped, vented, nor did it have a sea cock. We found that by tacking and slowing the boat's speed to reduce the quarter wave, the pump's outlet could be lifted from the water to stop the flow. Fortunately, the experience ended happily, but the point is that an inexperienced owner might have sunk if he had been in a bad seaway, had not noticed the boat's logginess, had not been able to locate the source of the trouble, or been unable to overcome the problem quickly. This story simply illustrates one of a great many examples of safety deficiencies seen today as a result of either poor design, poor construction, shoddy workmanship, corner cutting, or a combination of such factors.

Many design, construction, or equipment features that are desirable or essential for safety can be obtained on stock boats but often only as optional extras at additional cost, while non-essential frills, such as carpeting on the cabin sole are standard equipment on some boats. In my opinion, it should be the other way around, with vital safety features being standard on every boat, even if this means a higher base price, because many new boat buyers are complete novices who don't know what extras are important, and salesmen are often reluctant to inform them, presumably for fear of losing a sale from implications of possible dangers. As with many other products, one usually gets what he pays for in a boat. Although it is perfectly possible to buy a reasonably sound and safe boat at a moderately low price, with super bargains, the motto should be "caveat emptor."

Some faults seen on not all but many stock boats are: lack of or inadequate flotation in open boats; lack of rigidity or stiffness in vulnerable areas of many fiberglass and aluminum boats; lack of internal ventilation and accessibility to areas that should be serviced or inspected periodically; improper protection from electrolysis and galvanic action; improper grounding and bonding for lightning protection; potentially dangerous stove, fuel tanks, or engine installation; lack of watertightness on deck (seat lockers without latches, non-closing ventilators, etc.); lack of sea cocks on through-hull fittings; improper installation of W.C., bilge pump, or sink; inadequate installation of chain plates and weaknesses at other stress points; improper rigging practices; fittings that are too light; breakable or vulnerable windows, windshield, or cabin trunk; vulnerable companionway hatch allowing the possibility of flooding the cabin; cockpit drains far too small; life lines that are too low, and inadequate hand rails; sharp edges on tables, counters, etc. below; inadequate support at the mast step; weakness at the garboards; weak juncture of the deck and topsides; vulnerable, ineffective, or inadequately secured rudder; improperly bonded bulkheads; and so forth. Mind you, I am not saying that all boats have these defects. There are many well made, properly designed boats being produced, but there are too many modern craft that are carelessly designed and slapped together for the sake of making a "fast buck." After a spell of heavy weather or a rough ocean race, one hears too many horror stories of gear failures, of chain plates pulling out, of bows on some aluminum boats being dented in, of stress cracks and delamination in some fiberglass boats, of centerboards falling out, of rudders and steering mechanisms breaking, etc. I have even heard of a houseboat produced by a well-known builder that cracked in half during fair weather in a very moderate seaway, because the plywood boat lacked the customary sheer clamp and shelf construction and was held together only by thin wooden battens and fiberglass cloth.

It is a pity that some boat producers do not feel more responsible for the safety of their customers. I would hate to see rigid Federal safety regulations come into being, but it is becoming more and more apparent that the rapidly expanding boating public, which includes many rank beginners, needs protection. I don't think many sailors want strict controls on the boating industry, but there is little doubt that the public needs to be made aware of the faulty craft and equipment produced by some manufacturers who care little what happens after the initial sale has been made.

The best general advice I can think of to aid the prospective buyer in his boat purchase is, first of all, to buy a boat designed by a reputable naval architect and built by an established and respected builder. In my opinion, it is important to pick a designer and builder who are experienced seamen. The boats they produce should be the result of not only theory and professional experience, but also of knowledge gained from actually going to sea. If the prospective buyer is a greenhorn, I would strongly recommend that the boat under consideration be given a thorough inspection by a knowledgeable, experienced seaman. Of course, it is customary for the buyer to hire a professional marine surveyor to examine a used boat before she is purchased. New boats are seldom surveyed, but I think this is often a wise plan, especially when the buyer is a novice. A good professional surveyor can very often find faults or inadequacies that can be corrected before the owner takes delivery, and this procedure may avoid considerable trouble later on. Unfortunately, there is often a problem in finding a dependable, competent surveyor who is completely impartial. More will be said about this difficulty in Chapter 3 when we discuss preparation and inspection for sea.

In this chapter an attempt will be made to point out some basic construction and design features, both good and bad from a safety standpoint, seen on modern stock boats. Safety in rigging and equipment will be discussed in later chapters, but here we shall be concerned with the hull and most of its permanent fixtures, except plumbing and electrical systems and fittings relating to fire hazards, which will be discussed in later chapters.

*Safe Design for Small Craft*

Very small boats designed for sheltered waters obviously do not need the rugged construction and many safety features needed by larger boats that venture into unprotected waters. Nevertheless, it should be remembered that small open boats are often roughly handled because of their lack of size and weight, and this requires a certain robustness of construction. Then too, when considering safety features, thought must be given not only to the degree of protection offered by the waters of operation, but to the time of year and the temperature of those waters. An easily capsizeable boat with ample flotation used near a well-populated area might be perfectly safe in warm summer waters, but a capsizing in the same boat could prove fatal in the winter.

Perhaps the most glaring safety deficiency on many small boats is lack of flotation. Although this fault is not as common nowadays as it was formerly, there are still a great number of small, open (undecked) boats being produced or used today that are capable of capsizing or swamping and yet lack adequate flotation. Nearly all boats except some built of wood will sink when filled with water unless flotation is added. Even wooden boats with heavy keels or engines need extra buoyancy to remain afloat and support their crew when swamped. Furthermore, many small wooden boats float so deeply when swamped that self-rescue is virtually impossible. In other words, many boats in a swamped condition have so little freeboard or height above the water's surface, that they cannot be bailed out due to the fact that waves or even wavelets will slosh into the boat and fill her faster than she can be emptied. This problem is most critical in small sailboats with low centerboard wells which are open at the top (see Figure 1) or some outboard motorboats whose transoms are cut away to accommodate an outboard motor with a short shaft length.

Unless the stern is extremely buoyant, an outboard motorboat with a cutaway transom should be fitted with a self-bailing well just forward of the transom similar to the one illustrated in Figure 2. As can be seen in the drawing, a wave sloshing over the transom cut-out simply flows into and eventually drains out of the well without flooding the bilge. Designer Francis S. Kinney in the book *Skene's Elements of Yacht Design* points out the danger of a transom cut-out when two men move aft in a small outboard runabout to fuss with a stalled motor in rough waters. Their weight aft will raise the bow and cause it to swing downwind which will result in the cut-out transom facing the waves. Water can quickly slosh in and perhaps swamp a boat that lacks the aforementioned well.

Flotation may be in the form of a double skin (an inner and outer hull shell either unfilled or filled with very light material), air tanks, watertight

FIGURE 1: FLOTATION

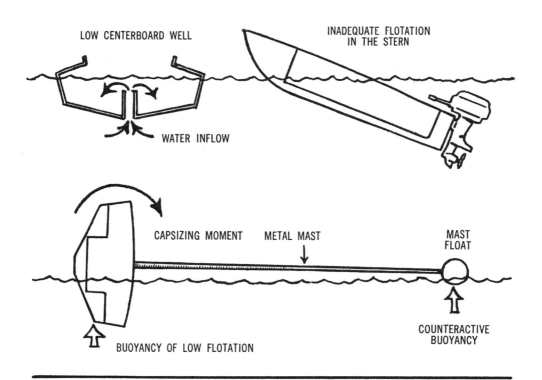

LOW CENTERBOARD WELL

INADEQUATE FLOTATION
IN THE STERN

WATER INFLOW

CAPSIZING MOMENT    METAL MAST

MAST
FLOAT

BUOYANCY OF LOW FLOTATION

COUNTERACTIVE
BUOYANCY

FIGURE 2: OUTBOARD WELL

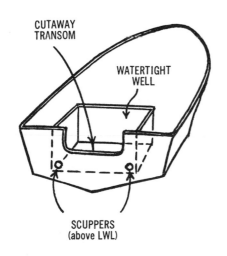

CUTAWAY
TRANSOM

WATERTIGHT
WELL

SCUPPERS
(above LWL)

FIGURE 3: STERN FLAPS
(on port & stbd.
side of transom)

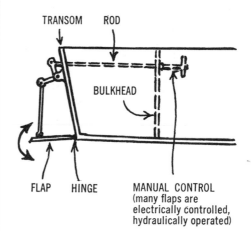

TRANSOM    ROD

BULKHEAD

FLAP    HINGE

MANUAL CONTROL
(many flaps are
electrically controlled,
hydraulically operated)

compartments, air bags, or expanded foamed-plastic materials. Of course air alone affords the greatest amount of buoyancy, but airtight areas between skins, in tanks, or in compartments may allow water to enter through even the smallest undetected hole and thus partially or entirely fail to buoy up the boat in an emergency. Air bags are effective, but they are not entirely satisfactory because of difficulties in securing them and they are vulnerable to punctures.

Foamed plastics such as polyurethane or styrofoam, a polystyrene, are a good solution to the problem of flotation because the aerated foam contains a myriad of plastic bubbles or closed cells and thus overcomes the danger of puncture or air leakage through one or a few holes. It is said that one cubic foot of this foamed material will support from 55 to 60 pounds in fresh water. Polystyrene may be subject to damage in conjunction with uncured polyester resin (used in most fiberglass boat construction) and from contact with gasoline and oil; therefore this type of foam usually should be protected with a coating of shellac or perhaps epoxy resin. Styrofoam comes in the form of rigid blocks and may be cut easily to fit under decks, seats, or any suitable space; but polyurethane in liquid form can be poured and expanded into solid foam inside an enclosed space.

Proper buoyancy not only depends on the adequacy of the flotation material but also on its location. Flotation should be distributed fore and aft in such a way that the boat floats level when swamped, not bow up and stern down or vice versa. Motorboats with their engines far aft will obviously need considerably more flotation aft than forward. Flotation placed low in the bilge or under the cockpit sole will make a boat float high when she is swamped, but there is the danger that the low placement will increase the boat's tendency to capsize or turn turtle, bottomside up (see Figure 1). This is especially true of a small centerboard sailboat. If she capsizes and lies on her beam ends, flotation located at the turn of her bilge will tend to turn her completely over, bottomside up. Boats with this tendency should carry air floats at their mastheads to avoid turning turtle (see Figure 1). Furthermore, I believe that any boat with a strong tendency to turn turtle should be fitted with some sort of hand grips on the boat's bottom. These might be in the form of small apertures cut out of the skeg in order to minimize any harmful effects that the hand grips might have on boat speed. Turning turtle is not always dangerous, but it is inconvenient to say the least. In the bottom-up position, many boats are extremely difficult to right, and furthermore in shallow water the top of the mast can become lodged in a soft bottom and possibly break.

Other highly recommended design features for small craft are:

• Ample beam and moderately low deadrise to provide high initial stability. A small boat, larger than the smaller dinghy size, should be suf-

*Although far from the best type to take on an extended offshore passage, this boat at least has a proper outboard motor well. These men were rescued by the Coast Guard after drifting for two days in the Straits of Florida when they attempted to reach Cuba in order to pick up relatives. (U. S. Coast Guard)*

ficiently stiff to support, without heeling excessively, one or two men standing on her gunwale.

• Sufficient freeboard to prevent shipping water in a chop. If the transom is drastically cut away for an outboard, it should be provided with a self-bailing well (as previously described).

• A small motorboat should be fitted with a *capacity plate*, a small, indelible information plate, fastened to the inside of the transom or in some conspicuous location, which gives loading capacity, an estimate of the number of people and the total weight (including the weight of people, fuel, motor, and gear) the boat can safely carry under normal weather conditions. When the boat is suitable for use with an outboard motor, the plate should specify the manufacturer's recommendation as to the motor size and maximum horsepower. In my opinion, the plate should also give flotation information, an estimate of how much weight the boat can support in a swamped condition, and also whether the boat's permanently installed equipment meets with federal requirements. Loading capacity should generally follow the formulas and standards developed by the American Boat and Yacht Council, Inc. (ABYC), 15 East 26th Street, New York, New York, 10010, as set forth in the book *Safety Standards for Small Craft*. One simple, rule-of-thumb formula recommended by the ABYC for the maxi-

mum number of persons (P) to be carried in a rowing boat or small craft
having a conventional shape is:

$$P = \frac{\text{length x beam}}{15}$$

If no information plate is provided, then obviously the boat buyer should
obtain the above information from the dealer or manufacturer.

• Open boats above the smaller sizes should have forward decks with
washboards (on sailboats) or windshields (on motorboats) and also side
decks with cockpit coamings to help prevent spray or waves from flooding
the cockpit.

• Windshields on powerboats should be adequately braced, made of
Plexiglass or safety glass, should be devoid of sharp corners or edges, should
be of such height that one's head will not strike the upper edge in the event
of a collision, and should be raked at the proper angle to avoid, as much as
possible, reflections that are harmful to visibility. The helmsman's seat
should be sufficiently high to prevent the bow from impairing visibility.
The ABYC suggests that the helmsman's eye be high enough to assure that
the impaired view of the water directly ahead is no more than X feet from
the bow as determined by the formula: $X = L [3- .02(L-16)]$, where L is
the boat's over-all length and X is the distance on the water from the bow
to the point ahead where the helmsman's view is obstructed by the bow.

• Some small motorboats designed for efficient planing at high
speeds have steering difficulties or a tendency to bury their bows when operating at slow speeds. These faults are often present when the hull form
is sharply V'd forward but extremely wide and flat aft. Such a form is usually suitable for planing, but when the boat is slowed in rough weather she
may become very difficult to manage. One partial solution to the dilemma
is to move weight aft to lift the bow, which also helps keep the propeller
submerged, but this tactic requires a high transom. The prospective boat
buyer should be sure that there is sufficient buoyancy forward even in a
high-speed boat, and if the boat will be used in exposed waters, it may be
advisable to have some deadrise aft with rounded chines or fairly deep V'd
sections carried back to the transom. This may allow the stern to squat
slightly, which will permit the bow to lift in a seaway. If stern squat is
excessive, however, it may be advantageous to add stern flaps (see Figure
3), or in some cases offshore racers use water ballast tanks at the bow. V'd
sections aft will usually require ample beam for sufficient stability. A skeg
is usually a great help to directional stability, but if it is too close to a high-
speed propeller there may be a problem with cavitation. In this case, the
skeg should end a foot or so ahead of the wheel, or perhaps twin skegs, one

on each side of the wheel would be an alternate satisfactory design.

- Extremely beamy, unballasted sailboats (multi-hulls especially) should be fitted with masthead floats and/or sponsons (buoyancy compartments or pontoons) at or outboard of the gunwale to counteract the tendency to turn turtle if capsized.
- It is essential that ballasted keel sailboats without self-bailing cockpits be fitted with sufficient flotation to buoy up the boat with a full crew aboard when she is swamped.
- To avoid personal injury from falls, all surfaces that will be stepped on or walked on should be skid-proofed (with abrasive paint, pads, raw teak, molded textures in fiberglass, etc.). Decks should not be excessively rounded, and there should be a low toe rail at the deck's edge. Hand grips should be placed wherever feasible, especially on a high-speed boat. There should be no sharp corners anywhere on the boat that one could fall against. A major cause of falls results from operators who start their outboard motors while a crew member is standing. Of course the crew should be sitting down and holding on, however, it would be highly desirable if motors could be made so that they could not be started with their throttles wide open. The Coast Guard is currently trying to devise such a standard that would be required by law.

## Designs for Unsheltered Waters

The primary concerns for boats that navigate unprotected waters are self-righting ability and watertight integrity. A monohull sailboat going offshore should be capable of recovering from a knockdown on her beam ends which lays her mast in the water. This means that she must have sufficient ballast, normally on her keel, to right herself from the beam-ends position, and her decks and cockpit well must be watertight to prevent swamping or flooding of the hull's interior.

Transverse or athwartships stability of a hull depends on its weight, form, beam, and ballast. The safest boats are those that have a high range of stability, or a tendency to self-right at very high as well as low angles of heel. Of course, a sailboat, especially a racer, needs high *initial* stability or "stiffness" to carry a large, efficient sail plan, but for maximum safety, she needs sufficient *ultimate* stability to avoid capsizing or turning turtle at extremely high angles of heel. For the normal, monohull, offshore sailboat, ultimate stability primarily depends on the amount and location of her ballast. The heavier the ballast and the deeper it is located, the greater the righting moment at high angles of heel. As a very general rule of thumb, the ballast-displacement ratio for such a boat should be above 33 per cent.

In other words, at least a third of the boat's total weight should be consigned to ballast.

In my opinion, it is also highly desirable that the draft of the average small, cabin sailer be at least one-seventh of her load waterline length in order that keel ballast can be kept low. Another important reason for this rule of thumb for draft is that it allows a sufficiently deep rudder for good steering control. Unless a boat is fitted with a complicated retractable rudder, the keel depth limits the depth of the rudder, because if the rudder were deeper than the keel, it could be damaged badly by a grounding. A keel-centerboard boat, especially, needs ample rudder depth, because a boat of this type with her relatively shallow keel is given extra beam to increase her initial stability and thus compensate for her relatively high keel ballast. When such a boat heels, she tends to "roll out" or lift up in the water as a result of submerging her buoyant leeward side. Of course, this roll-out lifts the rudder and lessens its effectiveness. Still another argument for reasonable draft in a keel-centerboarder is that centerboards are subject to jamming or loss of operation through broken pins or pendants, and in the event of an inoperable or lost board, the boat should have sufficient depth of lateral plane for satisfactory windward performance in heavy weather.

Although moderate draft is highly desirable, excessive draft is not. A large, deep lateral plane will minimize leeway, which is a great advantage in sailing to windward in average sailing conditions, but in extremely heavy weather when a boat must heave to or lie a-hull, such a deep lateral plane may be a decided disadvantage. Heaving to implies slowing headway and this is customarily accomplished with small counteracting sails while the boat lies beam-on or closer to the wind. Lying a-hull, a boat normally lies beam-on or with her bow a little further off the wind while she drifts under bare poles (these storm tactics will be discussed in some detail in Chapter 7). Both of these tactics seem most successful when the boat can make considerable leeway, for this allows her to sidestep and yield to the force of the seas. Additionally, leeway creates a drift wake to windward which may help smooth the seas and prevent them from breaking against the hull. Another point, not always realized, is that the deep-draft boat may heel further under normal sailing conditions than one of less draft, due to the fact that the deep boat has a lower center of lateral resistance (CLR), the geometric center of the lateral plane. The low CLR increases the length of the heeling arm (the distance from the center of effort, the geometric center of the sails, to the CLR of the hull as shown in Figure 4), and this creates a greater heeling moment as compared to a boat with a higher CLR. However, it should be pointed out that when there is no lateral force against the keel or at extremely high angles of heel, during a severe knockdown, the deep-draft boat with the lower center of gravity will have the greater righting moment for a given weight of keel ballast.

FIGURE 4: STABILITY

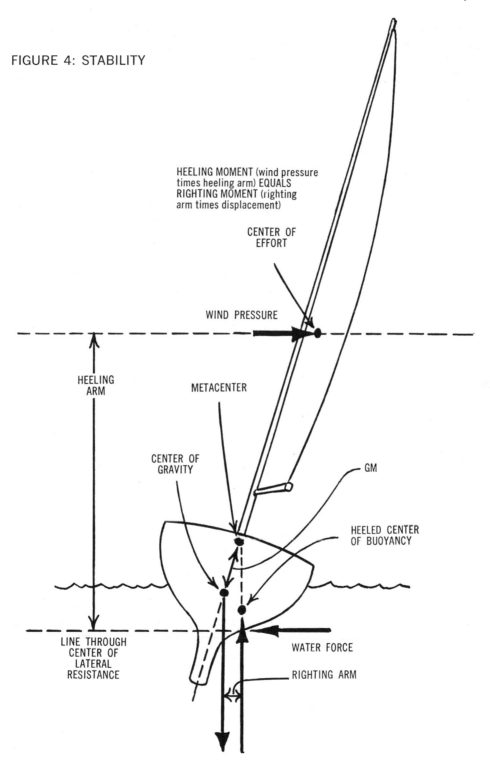

HEELING MOMENT (wind pressure times heeling arm) EQUALS RIGHTING MOMENT (righting arm times displacement)

CENTER OF EFFORT

WIND PRESSURE

HEELING ARM

METACENTER

CENTER OF GRAVITY

GM

HEELED CENTER OF BUOYANCY

LINE THROUGH CENTER OF LATERAL RESISTANCE

WATER FORCE

RIGHTING ARM

Keel ballast is usually not needed in the average fast powerboat, because she carries no sail and she relies on a large beam and flattish bilges for high initial stability. Then too, a large powerboat must not have an excessively high metacentric height (GM), the distance between the center of gravity and the metacenter (point M shown in Figure 4), for seakindly motion. As can be seen in the illustration, the metacenter is the point at which a vertical line through the heeled center of buoyancy intersects the plane of the vessel's centerline. Of course, adding or lowering ballast will lower the center of gravity and thus increase the GM. A long GM will increase a boat's stiffness and give her a quick roll. Considerable stiffness is tolerable on a racing sailboat, because she should be stiff enough to carry a lot of sail, and sails are effective roll dampers; but on a powerboat, whose hull form contributes to a relatively high metacenter, excessive and/or deeply located ballast could increase her GM to the point where a very quick, jerky rolling motion might be produced.

On the other hand, powerboats intended for extensive offshore work may very well require ballast, because such craft usually carry some sail, even if this is only a small steadying sail. Another possible reason for carrying some ballast is that most seagoing powerboats have less beam than those intended to plane in relatively smooth water, and of course, less beam means less stability. Another factor to consider is that the very lofty superstructures seen on some powercraft are affected by wind pressure almost like sails. Of course, the need for ballast will depend on the vessel's hull form and center of gravity. A hull having flattish bilges with little deadrise and with her engines and fuel tanks placed extremely low will normally be very stiff; but a relatively narrow, round bottom or deep V-bottom boat with tall superstructures, higher tanks and engine, and steadying sails will undoubtedly need some ballast.

Ample freeboard is important especially on sailboats, because this extends the range of stability. Once a boat heels beyond the point where she begins to submerge her rail, the heeled center of buoyancy (as shown in Figure 4) begins to move inboard with resulting loss of stability. Freeboard should not be excessive, however, because this would raise the hull's center of gravity and cause harmful windage. Furthermore, keel-centerboard sailers might suffer from excessive "roll out" which would be harmful to the control of a shallow rudder.

Adequate freeboard forward, combined with proper flare and buoyancy, is particularly important for powerboats in order that spray and seas will be thrown aside. In his book, *Seamanlike Sense in Powercraft*, the famous designer Uffa Fox describes what he considers a dangerous practice, "the ramping down of the foredeck" of many sharp-bowed motorboats. These craft, which have been designed to excell at high speeds, often lack proper freeboard far forward and buoyancy in the forefoot to negotiate a steep head sea at low speeds. With their "sloping down foredecks" which scoop up the seas, such boats can be what Mr. Fox describes as "death traps." These boats might be safe for careful operation in protected waters, but when distant runs are to be made, even just occasionally, in exposed waters, it would certainly seem prudent to choose a design with adequate freeboard, flare, and buoyancy forward. Proper flare, incidentally, will not only deflect spray but will add a reserve of buoyancy to the bow when it is deeply immersed in a steep sea.

Let us now turn to some considerations of watertight integrity. Cockpits should have scupper pipes of large diameter, located reasonably high above the waterline (see Figure 5), and the volume of the cockpit well should be minimal, because a large well filled with water can reduce freeboard and stability to a dangerous degree. The North American Yacht Racing Union (NAYRU) recommends a cockpit volume (for sailing yachts in unprotected waters) derived from the following formula: 6% (length over-all x maximum beam x freeboard aft) = maximum volume over lowest coamings. The NAYRU also recommends that the cockpit floor be at least .02 times the load water line length above the load water line, and that the cockpit drains have a combined area of drains not less than the equivalent of four ¾-inch drains. The ABYC recommends that scuppers or freeing ports should be located on both sides of the boat and should have a minimum total area determined by the formula: total area of the scuppers in square inches equals the cockpit length in feet times cockpit width in feet divided by fifteen. It is important that wide scuppers be covered with a coarse screen to prevent clogging. Obviously scuppers should be located at the well's low points, and normally, on a non-planing sailboat, these points should be at both sides of the cockpit's forward end in order that the well can't be flooded by the boat's quarter wave at fast speeds (see Figure 5). On a planing powerboat or any boat that lifts her bow at high speeds, however, scuppers should usually be placed at the cockpit's after end, or in some cases, usually on boats with abundant flotation, drains might be put through the transom. Quite often transom drains have outboard flaps that can be opened or closed with a cable leading to a control near the helmsman.

It is highly desirable, of course, that a large cockpit on a motorboat be self-bailing, but it should be pointed out such a cockpit is no guarantee against swamping or capsizing. A heavy sea breaking aboard could seriously weigh down a boat and affect her stability before the water is able to drain out. Furthermore, any heeling due to the boat rolling would cause the water to flow to the boat's low side, which would add tremendously to the tendency to capsize. In many powerboats, it is not possible for the sake of comfort and convenience to reduce the size of the cockpit, but it is important for such boats to have drains as large as possible, ample flotation, especially near the rails or gunwales, and care should be taken to avoid getting broadside to heavy breaking seas. (Management of powerboats in heavy weather will be discussed in Chapter 8.)

Commonly seen shortcomings in the watertightness of sailboat cockpits are: seat locker lids that are not watertight and are not provided with latches; ventilating holes in the sides of cockpit wells; and companionway sills too low. Most cockpit seats containing lockers that are accessible from the top have hinged lids. At extreme angles of heel these lids can fall or float open, and since most lockers of this type will allow water to drain into the bilge, the boat can quickly swamp or sink (see Figure 5). Thus it is very important for the locker lids to be fitted with dogs, hasps, or some kind of secure latching device. Lids should be well gasketed to prevent leaks even when they are completely submerged. In some cases seat locker openings are in the sides of cockpit wells. This arrangement is seldom satisfactory from a safety standpoint, because the openings are often left unclosed, and many covers for these openings are not really watertight. Quite often one sees ventilating holes in the sides of a cockpit well. Obviously, there must be a means of blocking off these holes when under way if they can admit water to the bilge.

Perhaps the most serious cockpit design fault seen on a surprisingly large number of boats being produced today is the low companionway sill. The sill height, the distance from the cockpit floor to the bottom of the companionway hatch, is often less than six inches. This distance is far from adequate for a boat sailing or especially racing in waters that are not entirely protected, because a knockdown or sea breaking into the cockpit could flood the cabin. Some boats with low sills are equipped with companionway slides that can be inserted in rough weather to raise the level of the sill, but most companionway slides I have seen lack the necessary strength to take the brunt of a heavy sea. It is preferable that an offshore boat have a high bridge deck between the companionway and cockpit well for maximum strength and minimal cockpit volume, but in the absence of a bridge deck there should be a strong sill or slide as high, at least, as the point at which water would begin to flow onto the deck from the flooded cockpit.

Another cockpit drainage detail relating less to safety than to comfort is that scuppers should be provided for the area between the edge of the cockpit seats and the coamings of a sailboat, because water can be trapped in that area when the boat is heeled. These upper scuppers are in the form of deep sloping gutters or pipes leading to the bottom of the cockpit as shown in Figure 5.

## FIGURE 5: COCKPIT WELL

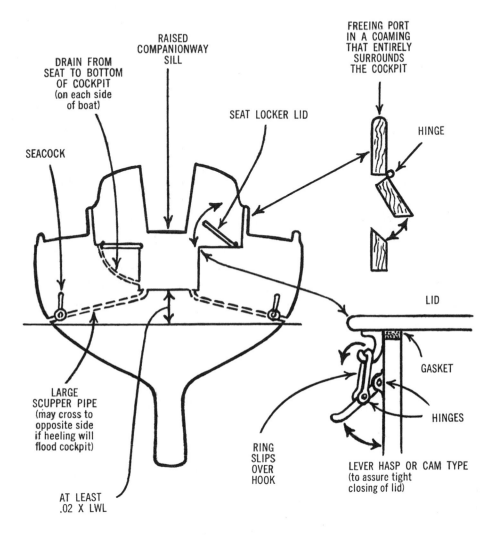

DRAIN FROM SEAT TO BOTTOM OF COCKPIT (on each side of boat)

RAISED COMPANIONWAY SILL

FREEING PORT IN A COAMING THAT ENTIRELY SURROUNDS THE COCKPIT

SEAT LOCKER LID

SEACOCK

HINGE

LID

GASKET

HINGES

LARGE SCUPPER PIPE (may cross to opposite side if heeling will flood cockpit)

RING SLIPS OVER HOOK

LEVER HASP OR CAM TYPE (to assure tight closing of lid)

AT LEAST .02 X LWL

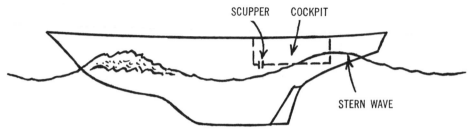

SCUPPER    COCKPIT

STERN WAVE

Watertight integrity below decks must be assured with the proper installation of sinks, head, permanent bilge pumps, and seacocks for all through-hull openings, intakes or outlets, below or near the waterline. It is surprising how many new stock boats are not fitted with seacocks or shut-off valves as standard equipment. They are usually offered as options only, and of course, many novice boat owners don't appreciate their safety value. In fact, it was recently reported to me that three stock, sailing auxiliaries of a well-known class sank in California waters when hoses slipped off through-hull fittings that lacked seacocks. Shut-off valves are especially important on underwater orifices, such as those for the head and the engine's water intake, but usually there should also be a means of closing those openings that are slightly above the waterline, such as scuppers, bilge pump outlets, and engine exhausts. Although some ocean racing requirements do not insist on seacocks on scupper outlets above the waterline, I know of an ocean racing sailboat that nearly sank because such a scupper pipe ruptured while the vessel was heeled during an overnight race well offshore.

A common failing on many stock boats is the inaccessibility of seacocks or through-hull fittings that need servicing. There must be a reasonably convenient means of reaching all seacocks, and even if some are rarely used, they should be lubricated and opened or closed periodically in order to prevent corrosion and jamming in the event of an emergency requiring their use. A fitting that is often difficult to reach is the stuffing box, the bronze gland with a large packing nut inside the boat through which the propeller shaft passes before penetrating the hull. This fitting is intended to prevent a significant amount of water from leaking into the hull at the point of the shaft's penetration. Stuffing boxes need periodic inspections for leaks and occasional servicing in the form of repacking, tightening the nut, or lubrication of the type that has a grease fitting. When such a grease fitting is hard to reach, some builders extend the grease cup with a copper tube to a point where it is readily accessible. Such tubes can be vulnerable to damage, however, through corrosion, vibration fatigue, or being struck with a falling object. A well-known ocean racer with this lubrication arrangement recently developed a dangerous leak from a ruptured grease cup tube. Another reason for periodically inspecting stuffing boxes is that many are the self-aligning type with a short length of rubber hose and two hose clamps which may need tightening or renewal. Clamps occasionally corrode, especially if they are not made of stainless steel, and the hoses have been known to tear. Naval architect Eric Steinlein has written that over-tightening an unlubricated packing nut can cause the packing to bind on the shaft and tear or loosen the hose. One hears frequent warnings, by the way, against over-tightening the stuffing box. A small drip while the engine is running is not serious, and such a leak will serve as a lubricant for flax packing.

Accessibility should not be limited to through-hull fittings. In my opinion every part of the hull's interior should be accessible for inspection. This is especially important for wood boats with seams that can leak and for inspection of areas that can catch fresh water that may cause rot. Furthermore, collisions with floating objects, broken-off fish net stakes, and the like are not uncommon, and such accidents require immediate accessibility to the damaged area for inspection and repairs. Other areas that must be reached for periodic inspection or servicing are: tanks, limber holes, keel bolts, chainplates, bilge pump strainers, all parts of the engine and fuel line, steering mechanisms (cables, sheaves, quadrant, worm gears, etc.), and every part of the plumbing and electrical systems. On some boats accessibility to certain areas is blocked by solid continuous ceilings or headliners, by access openings or doorways that are too small, or by the current building practice commonly referred to as "unitized construction," which often means that a major part of the boat's interior is molded or otherwise permanently bonded into one unit to lower production costs. In most cases, unitized construction seriously blocks accessibility to the hull shell, to fastenings such as the nuts for through-bolted fittings, to piping, wiring, and many other important places that sooner or later may need to be reached. In my opinion, the non-removable, structural part of ceilings should be in the form of longitudinal stringers spaced fairly widely to allow accessibility to all parts of the hull, and deep lazarets or lockers should have hatchways or openings large enough for a man to get his shoulders through.

In the earlier discussion of safe design for small craft, I mentioned the importance of skidproof decks, adequate handrails, and the danger of sharp corners anywhere on a boat. Of course, these features are even more important for larger craft designed for unsheltered waters. The latter point about sharp corners should be emphasized, because these sources of possible injury are often seen in the cabins of cruising boats: sharp corners or edges on tables, partitions, cupboards, stowage shelves, ice boxes, and elsewhere. Obviously, it is possible for a crew member to be thrown against a corner in rough weather, but even in smooth water one can lose his balance and fall in the cabin when the boat is rolled unexpectedly by the wake of an unseen passing powerboat.

Additional safety features for boats in unsheltered waters are: a hatch in addition to the companionway that is large enough to be used as an alternate exit; hatch covers fitted with strong dogs to assure secure latching; windows of safety glass or Plexiglass set in strong metal frames; a strong rudder of ample size located as far as possible abaft the vertical turning axis and preferably where it will receive propeller wash for effective steering under power; and, on a high-sided power boat, a transom platform or ladder to assist a swimmer or man overboard to board the boat. The alternate hatch may be needed for entrance or exit should the companionway become blocked by water, wreckage, or fire. When the well-known English yachtsman, Humphrey Barton, was pooped by a heavy sea in the 25-foot sloop, *Vertue XXXV*, the force of the sea jammed the companionway hatch cover, and a canvas cover over the forward hatch prevented an escape exit there. Barton might have been trapped in the cabin were it not for the fact that a broken doghouse window was large enough for him to crawl through. The lesson in this case is hardly the value of large doghouse windows, but to have a forward hatch that will permit exit.

Important safety items such as bilge pumps, pulpits, and life lines are more closely associated with equipment, and so they will be discussed in Chapter 3. Likewise, wiring, piping and electrolytic corrosion will be discussed in the same chapter, when we deal with inspections and preparation for sea. Gas tank installation and engine ventilation will be dealt with in Chapter 4, in the discussion of fire prevention.

### Construction Features

This section will not attempt a detailed discussion of construction methods and scantlings, but it will merely try to point out, in a simple way, some commonly seen, modern construction practices which are generally considered good or not so good.

First of all, it is well to examine the principle stresses to which a vessel is subjected. These are suggested in Figure 6. The size of the arrows show, in a very approximate way, the degree of stress; but, of course, exact loads would vary according to conditions, i.e. whether or not the boat is moored or underway, how hard she is being driven, the wind and sea conditions, and so forth. The stress labled H is caused by the propeller's thrust, and of course this would be considerable on an accelerating high-speed power boat. Thus engine beds and longitudinal stringers should be ample to resist the thrust and also the vibration of a powerful engine.

Of course, the downward thrust of a mast and the upward pull on the rigging put considerable strain on a sailing boat. The upward pull of the shrouds, which is considerable but only on one side of the boat when she is heeled, tends to hog or bend her rail upwards in the vicinity of the mast. Chainplates must be carefully designed with sufficient length and/or a means of spreading the load over a considerable area. Spreading the load might be accomplished by "beefing up" a large area surrounding the chainplates or by attaching them to frames or a transverse bulkhead secure-

FIGURE 6: HULL STRESSES

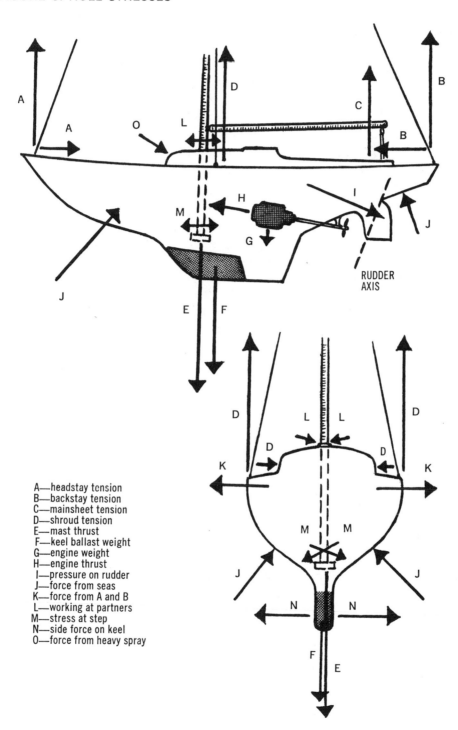

A—headstay tension
B—backstay tension
C—mainsheet tension
D—shroud tension
E—mast thrust
F—keel ballast weight
G—engine weight
H—engine thrust
I—pressure on rudder
J—force from seas
K—force from A and B
L—working at partners
M—stress at step
N—side force on keel
O—force from heavy spray

ly attached to the hull. The upward strain of stays at A and B can be enormous on a racing boat when she carries her jibstay tight for optimum windward efficiency. This strain not only causes the hull to bend up at her ends like a banana, but it may cause the hull to spread apart amidships as indicated by the K arrows. Here again, the securely attached bulkhead will help, as will the inward pull of lower shrouds shown at points D. Of course all the strain on the rigging tends to drive the mast through the bottom of the boat, and so the mast step must be well supported and the load distributed over a wide area with adequate frames and floors in the vicinity of the step. This is an area that is sometimes neglected as some boats with broken steps or leaking garboards can testify. Boats with masts stepped on deck should have an adequate post (or two posts with a strong metal spanner at the top) to transmit the mast's load to the floors and keel.

The stresses shown at J and even O in Figure 6 can be severe in a seaway. Flat surfaces are subject to greater strains than those which are convex; therefore V-bottom boats must normally be more strongly constructed than those with round bottoms when they are to be subjected to similar conditions. The bottom's angle of deadrise will also affect the extent of stresses at J. Slack, easy bilges and deep, rather than flat, bow and stern sections will minimize harmful pounding.

A source of weakness on many offshore boats is the shape of the cabin trunk. Flat, slab-sided deck houses have been severely damaged in heavy weather. In my opinion, cabin trunks or similar structures on offshore boats must not only be very strong, they should be slanted and curved or rounded to resist boarding seas or impact with the water during an extreme knockdown. Wood cabin trunk sides should usually be secured to the deck carlins or headers with long verticle bolts or tie rods.

Arrows G and H shown in the illustration signify keel stresses. These can be considerable, especially in heavy seas, because of the ballast's heavy weight and the side forces and twisting action imposed on the keel by leeway, and the boat's yawing, swaying, and pitching while heeled. Integral keel boats with bolted-on ballast or ballast sealed inside the keel, and the garboards faired into the keel (rather than bolted-on metal fins) normally are the most strongly constructed.

Modern stock boats are made from a variety of materials, such as aluminum, steel, wood, plywood, and ferro-cement, but by far the greatest number of craft produced in the United States at the present time are of fiberglass.

Fiberglass, commonly referred to as GRP in England, is actually fiberglass reinforced plastic. In much the same way that steel rods are used to reinforce concrete, fiberglass uses glass filaments to strengthen the plastic, which is generally in the form of a thermosetting resin. The actual fiberglass skin of a boat is a laminate built up of alternating layers of woven or bonded glass materials that are stuck together with resin. In some cases, chopped glass fibers are sprayed with resin onto the hull or hull mold with a special gun. Glass materials used for reinforcement are in the form of mat (random glass strands loosely bonded together), cloth (a finely woven fabric of glass strands), and woven roving (a coarsely woven fabric). A typical laminate combination for a small boat might be a gel coat (the thin, smooth outer layer of the hull composed of pure resin and pigment), a layer of cloth, a layer of mat, woven roving, another mat, and a final layer of woven roving. Well constructed larger boats use more plys of roving, seven or more below the waterline in some cases. Resins are sometimes epoxy, which are relatively expensive and extremely strong, but far more often the more economical, easier to work with, and weaker (but in most cases adequately strong) polyester resins are used.

Although fiberglass boats are built by several different methods, the most usual one for the stock hull is to build it on the inside of a female mold. Gel coat is sprayed or painted on the mold first, and then the alternating layers of fiberglass reinforcement and resin are applied. There is a good deal of controversy about the quality of the manufacturing method which uses chopped glass fibers sprayed on with a "chopper gun," as opposed to the "hand lay-up" method which uses alternating layers of glass cloth, mat, and roving. Of course, most manufacturers extol their own systems and sometimes criticize those of competitors. It seems reasonably certain, however, that either the spray-on or lay-up method can be satis-

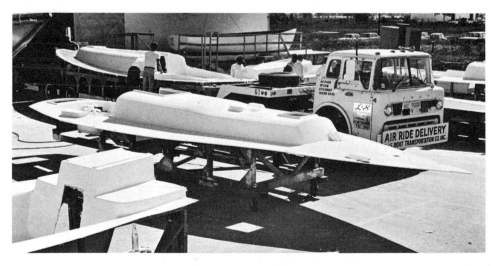

*Fiberglass deck, cockpit, and cabin trunk molded in one piece at Morgan Yachts. (Fenno Jacobs)*

factory when they are properly done, but most authorities agree that it takes greater skill to use the chopper gun. With the latter method, great care must be taken to see that the fiberglass has even, uniform thickness or greater thickness in areas of extra stress. In the hand lay-up method, strength can be assured with the use of fabrics made of long, woven, twisted and untwisted fibers, but care must be taken to see that the correct amount of resin is applied and that voids and air bubbles are removed as much as possible by squeegeeing the laminations.

Fiberglass construction has many advantages in compressive and tensile strength and freedom from corrosion, rot, and destruction from worms, but the material will abrade, and it is highly flexible. To assure adequate stiffness, fiberglass hulls should be sufficiently thick especially in stress areas to inhibit excessive flexing or "oil-canning," and stiffeners should be provided in the form of frames, bulkheads, longitudinal stringers, and stowage shelves, tanks, or bunks, which are built in to serve double duty as stiffening members. Bulkheads and other stiffeners must be very securely attached to the hull shell, usually with continuous fiberglass strips or tape on both sides of the stiffener where it meets the shell. I recently heard of a transverse bulkhead being popped loose from a fiberglass hull due to excessive strains at points K, shown in Figure 6, when the boat's headstay and backstay were carried extremely taut.

Another potential source of weakness is "hardspots," small areas of stiffness that are surrounded by flexible areas. These spots are normally caused by the pressing of a rigid stiffener on a small area of the flexible shell. Hardspots can create serious stress concentrations or fatigue from constant bending where there is an abrupt transition from stiffness to flexibility, and the condition should be avoided by distributing the pressure of stiffeners over wide areas with the use of extra plies of laminate or preferably wide plates between the shell and stiffener to disperse the stress.

One of the great advantages of fiberglass construction is that it produces a nearly monolithic hull with minimal joints or seams. The few joints that do exist, such as where the deck joins the hull, however, require very careful, strong connections, perhaps with epoxy resin in many cases. When the deck and hull laminates are butted and held together with layers of fiberglass reinforcement on the inside of the seam, there is a tendency for the hull and the deck laminate to peel apart near the outside of the seam. In some cases the hull laminate can be rolled over at its top edge so that the seam can be covered with a toe rail to mitigate the tendency to peel, or the deck and hull edges can be flanged or given lips which may be bolted together and then covered with a rubbing strip. Decks and other relatively flat surfaces, such as transoms, or bulkheads, need to be quite rigid; thus they are often of plywood covered with glass cloth or plywood sandwiched between layers of fiberglass or, in some cases, fiberglass with molded-in stiffeners.

Sandwich construction is even used for the hull in many cases. Although a good grade of marine plywood is often suitable for the core material, solid hard wood should be avoided because of the possibility that it might swell and crack the laminate. Quite often balsa wood or foamed plastics are used for the core. Advantages of this construction are not only in the rigidity it affords but also in its light weight, which may even be sufficiently light to provide flotation in some cases. It is very important, however, that the core materials have the strength to resist impact and sheer stresses, and also that the outer laminate skin is sufficiently thick and strong to resist puncture or leakage of water through minute holes in the laminate. Water leaking into the core can sometimes cause serious problems.

Ballast is secured to an integral fiberglass keel in one of two ways: by bolting the ballast to the outside of the keel, or by placing the ballast inside of the hollow keel. There are advantages and disadvantages in each method. External ballast assures the lowest possible center of gravity for a given weight and affords good protection when grounding on rocks or hard bottoms, but such ballast usually detracts from the keel's smoothness and fairness, and also keel bolts will corrode or erode in time. With external ballast, it is essential that the design allows for the inspection, tightening, and replacement of the bolts and nuts, but accessibility is lacking on some boats. Internal keel ballast assures smoothness and avoids the complication of keel bolts, but the keel is more vulnerable to groundings, and if the ballast is not tightly fitted and bonded in place, it may shift or move slightly, and any movement may lead to fatigue or abrasion. If the keel should happen to be holed from a grounding on rocks, it may fill with water or even drop ballast when it consists of individual, small pieces of metal. This has happened on several occasions. Pockets of water allowed to remain between the keel shell and the ballast could freeze and swell, possibly cracking the laminate in northern waters. The most satisfactory internal ballast is generally the one-piece lead casting that exactly fits the hollow of the keel. Internal keel ballast requires ample laminate thickness at the garboards as well as in the keel itself and the ballast should be sealed with fiberglass at its top to firmly hold it down and to prevent water from entering the hull in case the bottom of the keel happens to be punctured.

A few additional, miscellaneous thoughts on fiberglass construction are as follows: sharp, right-angle corners should be avoided in favor of curved or rounded corners to mitigate cracking the laminate; stress areas at winches, cleats, chainplates, chocks, etc. should be thickened and rein-

## FIGURE 7: FIBERGLASS HULL CONNECTIONS AND FITTINGS (GIBBS & COX)

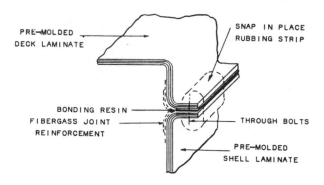

DECK EDGE CONNECTION — SMALL
BOAT TYPE WITH SNAP IN PLACE RUBBING STRIP

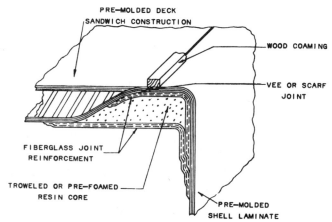

DECK EDGE CONNECTION — SANDWICH
DECK WITH WOOD COAMING AND JOINT IN DECK

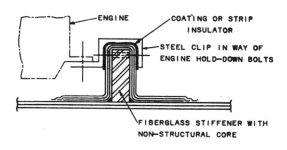

ENGINE BEARER — STEEL
CLIP BOLTED TO HAT STIFFENER

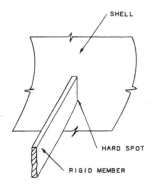
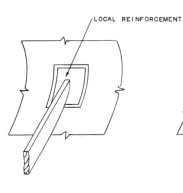
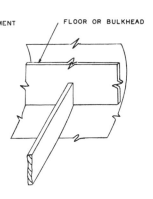

a. <u>NOT ACCEPTABLE</u>
FULL DEPTH FRAME ENDING
IN UNSUPPORTED PANEL

b. <u>BETTER BUT TO BE AVOIDED</u>
FRAME TAPERED TO REDUCE
RIGIDITY. LAMINATE REIN-
FORCED LOCALLY AT HARD
SPOT.

c. <u>BEST</u>
FRAME ENDS AT
STRUCTURAL MEMBER

## HARD SPOT — FRAME ENDINGS

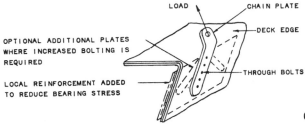

## CHAIN PLATE ATTACHMENTS

a. SIMPLE EXTERIOR SIDE STAY CHAIN PLATE. SIMILAR
DETAIL IS USED AT THE BOW FOR FORE STAY CHAIN PLATES
AND AT THE STERN FOR BACK STAY CHAIN PLATES

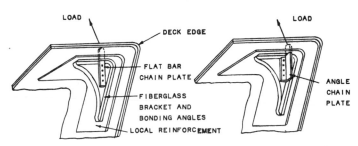

b. INTERIOR SIDE CHAIN PLATE. CHAIN PLATES MAY BE CONNECTED
TO A TRANSVERSE BULKHEAD, OR THE BOTTOM OF THE BRACKET MAY
BE CONNECTED TO A LONGITUDINAL FRAME. BOTH ARE IMPROVED
CONSTRUCTIONS. CONSTRUCTION SHOWN IS CONSIDERED THE MIN-
IMUM ACCEPTABLE. A SIMILAR DETAIL IS USED ON THE TRANSOM
FOR BACK STAY CHAIN PLATES.

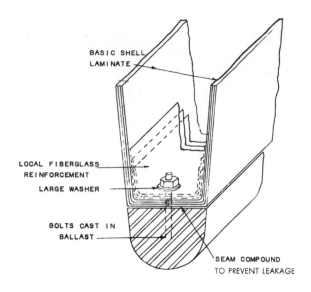

BASIC SHELL LAMINATE

LOCAL FIBERGLASS REINFORCEMENT

LARGE WASHER

BOLTS CAST IN BALLAST

SEAM COMPOUND TO PREVENT LEAKAGE

## BALLAST TO HULL CONNECTION

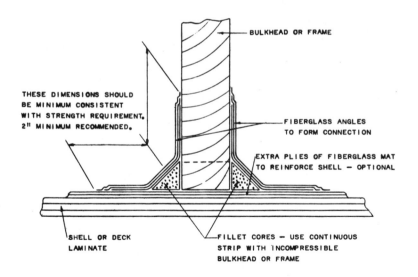

BULKHEAD OR FRAME

THESE DIMENSIONS SHOULD BE MINIMUM CONSISTENT WITH STRENGTH REQUIREMENT. 2" MINIMUM RECOMMENDED.

FIBERGLASS ANGLES TO FORM CONNECTION

EXTRA PLIES OF FIBERGLASS MAT TO REINFORCE SHELL — OPTIONAL

SHELL OR DECK LAMINATE

FILLET CORES — USE CONTINUOUS STRIP WITH INCOMPRESSIBLE BULKHEAD OR FRAME

## CONNECTION — BULKHEADS AND FRAMING TO SHELL OR DECK

forced with extra laminate plys; these plys should add thickness gradually with the reinforcement laid in patches of diminishing size, one on top of another; when strains are mostly in one direction, the reinforcing fabric should be aligned so that the stress is in the direction of the cloth's weave and not on the bias; and extra roving and stiffeners should be used when the laminate is subject to fatigue stress produced by continually alternating or repetitive loads. Fatigue stresses, which can be very dangerous, are most often produced by the pounding of seas under the bows of high-speed, flat or V-bottomed craft and by the vibration of powerful engines. Although not very often found on mass-produced American sailing boats, many of the better-built European boats have longitudinal stringers inside the hull that provide extra longitudinal stiffening, assure hull fairness, resist oil-canning and fatigue stresses from head seas, and also resist the strains on a hull imposed by taut rigging. More will be said about inspec-

*Fiberglass is not indestructible. Prolonged pounding in head seas at high speeds can cause fatigue cracks and perhaps massive failure if the boat is not built to the highest standards. This boat was damaged in a race at Fond du Lac, Wisconsin. (Milwaukee Sentinel)*

tions and looking for flaws in fiberglass and other forms of construction when we discuss preparations for sea in Chapter 3.

As for other boat construction materials, a few brief comments on desirable construction methods and practices will follow. To begin with, any boat built in accordance with the rules and scantlings recommended and set forth by Lloyd's Register of Shipping will very likely be exceptionally strong and sound. It should be pointed out, however, that in some instances Lloyd's standards may be heavier than necessary. For instance, the noted English designer-author, Douglas Phillips-Birt, tells us that it is common practice to make greater reductions in the thickness of canvas or plastic covered decks than that allowed by Lloyds.

*There is great inherent strength in the structure of conventional plank-on-frame wood construction, provided the scantlings and fastenings are reasonably heavy and the joinery is accurate. (W. H. Ballard)*

A primary consideration with wood construction should be the inhibition of dry rot. Of course, suitable woods such as teak, mahogany, Douglas fir, longleaf yellow pine, and white oak (for structural members) should be used, and they should be well dried and treated with a wood preservative. It is of the utmost importance that adequate ventilation is provided below decks and that all dead air pockets are eliminated to discourage rot. There should be ventilation holes in all lockers and closed spaces, ceilings or inner skins should be open at the top or preferably slotted, and forepeaks and after lazarets should be aired with cowl or venturi type ventilators. There should be no pockets to trap water such as at the top of butt blocks, at floor-timbers, or in mast steps. Such areas should be beveled or provided with adequate drains or limber holes to avoid the collection of fresh water from condensation or leakage of rain water.

An adequate ceiling inside of a boat adds considerably to her longitudinal strength. For this reason and others, bilge stringers are often omitted from modern ceiled boats of conventional wood construction. Yet the famous Swedish designer-builder, Gustav Plym, believes that for the very roughest weather offshore, a sailing yacht may need the extra support afforded by a bilge stringer. In his book, *Yacht and Sea*, Plym describes how his *Elseli IV* suffered broken frames and superficially split planks during the very rough Fastnet race in 1957. He came to the conclusion that this damage resulted from the planks and ribs flexing on either side of a rigid bulkhead and that bilge stringers were needed to distribute the stress. Of course, steel frames and/or floors are sometimes used to assure rigidity, but they may present a problem with rust or galvanic corrosion, particularly when fastenings of dissimilar metals are used.

Boats with glued seams, especially those strip-planked and edge-fastened, generally have rigid, almost monolithic, watertight hulls, but this construction may be somewhat risky in areas of extreme dry heat or where there are extreme changes in temperature. Glued-seam hulls with fairly wide planks should be planked with well dried wood and it is the safest plan to paint the exterior of the hull white to avoid absorption of heat that might cause the wood to split. Such hulls have good longitudinal strength, but Gustav Plym warns that this is no excuse to decrease the strength of longitudinal members such as the keel, stern post, stem, deck shelves, and bilge stringers.

With the advent of modern, waterproof glues after World War II, many boats were built of plywood, either molded or with flat sheets. Round-bottomed boats usually must be molded or built up in layers of thin veneer, bent, either hot or cold, over a mold. This construction, using veneer strips laid diagonally, with each layer alternately crossing the one beneath at nearly right angles, has one of the highest strength-to-weight

*Strip plank construction. Gluing and edge-nailing wood strips one on top of the other makes a strong, bottle-tight hull that requires a minimum of frames. (W. H. Ballard)*

ratios of any boatbuilding material. Sheet plywood has many advantages for the amateur builder, but the hull must be especially designed (usually with a hard-chine form) for the material, because the sheets cannot be bent into compound curves. Top grade, exterior, marine plywood should be used for boatbuilding, and the wood must be kept well painted, especially any exposed ends that are sometimes vulnerable to delamination from water seepage. Plywood is often covered with fiberglass cloth bonded with epoxy resin, which generally makes a very tough, strong, and rigid construction, but it should be kept in mind that the bonding of fiberglass to plywood is not as strong as that of fiberglass to fiberglass if there are stresses which tend to pull the laminations apart. Naval architect Robert Harris tells us that when the load is at ninety degrees to a fiberglass-plywood bonded surface, the glass should be through-bolted, otherwise the bond might fail as a result of the wood surface fibers pulling apart. Sheet plywood is often suitable for stiffening and for structural members, such as knees and bulkheads regardless of the hull material. Oval openings or doorways with rounded instead of square corners will avoid stress concentrations.

Welded metal hulls have some advantages in strength, resistance to abrasion, and of course, freedom from rot and worm destruction. A possible problem with most metal hulls however, is deterioration by galvanic action and electrolysis. Particular attention should be given to electric wiring (which should be done by a qualified marine electrician), and fastenings or other metals used in construction and the metal in bottom paints should be electrolytically compatible with the hull shell.

When it is necessary to use dissimilar metals, they should be as close as possible together on the galvanic scale (see Figure 13), or they might be insulated with a barrier material, such as neoprene. Steel hulls have the disadvantage of relatively heavy weight and susceptibility to rust. To cope with the latter problem, hulls must be kept well painted, and, of course, all means should be taken to prevent leaks and excessive condensation below decks. Aluminum construction is light and strong, and the newest alloys are highly resistant to corrosion, but the material is subject to being dented quite easily; thus it should be adequately supported by structural and stiffening members. Indeed, several aluminum ocean racers have had their bows bent in by the force of head seas in rugged offshore conditions.

A surprisingly old boatbuilding material, steel reinforced concrete, commonly called ferro-cement, is currently enjoying a great revival. In modern construction with this material, thin layers of cement are applied to both sides of a metal skeletal form of the boat comprised of bent pipe frames connected with longitudinal steel rods and wire mesh. The advantages of ferro-cement are its tremendous strength that increases with age due to slow curing of the cement, great rigidity, freedom from rot and worm damage, fire resistance, low maintenance, and insulation from sound and temperature. Disadvantages of the material are few, but they are: poor resistance to certain acids; moderately heavy weight (about equal to or slightly heavier than modern conventional wood construction) despite claims to the contrary, which often makes it unsuitable for small or light-displacement craft; the difficulty in obtaining a smooth, fair surface as compared to other building methods; and the problem of eliminating and detecting voids in the cement. Because of the considerable weight of a conventionally built ferro-cement boat, it is often desirable that the cabin trunk and decks be made of plywood or some lighter material in order to keep the center of gravity low. The difficulty in achieving hull fairness is sometimes attributed to the sagging or deflection of the wire mesh under the weight of the mortar. Voids result from the difficulty of

*Pipe frames and longitudinal rods partially covered with wire mesh shown during the construction of a ferro-cement boat.*

making the cement fully penetrate the closely spaced layers of mesh, and sometimes these voids lead to water penetration and leaks. Ferro-cement seems a very promising material indeed, and it is often highly touted as the ideal boatbuilding method for amateurs. However, authorities such as naval architect Arthur Drilling, Jr. warn that this construction must be competently engineered, and there must be the highest quality control in production. He advises leaving ferro-cement construction to the professionals. Two other authorities with impressive credentials, Raymond L. Waddell and Thomas W. Beckett, also advise great care and caution with this construction method. They warn against slap-dash procedures and short-cuts, such as the sometimes recommended use of fox or chicken wire

*Mesh being wired in place over pipe frames prior to the application of cement during the building of a small ferro-cement boat.*

*Applying the cement. It is important that cement of proper consistency is forced entirely through the wire mesh in such a way that there are no air pockets or voids.*

for the hull mesh. Of course, many details of this construction are controversial, but it certainly seems prudent for the prospective buyer of a new ferro-cement boat to read all available literature on the subject and to use a reputable designer and a builder who has considerable experience with the material.

In conclusion, a boat owner must be certain his craft is entirely suited in design and construction to her intended use, and at the same time he should be sure that she is not used for a purpose beyond that for which she is intended. But in addition, there must be a considerable margin of safety for the unexpected, because one cannot always count on certainties where the sea is concerned.

# 2 / TYPES OF SEAGOING CRAFT

What type of boat is the safest to take offshore? This question is often the subject of lively debates and discussions around the cabin table, or elsewhere. Typical opinions range from: a replica of Captain Joshua Slocum's *Spray*, to a modern ocean racer, to a heavy, fisherman-type power-boat, to a cruising catamaran or trimaran, or to a Colin Archer type double-ender. Sailors who ruminate on this subject might be grouped in one of three camps: the traditionalists, the modernists, or the moderates, those whose ideas lie somewhere between the two extremes.

My own thinking belongs with the latter school. To put it very briefly, I believe that a monohulled, ballasted keel sailer of normal, moderate dimensions and proportions, having good performance, a high range of stability, watertight integrity, and strong but not necessarily heavy construction is the safest kind of boat to take to sea. Furthermore, I feel that a boat *specifically designed by a reputable naval architect for cruising offshore* is nearly always superior to a converted work boat type such as an oyster dredger, fisherman, trawler, pilot vessel, life boat, and so forth, although it must be admitted that the latter boats often can be obtained at a low price and some types might be and have been converted satisfactorily. The design or development of a work boat type is always influenced by the work she is to perform, and she is given capabilities that usually detract from pure passagemaking.

It is often a mistake to judge a boat's seaworthiness by her performance record only, especially for one particular passage. The success of a passage may be due to good weather, good luck, or unusually good seamanship, rather than to the inherent seaworthiness of the vessel. The Atlantic has been crossed by rafts, a rubber kayak, a canvas folding boat, an amphibious jeep, and a boat only six feet long, but surely few knowledgeable sailors would recommend such craft as the safest to take offshore.

## Offshore Sailing Craft

Sailboat traditionalists generally prefer a rather heavy displacement hull with a long keel, deep forefoot, generous beam, and perhaps a pointed stern for offshore work. Examples of this type are North Sea pilot cutters typical of designs by Colin Archer or the so called Tahiti or *Carol* ketches designed by John G. Hanna (see Figure 8 for the general type). These or similar double-enders have made many celebrated deep water passages, which include the circumnavigations of: Erling Tambs' *Teddy,* Al Petersen's *Stornaway,* Jean Gau's *Atom,* Tom Steele's *Adios,* J. Y. LeToumelin's *Kurun,* Vito Dumas' *Lehg II,* and Robin Knox-Johnston's *Suhaili* (the latter three are quite similar to Colin Archer types). These vessels are seakindly

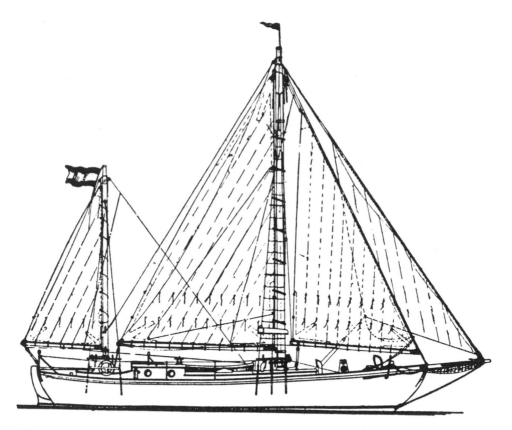

*Plans of the* Gaucho, *a Colin Archer type, similar to Type A in Figure 8. She was built by Manuel Campos in Buenos Aires for Ernesto Uriburu, who made several notable ocean passages in her in the Forties. Dimensions are: LOA—50 feet; LWL—42 feet; beam—14 feet; draft—7 feet, 5 inches; displacement—28 tons; and sail area—969 square feet. (Dodd, Mead)*

and generally very able, but in boat design compromises are nearly always necessary, and so the heavy double-ender concept also has weaknesses.

A decided drawback of this general type is poor to mediocre sailing performance, especially to windward and in light airs. Speed and weather-liness are not only characteristics that make a boat fun to sail, but they can be very important safety factors, such as, for example, when it becomes important to make port in good time against a head wind or to claw off a lee shore in heavy weather. Another possible disadvantage is sluggish maneuverability. Most vessels with extremely long keels are slow to turn and subject to getting in irons when tacking. Smart maneuverability is becoming increasingly important on today's crowded waterways.

As for the desirability of a pointed stern, I think that the majority of the leading designers now agree that the double-ender enjoys little if any special advantage when running off in a seaway. It has often been said that a sharp stern will "part" a following sea, but the behavior of a vessel when running off will depend on her hull form (forward as well as

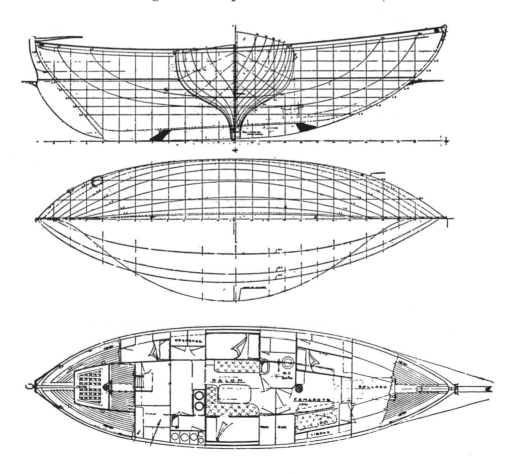

aft), her buttock lines and run, the distribution of her displacement, the shape of her ends, and the amount of buoyancy in her bow and stern, whether the stern is pointed or square. In other words, there have been good and bad downwind performers with sharp sterns, with counters, and with transom sterns. An important consideration seems to be in having sufficient (but not excessive) buoyancy aft so that the stern will lift to a following sea. The designer of a double-ender must be especially careful to keep sufficient fullness aft, because obviously there is less volume in a pointed (or canoe type) stern than in one that is square. The Colin Archer and Tahiti type sterns are usually well rounded and thus have ample buoyancy aft. It is worth noting that the double-enders that have been developed to cope with the short, steep seas of the Baltic, have even more fullness aft above the waterline than either the Colin Archer or Tahiti types.

Whether the stern is sharp or square, the traditional heavy hull is usually given generous beam and a deep forefoot. This combination of design characteristics can lead to problems when scudding (running off) in heavy weather if the entrance is fine, because the vessel may tend to root or bury her bow and trip on her forefoot, and this might create a tendency to pitch-pole (turn end over end) or broach to (turn uncontrollably beam to the wind and seas). Roderick Stephens, Jr., famous seaman and authority on yacht design, writes, "I presume the tendency to pitch-pole is stimulated by excessive beam." The noted naval architect and design critic, Robert G. Henry, Jr., reinforces this theory and elaborates by saying: "I agree with Rod's statement that excessive beam may contribute to the tendency to pitch-pole. Two boats of the same size and displacement, the one with the greater beam would have more displacement amidships and less in the ends. I think this loss of buoyancy in the bow tends to encourage rooting and possible pitch-poling. That is also why I like to have a fairly high prismatic coefficient in my designs, because a low prismatic is an indication that the midship section is too big compared to the other nine sections." (The prismatic coefficient is a measure of how the displacement is distributed longitudinally in a boat's underbody. A high coefficient, perhaps about .60, means that there is abundant fullness in the ends.) Normally, the Colin Archer type double-ender has sufficient buoyancy in her ends, but it is worth noting that one of these vessels, the very beamy *Sandefjord*, pitch-poled while running before a blow in the mid-Atlantic in 1935. She survived but lost one crew member and her mizzen mast.

For many traditionalists, Captain Slocum's *Spray* or a similar type represents the ultimate in small boat seaworthiness. Of course Slocum was the first solo circumnavigator, and his classic book, *Sailing Alone Around*

FIGURE 8: OFFSHORE SAILERS

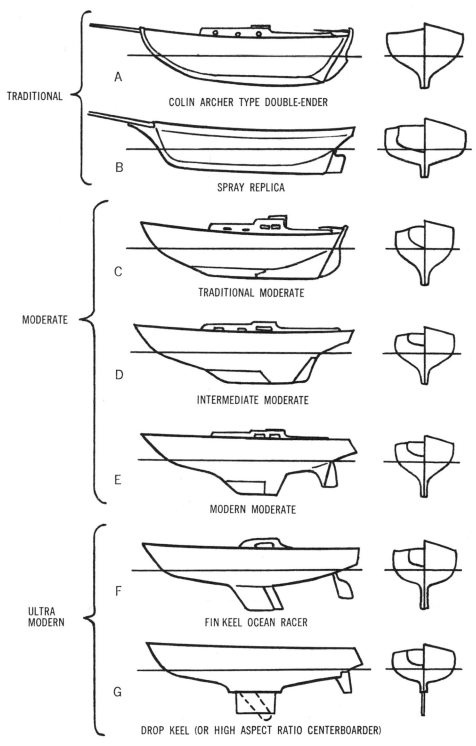

TRADITIONAL

A — COLIN ARCHER TYPE DOUBLE-ENDER

B — SPRAY REPLICA

MODERATE

C — TRADITIONAL MODERATE

D — INTERMEDIATE MODERATE

E — MODERN MODERATE

ULTRA MODERN

F — FIN KEEL OCEAN RACER

G — DROP KEEL (OR HIGH ASPECT RATIO CENTERBOARDER)

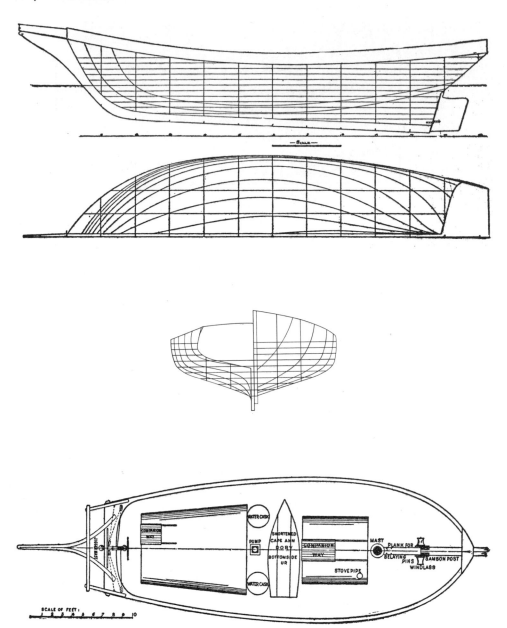

*Plans of Joshua Slocum's* Spray, *the first boat to be sailed around the world single-handed. The dotted lines in the sail plan show the rig changes made by Slocum in South America after crossing and recrossing the Atlantic. Her dimensions were: LOA—36 feet, 9 inches; LWL—32 feet, 1 inch; beam—14 feet, 1 inch; draft—4 feet, 1 inch; displacement—16 tons; sail area (yawl rig)—1,161 square feet.*

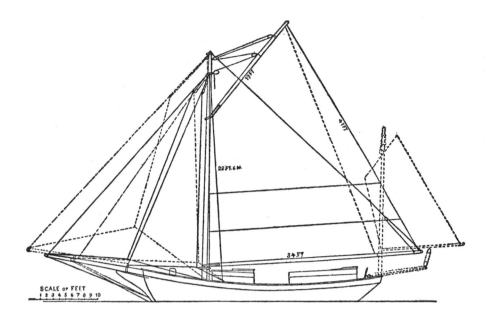

*The Spray steering herself on the wind with the jib trimmed in flat and the main sheet eased just a bit. Her mizzen is not bent and her portable jibboom is run in. (The Peabody Museum of Salem)*

*the World,* which kindled the spirit of adventure in so many sailors, also created a legion of *Spray* devotees. Many admirers of Slocum, including myself, have developed a real sentimental affection for the old *Spray,* which began her career as an oyster sloop many decades before she rounded the world. Although this vessel served her master well and had many virtues, we should not be blind to her faults. Some of her advantages were that her long keel and outboard rig (especially the long bowsprit) helped give her a remarkable balance that permitted self steering, which is nearly essential for single-handing. Also, her heavy displacement and great beam gave her high initial stability, roominess, and the capacity and ability to carry quantities of supplies without detracting a great deal from her performance. Despite her abundant beam, she had ample buoyancy in her ends with a prismatic coefficient of .65. Disadvantages of the *Spray* were that her rig was large, heavy, and less safe from the standpoint of handling than an inboard rig; she was a sluggard to windward (despite occasional arguments to the contrary) as compared with typical modern boats, and she had a less-than-desirable range of stability.

To elaborate on the latter point, a sailing craft intended for extensive offshore work should have as much ultimate stability as possible to assure recovery from an extreme knockdown. Stability curves calculated for the *Spray* show that her maximum righting moment occurred at about 35 degrees angle of heel, while positive stability was zero at from 95 to 100 degrees. Many ocean racers have maximum righting moments close to 90 degrees with positive stability to 140 degrees or higher. In my opinion, an offshore monohull sailer should have positive recovery from a 110-degree knockdown *at least.* It is often argued that since the *Spray* and a few replicas had successful voyages, therefore the type must be extremely seaworthy, but it should be pointed out that Slocum was an unusually masterful seaman and also that one of the replicas, the *Pandora,* did capsize, and right again when the masts snapped, in the South Atlantic shortly after rounding Cape Horn in 1911. Of course, other craft with greater reserve stability have also capsized, and I do not mean to give the impression that I think the *Spray* is the worst type to take offshore. In my opinion, however, there are presently better and safer designs for blue water sailing.

Traditional vessels similar to the *Spray* or the aforementioned double-enders usually carry little (and sometimes no) keel ballast, and they depend on their great beam, internal ballast, and heavy displacement for their stability. Despite the fact that many of these craft have made remarkable passages and have weathered severe storms, some have turned turtle. In addition to the *Pandora* and the Colin Archer designed *Sandefjord,* the Tahiti double-enders *Adios* and *Atom* rolled over, and also

*The* Spray, *formerly* Sojourner, *a slightly enlarged (44-foot), ketch-rigged replica of Joshua Slocum's* Spray, *Type B in Figure 8.*

*Lehg II* capsized. Perhaps any other small craft would have done the same thing under similar conditions, but it seems to me that a greater range of stability and thus a greater margin of safety could be achieved with equally strong but less massive construction in order that the ballast-displacement ratio might be increased. Weight saved in the lighter (but equally strong) construction could then be consigned to outside keel ballast without increasing displacement. This is perfectly possible with the technology, materials, and construction methods that we have today. Of course, in a very beamy cruiser especially, care must be taken not to add so much ballast that the metacentric height would be increased to the point where it would produce an excessively quick and uncomfortable rolling motion.

Traditionalists feel that a long keel is necessary on an offshore cruiser to facilitate self steering. In former days self steering had to be accomplished with the trim of sails alone, and this often required the directional stability of a long keel, but today, with the advent of wind-vane steering, it is possible to make most boats with short keels steer themselves on all points of sailing. In fact, the majority of single-handed ocean racers produced today have fairly short keels. Wind vane steerers come in a variety of styles, but the principle of one simple type is illustrated in Figure 9. Of course the short keel has great advantages for a racing boat in lateral plane efficiency to windward and sensitive maneuverability, but there are also advantages for the cruising boat in that a short keel and cutaway forefoot lessen wetted surface drag and thus allow the use of a small, easy-to-handle rig. I do not believe in extremely short keels for seagoing craft, however, because there is a point of diminishing returns when directional stability becomes too sensitive and steering becomes very difficult under certain conditions. My choice for keel length in an offshore sailer would be D or E shown in Figure 8. Both boats have moderately short keels and hence reasonably low wetted surfaces. Also, each keel is integral and is faired into the hull for maximum strength and to allow a hollow space above the keel ballast for tanks (for effective ballast so long as the tanks remain filled) and a sump to hold the bilge water (to prevent it from sloshing up under the bunks and cabin sole when heeled or in a seaway).

For those offshore sailors who want reasonable but not necessarily outstanding speed or performance to windward in conjunction with a seakindly hull that can be balanced for self-steering on many points of sailing without dependence on a wind vane, then type C (Figure 8) may well be the best choice. Of course this type may use vane steering, but without it, her helm is reasonably steady, and usually she can be made to self-steer more easily than a very short keeled boat with various sail combinations, such as twin headsails (two similar-sized headsails boomed out on opposite sides with their sheets attached to the tiller). Type C, which I have termed traditional-moderate, is quite similar to the famous British, Laurent Giles designed, Vertue class. These small cruisers (or boats with similar lines) have probably made more extended offshore passages than any other small class boat. Some famous Vertues are: *Salmo, Speedwell of Hong Kong, Vertue XXXV, Icebird, Easy Vertue, and Cardinal Vertue,* the latter having been sailed around the world via Cape Horn by Bill Nance, an Australian. The well-known circumnavigator and author, Eric Hiscock, has written that he considers the Vertue as the "finest of all small cruisers," and his *Wanderer III* was a similar but slightly larger version of a Vertue.

Hull types F and G (Figure 8) represent ultra modern ocean racers of very light displacement and low wetted surface. They may have the advantage of being very fast and perhaps close-winded, but in my opinion they are not the best type for extended offshore cruising. The extremely short keel can lead to steering difficulties (even when the rudder is de-

FIGURE 9: SIMPLE WIND VANE FOR A SMALL BOAT

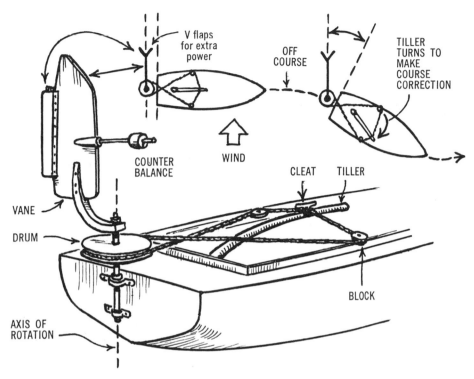

NOTE: Medium to large size cruisers will probably need a vane with a horizontal axis or the vane linked to an auxiliary rudder, underwater pendulum, or rudder trim tab for sufficient power.

tached from the keel and moved aft) when reaching or running in strong winds and confused following seas. This may not present too much of a problem to an ocean racer with a large crew taking short tricks at the helm, but the problem can be serious for a short-handed cruiser. Although very light displacement and hard, flat bilges are conducive to speed and high initial stability for sail carrying ability, this type of hull may have a quick, uncomfortable motion and may pound in head seas. If strongly built, such a boat can be seaworthy from the standpoint of constructional safety, but she will probably not be seakindly or conducive to crew comfort. Of course, when the crew becomes excessively uncomfortable (overly fatigued, seasick, or injured from falls), the over-all safety of the vessel is very much jeopardized. Another disadvantage of extreme light displacement for extended cruising is that the weight of stores may seriously hamper performance. However, moderately light displacement may be desirable for buoyancy and because a light boat requires less sail area than a heavy one.

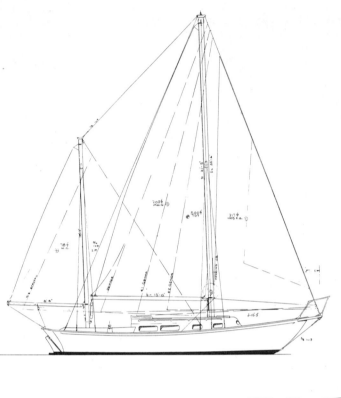

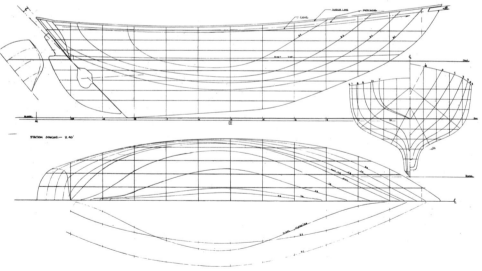

*Plans of the* Seawind-*class ketch, designed by Thomas C. Gillmer, typical of Type C in Figure 8. Her dimensions are: LOA—30 feet; LWL—24 feet; beam —9 feet, 5 inches; draft—4 feet, 3 inches; sail area—500 square feet. (Allied Boat Co.)*

Seawind *ketch, the* Ode, *on a close reach. One of these 30-footers, the* Apogee, *skippered by Alan Eddy, is said to be the first fiberglass boat to sail around the world. Her robust construction was sufficient to withstand severe jostling from a pod of whales at one point during her circumnavigation. (Mrs. Fred Thomas)*

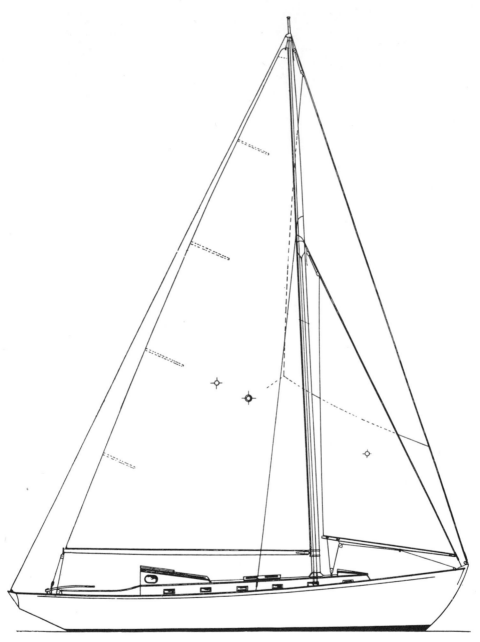

*Plans of the* Barnswallow, *a moderate-draft cruising sloop designed by Starling Burgess for Paul Hammond, representative of Type D in Figure 8. Her dimensions are: LOA—39 feet; LWL—30 feet; beam—10 feet, 6 inches; draft—5 feet; displacement—9.8 tons; sail area—585 square feet. She was designed especially for single-handed sailing with all her halyards leading to the cockpit. (Uffa Fox)*

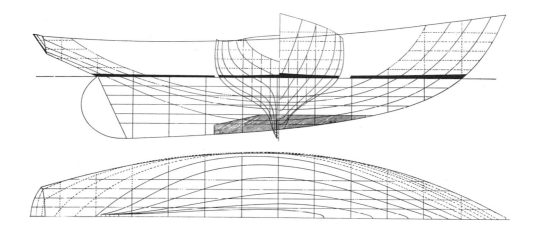

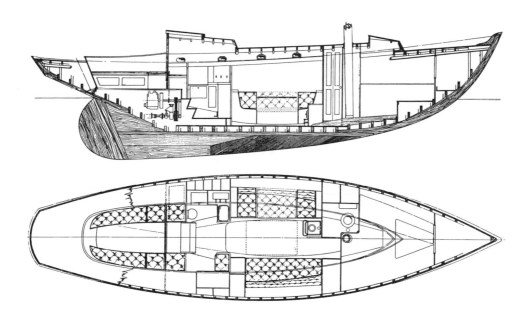

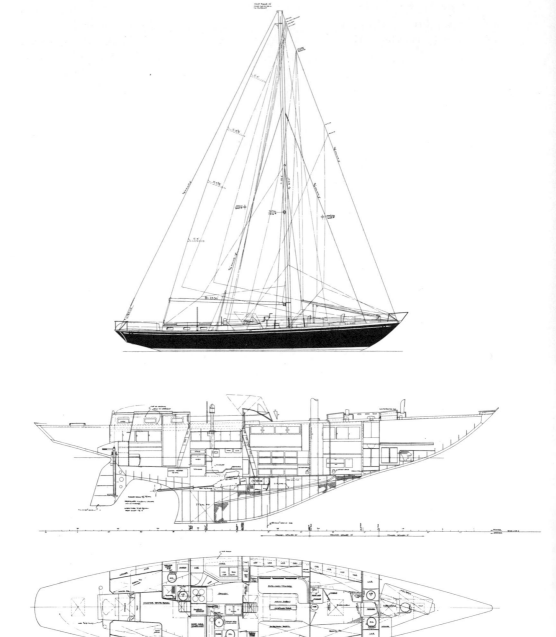

*Plans of the* Palawan, *designed by Sparkman and Stephens and similar to Type E in Figure 8. Her dimensions are: LOA—58 feet; LWL—40 feet; beam—12 feet, 4 inches; draft—8 feet, 1 inch; displacement—23 tons; sail area—1,308 square feet.*

Hull type G represents the very modern, high-aspect-ratio, ballasted, drop-keel boat. In many respects this type is similar to some modern keel-centerboarders, the advantages and disadvantages of which we discussed in the previous section (Designs for Unsheltered Waters). A drop-keel boat, like a centerboarder, may have an advantage when lying a-hull in that she will yield to seas and is not subject to tripping on a deep keel. However, I would be concerned about the ultimate stability of such a vessel. Before taking this type of craft to sea on an extended passage, consideration might be given to having her stability at high angles of heel calculated by a naval architect, and if the righting moments were questionable, it might be a wise plan to fix the keel in its lowered position.

A boat with a moderately short fin keel may have an advantage when lying a-hull in that her keel will be stalled (not supplying lift for lateral resistance) when the boat is not forereaching, so that she will yield to beam seas and avoid tripping on her keel. On the other hand, the long-keeled boat may have considerable lateral resistance even when she is not forereaching. This point will be dealt with in Chapter 7 when we discuss the storm tactic of lying a-hull. It should be said here, however, that the extremely short-keeled, high-performance boat may not be so successful with this storm tactic, because her bow might blow off and she would tend to make considerable headway, which would lessen leeway and the ability to yield to breaking seas.

The modern trend towards low-wetted-surface, short keels has produced some steering control problems. For an offshore sailer used solely for cruising, I think it is best to have sufficient length of keel to allow the rudder to be attached to the keel's trailing edge for maximum rudder strength and protection. However, if the trailing edge of the keel is quite far forward of the after end of the waterline, the rudder must be detached from the keel and moved aft (as shown in E, F, and G in Figure 8) in order to obtain a sufficiently long lever arm between the rudder's center of pressure and the boat's vertical turning axis for adequate steering control. Moving the rudder aft is often accomplished with a free-standing spade (see F and G in Figure 8) or by attaching the rudder to a skeg (E in Figure 8). An advantage with the spade rudder is that it may be balanced (with its turning axis slightly abaft its leading edge) to let the water force assist in turning it. This allows the use of an unusually sensitive tiller, even on a fairly large boat. An advantage with a skeg-attached rudder, however, is that the skeg directs water flow onto the rudder, and this delays stalling or sudden separation of flow and loss of rudder lift.

Some free-standing spades have caused steering problems. A typical difficulty is often encountered on a broad or beam reach in heavy weather when the rudder stalls and the boat uncontrollably rounds up into the

*Plans of the* Black Velvet II. *She was designed by Ted Brewer as a fast cruiser. Her dimensions are: LOA—43 feet, 2 inches; LWL—35 feet, 4 inches; beam—12 feet, 9 inches; draft—6 feet, 4 inches; displacement—12.4 tons; sail area—895 square feet.*

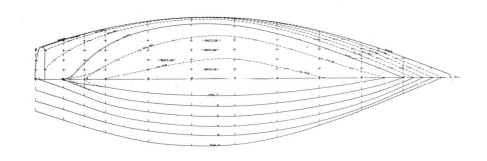

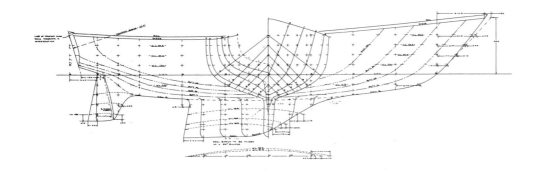

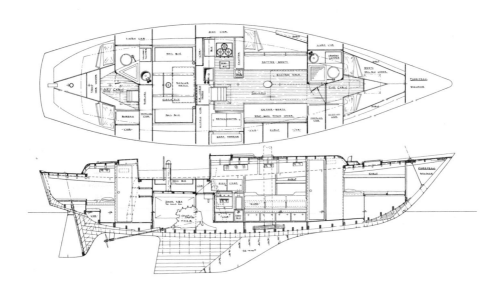

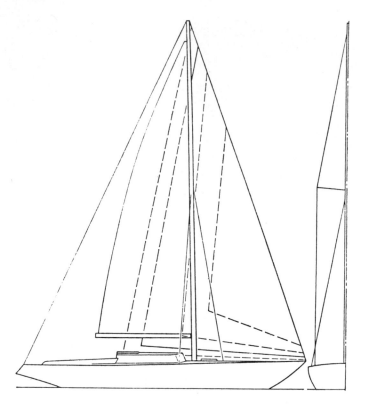

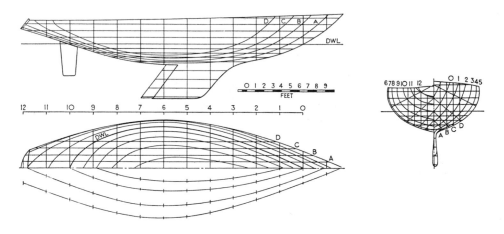

*Plans of the* Tina, *a Dick Carter design similar to Type F, Figure 8. Her dimensions are: LOA—36 feet, 10 inches; LWL—26 feet, 8 inches; beam—10 feet, 9 inches; draft—6 feet, 2 inches; displacement—6.1 tons; sail area—530 square feet.* (Yachting World Annual)

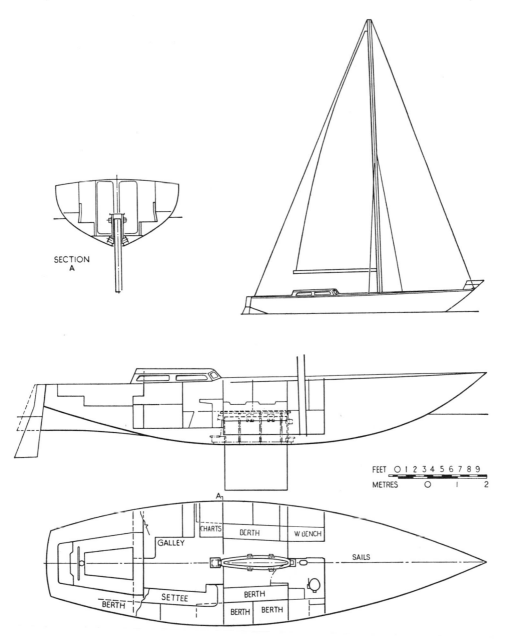

*Plans of the* Noryema VII, *an ocean racer with a drop keel and outboard rudder, representative of Type G in Figure 8. She is from Dick Carter's board. Her dimensions are: LOA—49 feet, 5 inches; LWL—38 feet, 4 inches; beam—13 feet, 8 inches; draft—3 feet, 3 inches with keel and rudder raised, 8 feet, 2 inches with keel lowered; displacement—14 tons; sail area—958 square feet.* (Yachting World)

wind. In my opinion this problem is aggravated by: an extremely short keel, in some cases by positioning the rudder so far aft that it cavitates (or ventilates) sucking air down from the surface, and by overly raking the rudder axis in the same direction as the leading edge of the keel, as shown in Figure 10. It is surprising how often one sees a spade rudder raked in this manner. Of course, such a rake helps move the rudder's center of pressure aft for leverage, but when the boat is heeled and has weather helm, the side force of the water on the rudder acts in an upward rather than in a lateral direction, as shown in the illustration. Actually, some spade rudders, having little if any of this rake, work well downwind when the boat is not heeled excessively and has good directional stability. Scott Allen, who helped his brother, Skip, sail a Cal 40 (a well-known class with a spade rudder) to victory in the downwind Honolulu Race in 1967, told me that the boat surfed under spinnaker for day after day, and there were never any steering problems even in strong winds. Naval architect Halsey Herreshoff attributes the Cal 40's steering control at least partially to the fact that "they have relatively long keels fore-and-aft, compared to the newest hot boats." The particular trapezoidal shape of the Cal 40's keel (not unlike E in Figure 8) is long at the top for directional stability, but short at the bottom to reduce wetted surface area, and this shape also gives a fairly high center of lateral resistance to minimize heeling.

Regardless of the effectiveness of this trapezoidal keel on ocean racers, however, for an offshore cruiser with a moderately short fin-type keel, I would prefer a skeg aft, faired into the hull, and the rudder's entire leading edge attached to the skeg (see E, Figure 8). As mentioned previously, this arrangement not only delays stalling, but also provides rudder protection and greater inherent strength as compared with a free-standing spade.

An offshore, monohull sailer should, of course, have all the safety characteristics discussed in the preceding section [Designs for Unsheltered Waters] such as: water tight integrity, self bailing cockpit, proper ballast, suitable bilge pumps, adequate freeboard, proper piping and wiring, skid proof decks and adequate hand rails, toe rails, an alternate exit hatch, unbreakable windows, a raised companionway sill, and so forth. But in addition to these, a true seagoing boat should have moderate overhangs, a low and preferably rounded cabin trunk, small windows, large freeing ports if she has bulwarks, hatches and companionways located near the centerline, and preferably an inboard rig. The latter point will be discussed in Chapter 6 which deals with sails and rigging.

Overhangs should be moderate to avoid violent pitching and pounding in heavy seas. Of course, slight overhangs are often advisable for reserve buoyancy when the ends are submerged in seas, but a long, overhanging bow may slam into a sea, and even the stern can pound when there is a

FIGURE 10: RAKED RUDDER AXES

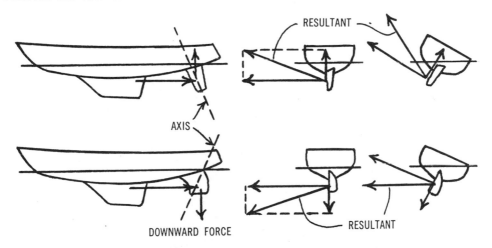

long flat counter. In addition, the extra weight of long overhangs at the boat's ends may adversely affect her moment of inertia and consequently increase her tendency to pitch. Rod Stephens writes in regard to the safest seagoing yacht, "certainly the weight should be concentrated, which makes for a much drier boat reducing the amplitude of pitching." Although the bow sections are often sharper or slightly more V'd than the stern sections, the ends of an offshore displacement yacht should be reasonably matched for good helm balance under all conditions.

A few blue water sailors believe that the ideal offshore boat should be flush-decked, without any cabin trunk. I don't go this far, but I believe the cabin trunk should be as low as possible, rounded, and immensely strong. Such a trunk can actually be a benefit in my opinion, because it affords the helmsman and those in the cockpit some protection against spray or seas breaking aboard, and its edge provides a convenient location for hand rails to assist a crew member moving along the deck.

A pet peeve of mine is the large "picture" windows seen on many stock boats. Of course, as said in the last section, glass should be unbreakable (safety or Plexiglass) and should be set in strong metal frames, but even so, the area should be small. The North American Yacht Racing Union recommends that windows with an area over two square feet should be fitted with rigid and strong coverings (storm shutters). Some sponsors of ocean races, however, require rigid covers for windows exceeding eight inches in height regardless of area. On many occasions windows have been smashed not only by seas breaking aboard, but by impact with the water on the boat's lee side when she takes a sudden knockdown. A well-known example of smashed leeward windows (one window was consider-

*An offshore, gaff-rigged, double-ended ketch with a Baltic type stern. Notice her mizzen gallows frame, her small portholes, ample freeing ports, ratlines to facilitate going aloft, low hawsehole which minimizes chafe on the bobstay, self-tending jib, abundant reef points, and safety net under her bowsprit.. This is the* Lille Dansker, *designed by Murray Peterson and K. Aage Neilson. (Douglas Photo Shop)*

ably smaller than two square feet, by the way) is the aforementioned case of Humphrey Barton in the *Vertue XXXV* when the twenty-five foot Vertue Class sloop was pooped north of Bermuda in 1950. Barton describes the incident in his book, *Vertue XXXV*, and in the same book he shows plans of a standard Vertue modified for "extended ocean cruising." This boat has a lower cabin trunk with four small, round portholes on each side. Small ports may look old fashioned, but they are very sensible and can be seen on such well-known blue water cruisers as Eric Hiscock's *Wanderer III*, Marcel Bardiaux's *Les 4 Vents*, Edward Allcard's *Sea Wanderer*, H. G. Hasler's *Jester*, Dr. Joseph Cunningham's *Icebird*, and many others.

Occasionally sailing cruisers have their companionways or hatches located off center, usually for the sake of solving some problem associated with the accommodation arrangements. For seagoing vessels, however, this practice can be dangerous, because a knockdown which submerges the rail nearest the off-center hatch could allow flooding or leakage through the hatchway. Such a dilemma happened to Captain John C. Voss when he rode out a typhoon in the twenty-five-foot yawl *Sea Queen* off Japan in 1912. The yawl heeled over and began shipping water through her companionway to such an extent that Voss was forced to wear ship onto the other tack in a storm of nearly one hundred miles an hour in order to keep his boat afloat.

Quite often one hears talk about the harmful influences of handicap rating rules on yacht design. Perhaps there is a slight justification for this thinking, and it is very true that rating rules have had and continue to have a tremendous influence on racing sailboat design, but by and large I think the influence of the major ocean racing rules has been more healthy than harmful in regard to safety. For instance, the Cruising Club of America Rule and the Midget Ocean Racing Club Rule, long the most popular measurement rules in the United States at the time of this writing, compare a yacht's measurement with an imaginary "base" or ideal boat, one that designers generally agree is a reasonably sound, safe, and wholesome type. In most instances, the rating formulas are developed to encourage dimensions and other characteristics that are fairly close to those of the base boat. Robert G. Henry, Jr., wrote me about one of his own designs: "Bob Ayer's International 600 *Premise* has crossed the Atlantic about four times and he says she is a wonderful sea boat and but thirty-six feet over-all. In fact here is a boat that takes practically no penalties or premiums under the CCA (Cruising Club of America) rule except a sail area penalty and this is the one item that can be reduced in heavy weather. It bears out my contention that in spite of adverse opinions the CCA rule develops a very wholesome type of offshore cruising boat." I agree with Bob Henry, although I do feel that soon the major rules might have to be modified to penalize extremely low wetted surface, which, in some cases, has led to overly short keels and consequently serious steering control problems. Also we have to be careful that the rules don't encourage scantlings that are dangerously light. In addition, I would like to see the International Offshore Rule modified somewhat to encourage higher prismatic coefficients, especially to encourage more buoyant sterns. There are often serious faults with rigging, fittings, and construction on today's ocean racers, but in most cases I don't think we can blame the rating rules for these failings. Usually the blame should be put on the manufacturers or boatbuilders or occasionally on the owners for poor seamanship or poor judgment in the selection of boat or gear which, perhaps, was not intended for use offshore.

*Richard Bertram's* Lucky Moppie, *a nearly-constant-deadrise, V-bottom, offshore racing powerboat designed to withstand severe pounding in a chop. (Roland Rose)*

### Offshore Powerboats and Motor Sailers

Heavy fishing type power craft have long been regarded as the safest kind of motorboat for extended passage offshore. This type might be described in a very general way as being deep-bodied, full-ended, and heavily built, with moderate beam and draft, short overhangs, ample sheer, and round bilges. Such a heavy displacement, non-planing hull cannot readily be pushed above a speed of 1.34 times the square root of its waterline length without a tremendous waste of power and the creation of a formidable wave system. Deep water commercial fishing craft have exerted a strong influence on the design of offshore motorboats. In fact pleasure craft of this kind are often called MFV (Motor Fishing Vessel) type yachts.

Although it is generally agreed that MFVs are very suitable for continual offshore work, seagoing boats should not necessarily be slavish, exact imitations of fishermen, because of the considerable difference in purpose between a work boat and a pleasure craft. In an interesting article (in *Yachting World Annual*—1964) on MFVs, the well-known British designer-author, Douglas Phillips-Birt suggested slight variations on the typical fisherman design that might improve it for yachting purposes. Those variations or modifications included a somewhat lighter displacement, slightly finer ends, greater overhangs with some flare forward, and more freeboard amidships.

A reasonably deep forefoot and deep V'd bow sections with rounded sections further aft lessen pounding in head seas, but the designer of an MFV type has to be careful to keep the stern reasonably narrow to avoid excessive buoyancy aft, which might tend to make the bow root (bury) in a following sea. As designer Bob Henry wrote, "The powerboats that seem to perform well at sea are the round bilge displacement type with a narrow stern to prevent broaching in a following sea. However, one needs the opposite for good performance in calm water — a broad stern to prevent squatting and a hard chine to induce planing. I really think seagoing powerboats are more of a compromise than seagoing sailboats."

As a matter of fact, the typical planing hull with a sharp V bow, a wide, flat stern, and hard chines is unsuitable for extended passages offshore not only because of difficult steering tendencies in rough following seas, but because steering may be difficult under any condition at low speeds when the submerged fine bow causes the boat to lose directional stability. Furthermore, in some sea conditions there may be pounding under the chines when the deadrise is flat. Also, as said in the last chapter, when this type of hull lacks adequate flare and freeboard forward and has a ramped or sloping down foredeck, it could become what Uffa Fox calls a "death trap" in steep head seas.

One solution to the problem of achieving speed without great sacrifice to seaworthiness is the deep V'd hull with longitudinal steps and the V sections carried aft, all the way to the transom. This is the famous *Hunter* or *Moppie* type designed by Raymond Hunt and produced by Richard Bertram, which is used extensively in offshore races. Such a hull form produces reasonably matched ends, gives a fairly soft ride without excessive pounding, and generally permits advantageous fore and aft trim over a wide range of conditions when sufficient beam is carried aft to inhibit squatting. However, this concept also involves compromises, for there is some sacrifice in speed and quickness to plane in smooth water, as compared to a form with less deadrise, and there is some loss of sea-kindliness as compared to an MFV type. Another compromise is the so-called semi-planing, round-bottom type, which has little deadrise but is rounded at the turn of the bilge. This type is a good blend of speed and seaworthiness in moderate conditions, but for the worst conditions far offshore (where shelter cannot be reached), there seems to be little doubt that the deep, round-bilged, moderately heavy displacement, slightly modified MFV type affords greater comfort and safety than the other motor boat types.

Offshore powerboats should have many characteristics in common with offshore sailboats, such as: watertight integrity, unbreakable windows of minimal area, generous freeboard, reasonably low superstructures, life rails or bulwarks with large freeing ports, a low center of gravity (often assured with the use of inside ballast), and perhaps even some sail to mitigate rolling or to serve as emergency propulsion. Of course, offshore power craft and sailing craft have differences in safety requirements, but it is not so much that different characteristics are required, as that the same characteristics often need to be more extreme in sailing craft. For instance, a powerboat does not need the same amount of reserve stability as a sailboat, because the former is not subject to extreme knockdowns from wind pressure on a lofty rig. Also, a powerboat's windows can be larger than a sailboat's, because they are not subject to the impact imposed by a beam-ends knockdown; nevertheless glass area on any offshore boat should be kept reasonably small, windows and windshields should be strongly framed with adequate bracing, and the panes should be of safety glass. Time and again power craft have had their windows smashed by seas or heavy spray breaking aboard, and in more than a few cases it has been reported that the windows were of ordinary, single-thickness, breakable glass. One problem with offshore powerboats is the vulnerability of windshields. Obviously, the helmsman must have a reasonably large area of glass ahead of him for good visibility. One supposedly effective method of preventing damage to windshields or pilot house windows is to attach, temporarily, when the seas are heavy, a fine-mesh wire screen mounted on a rigid frame in front of the windshield or window, about one inch away from the glass. The theory behind this method is that solid water striking the screen will be divided into tiny particles that will lack the power and velocity to break the glass.

Superstructures or deckhouses can be higher on power vessels than on sailing craft, but extreme height can be dangerous, because this raises the center of gravity and presents an area to the wind that acts almost like a sail, to produce a side force and consequent heeling if the boat is caught beam to a squall. Needless to say, deckhouses should be tremendously strong in all cases. While generous freeboard in an offshore motorboat is desirable, excessive freeboard should be avoided for the same reasons that should prohibit high deckhouses and extremely lofty superstructures, such as flying bridges and conning towers.

*A small offshore cruising powerboat. Notice her small portholes in the cabin trunk instead of the customary large glass windows and also the large freeing ports through her bulwarks. Her small, two-masted rig gives versatile sail combinations for the purposes of steadying, lying-to with the bow held up, or scudding.* (National Fisherman)

Although it is necessary to keep the center of gravity fairly low on a seagoing motorboat, she should not be excessively ballasted, as said earlier, because of the possibility of increasing the GM to the point where it would produce a violent rolling motion. However, MFV types usually need some inside ballast, primarily because they are often fitted with riding or steadying sails. As the noted designer of offshore powerboats, Edwin Monk, has stated, "The steadying sail should be used with a little caution, and the boat should be ballasted." Of course, the more sail the boat carries, the more ballast she will need.

All inside ballast should be securely fastened so that it cannot possibly shift. There have been many cases of vessels being lost through shifting ballast, but one of the most dramatic examples took place in 1867 when the small ketch *John T. Ford* capsized far off the coast of Ireland. Her ballast shifted in such a way that she could not be righted and as a result three people drowned. The sole survivor was a man who was finally rescued after clinging to the bottom of the upturned boat for three days and four nights.

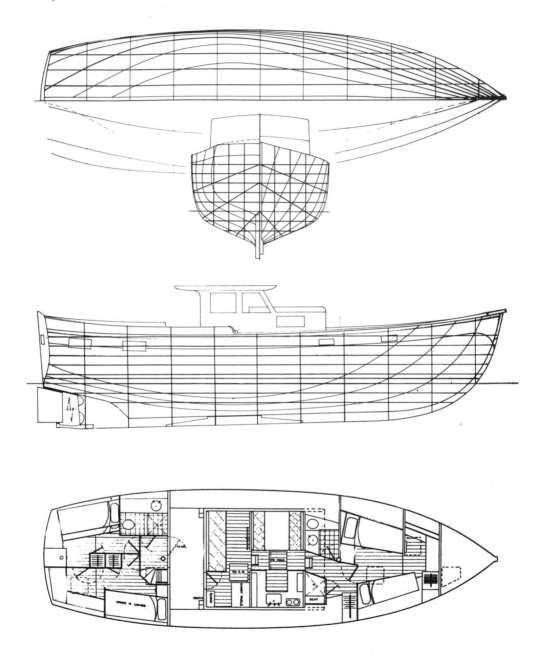

*The plans of Robert P. Beebe's seagoing powerboat,* Passagemaker. *She is a heavy, modified MFV type, with a round-bottomed hull of moderate speed. She has fairly deep draft and a single screw that is well protected by the keel. Her dimensions are: LOA—50 feet; LWL—46 feet; beam—15 feet; draft—5 feet, 4 inches; power—Ford 330 diesel; range—3,300 miles at 7½ knots on 1,200 gallons.* (Robert P. Beebe *and* Motor Boating and Sailing).

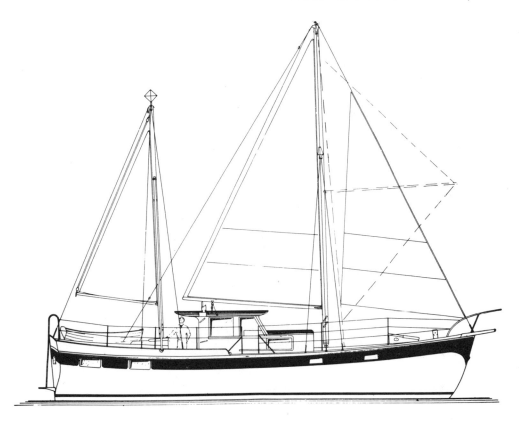

The center of gravity on a seagoing powerboat is usually kept low partly by the placement of water and fuel tanks deep in the bilge. Quite often the engine is placed very low also, but care should be taken that it is not placed so low as to allow the possibility of its being drowned in the event the bilge becomes flooded. On some offshore boats, ocean racers especially, the engine is placed right down in the keel, but in my opinion this practice is not sound. Aside from the fact that such an arrangement often makes servicing difficult and oil or fumes may accumulate deep in the keel, gasoline engines can suffer from wet ignition systems, and even diesels may be subject to severe damage if water gets sucked into the air intake. In fact, according to W. S. Amos, in an article written for the July, 1969, issue of *Yachting World*, a diesel engine drowned in this manner could actually "explode" as a result of a "hydraulic lock" in the combustion chamber with such force that the hull as well as the engine could be damaged. Mr. Amos speculates that this kind of damage led to the loss of the thirty-four-foot MFV *Mhairi Dhonn* when she foundered in Scottish waters during a gale in 1968.

Another factor that may have contributed to the loss of this fisherman,

*The* Passagemaker *leaving Bermuda for Newport, R.I. She has made many ocean passages. Rolling is minimized with paravane, "flopper-stopper" stabilizers. (Norris D. Hoyt)*

according to Mr. Amos, was the fact that the boat had very high bulwarks without properly designed clearing ports. He suggests that a heavy sea broke aboard, deep water lingered on deck when the narrow, slit-like clearing ports became clogged with ropes, nets, or fish and this allowed water to leak through the hatches, which were not designed to withstand total immersion. Consequently, the engine sucked in more than enough water to cause the hydraulic lock which blew apart the engine and damaged the hull. Of course, high bulwarks with inadequate freeing ports can also contribute to a capsizing, as the free surface liquid rushes to leeward when the vessel rolls. Thus the lessons seem clear: that engines should not be placed where they can be drowned, air intakes must be high out of the bilge and protected, hatches should be watertight, and bulwarks must be low with ample, large ports, or else open stanchions and railings should be fitted.

Powerboats with a large fuel capacity should not have tanks that are extremely wide and flat, as the free surface movement of the fuel in a partially filled tank when rolling produces sizable heeling that could contribute to a capsize. Tanks should be well baffled, of course, and the baffling should be designed with the intent of keeping the free surface movement out of phase with the vessel's period of roll, otherwise a possibly dangerous rhythmic rolling could develop. When a vessel has many tanks, it is advisable to keep them topped and to use only one tank until it is depleted in order to minimize free surface. Keel tanks should be used last of all because of their low placement, which increases stability, and deep, narrow shape, which minimizes the effect of free surface.

Most MFV types are powered with diesel engines because of their fuel economy, reliability, and safety, due to using a non-explosive fuel. Normally these boats have a large single propeller on center which can be well protected by the keel. The MFV's relatively deep draft allows ample rudder depth and deep immersion of the propeller. One problem with a single-screw offshore motorboat lacking propulsion sail, however, is the possibility of engine failure. From this point of view twin engines with twin screws are safer, but with such an arrangement propellers and shafts are usually more vulnerable to damage from striking driftwood or grounding and cannot be immersed as deeply as can a single screw. If the propeller is too shallow, it will race, and lose power, both when the vessel is plunging into a head sea and running before a high following sea. Some single-screw offshore yachts are equipped with standby power in the event that the main engine breaks down. Quite often the secondary power is supplied by the generator with a belt or chain linking it to the main shaft, or in some cases the generator may have its own shaft and small auxiliary propeller which might be located above the main prop, behind the keel deadwood and forward of the rudder. An interesting article on emergency engine propulsion, written by naval architect William Garden, appeared in the December, 1968, *Motor Boating* magazine. Of course, many seamen would prefer to rely on some sail for standby propulsion, but usually true powerboats cannot be made to sail to windward.

As said before, sails effectively damp rolling, and most offshore powerboats need some means of lessening this motion when the seas are on the beam. If the boat has no sail, she will need some other form of roll damping, such as keel-end plates, bilge keels, or fin stabilizers (See Figure 11). The theory behind the end plates or angle irons is that they help stabilize the boat by blocking the flow of water from one side of the keel to the other when the boat rolls. This method is undoubtedly helpful, but

## FIGURE 11: PERMANENT POWERBOAT STABILIZERS
(non-permanent stabilizers are shown in Figure 47)

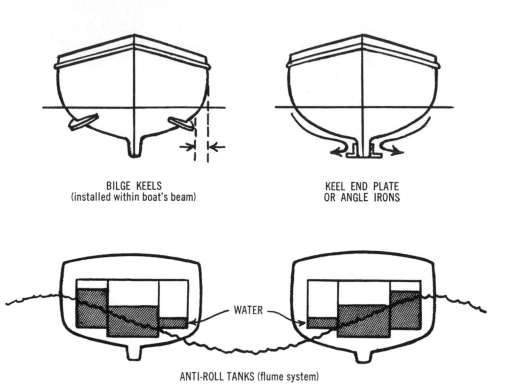

BILGE KEELS
(installed within boat's beam)

KEEL END PLATE
OR ANGLE IRONS

ANTI-ROLL TANKS (flume system)

WATER

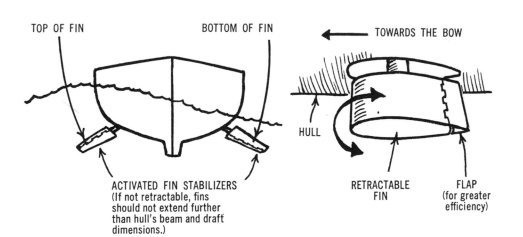

TOP OF FIN

BOTTOM OF FIN

TOWARDS THE BOW

HULL

ACTIVATED FIN STABILIZERS
(If not retractable, fins
should not extend further
than hull's beam and draft
dimensions.)

RETRACTABLE
FIN

FLAP
(for greater
efficiency)

to what extent is open to debate. Bilge keels are also helpful, but they should not extend very far forward because of the likelihood of emersion and pounding in head seas. Probably the most effective means of reducing rolling is with fin stabilizers. These are short hydrofoils projecting from each side of the hull below water, and they are alternately twisted mechanically to vary the angle of attack and thus cause an upward or downward force that opposes the direction of roll. Mechanical twisting is controlled by sensing gyroscopes, and some systems allow the fins to retract or fold into the hull when they are not in use. One drawback of fin stabilizers is that they are not effective unless the vessel is moving ahead with considerable speed. Anti-rolling tanks, on the other hand, can be effective regardless of speed, but these are not usually very practical on a small boat because of her quick period of roll and the fact that transverse tanks take up valuable room. Such tanks are partially filled with water and the free surface flow is controlled with baffles so that it is out of phase with the period of roll. As the vessel rolls, the greatest amount of water is held temporarily in the high tank to produce a stabilizing effect (see Figure 11). The anti-rolling methods that have been mentioned might be considered

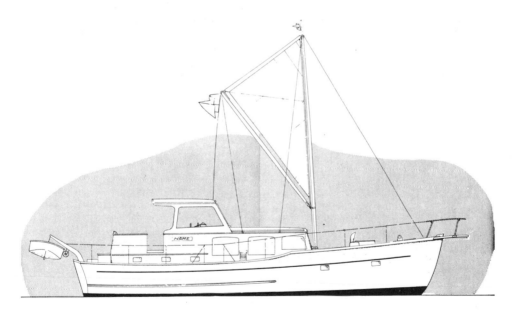

*An offshore powerboat with steadying sail. Notice how maximum sail area is kept high to avoid being blanketed in the troughs of ocean waves. I would prefer that the forward windows in the superstructure were considerably smaller. The dinghy in the stern davits should be brought aboard in heavy weather at sea. (Palmer Service, Inc.)*

permanent or built-in, but an effective temporary or removable method is the use of fisherman paravane stabilizers often called "flopper-stoppers." These will be discussed briefly in Chapter 8, when we deal with power-boat management at sea.

When an MFV type is rigged with small steadying sails for roll-damping, the sails may be used for emergency propulsion when the destination lies to leeward or across the wind. However, as mentioned earlier, powerboats seldom can make progress to windward under sail. To sail to windward, the vessel must have a fairly large, efficient rig and also ample lateral plane and draft to prevent leeway. The powerboat with such characteristics may then be termed a motor sailer. Definitions of this type of vessel vary, but to my way of thinking, a powerboat with sails is not a motor sailer unless she can make at least some progress to windward, and usually this vessel is fairly close to the type known as a fifty-fifty, meaning that about half the propulsive power is allotted to the engine and the other half to sails.

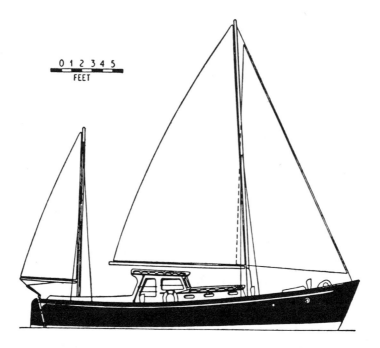

*The plans of a twin-screw launch designed by J. Francis Jones. Her dimensions are: LOA—31 feet, 6 inches; LWL—28 feet, 6 inches; beam—10 feet; draft—4 feet; displacement—7.4 tons; sail area—335 square feet; power—two B.M.C. Commodore 46-h.p. diesels; speed—8 knots. She has enough sail to make port across the wind or to leeward in case of mechanical failure. She has 1.3 tons of outside lead ballast on the keel. (Yachting World Annual)*

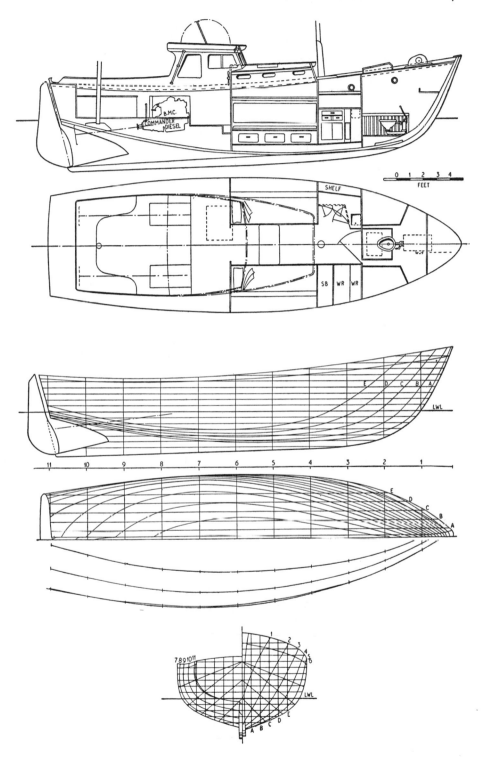

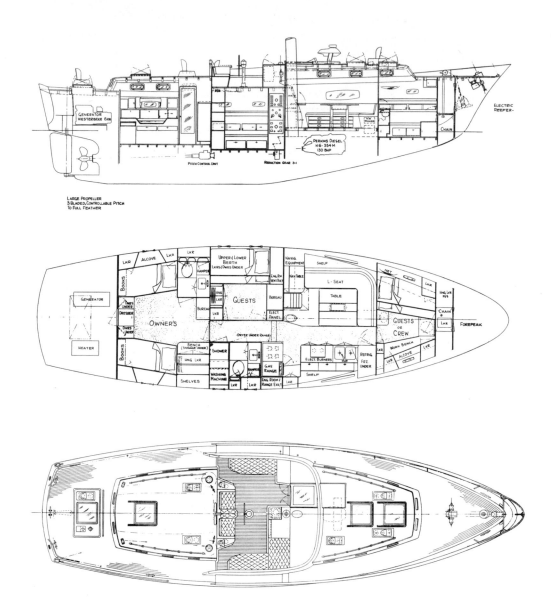

*Plans of the* Delfina, *an ocean-cruising motor sailer designed by MacLear and Harris. Her dimensions are: LOA—52 feet, 4 inches; LWL—45 feet, 10 inches; beam—15 feet, 3 inches; draft—5 feet, 9 inches; sail area—1,270 square feet.*

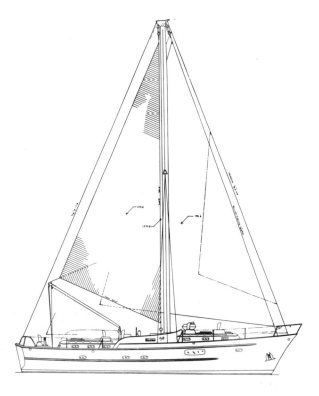

Motor sailers have many advantages over powerboats for long range cruising and passage making in that a reasonably efficient sail plan provides: economy of fuel; roll damping; emergency propulsion; greater versatility for heavy weather management; and the alleviation of annoying engine noises, smells, and vibrations over lengthy periods of time. Advantages of this type over pure sailers with auxiliary power are: normally greater space for comfort; fuel capacity for long-range powering; the ability to escape the doldrums or lengthy calm spells; and the ability to make progress to windward under adverse conditions by using the engine and sails simultaneously. Of course, as with all other boats, some compromises are necessary with motor sailers. Their chief disadvantage is in poor sailing ability, especially in the fifty-fifty type. Personally, I would prefer the so-called seventy-thirty type, which is really a heavily powered sailer. Such a vessel has a comparatively tall, efficient rig, with fairly deep draft, and a relatively high ballast-to-displacement ratio; and, at the same time, she has reasonable fuel capacity, and a slow-turning engine directly driving a large two-bladed propeller, which can hide behind the keel deadwood to reduce drag under sail. Although not a racer, she should be a fairly smart sailer having sufficient engine power to escape calms and drive the vessel into strong winds and heavy seas.

*The* Delfina *stepping along under sail and power. Both sails are roller furling. She has a three-bladed, 30-inch, controllable pitch propeller driven by a 130-h.p. Perkins diesel. Being able to adjust the propeller pitch is especially useful when using the engine to increase slightly the speed under sail. (Brian Manby)*

## Offshore Multihulls

One of the most controversial subjects in the world of offshore cruising concerns the seaworthiness of sailing multihulls (catamarans, trimarans, proas, and the like). More and more of these craft are taking to the open sea, and many have made remarkably successful passages, but more than a few have been lost. Opinions of knowledgeable designers range from that of catamaran designer Roland Prout, who says, "I believe that a forty-five-foot catamaran is the safest possible craft, with few of the dangers of conventional ballasted boats," to the other extreme expressed by single-hull designer Olin Stephens, who has "no use for them [catamarans] at all as seagoing boats." Arguments in favor of the multihull concept for safety are that, being unballasted, they will not sink; some types may not have as great a tendency as some single-hulled boats to broach to while running off; and their very shallow draft allows the possibility of beaching if caught on a lee shore in a blow. Arguments against multihull safety include: their extremely high initial stability, which puts a tremendous strain on the rigging and may cause a very quick, uncomfortable motion under certain conditions; the great strain imposed on the attachment of the hulls in extremely heavy weather with confused seas; and their lack of ultimate stability.

The most serious consideration with respect to multihull safety is the matter of stability. Their very high initial stability does indeed put a considerable strain on the rig, which means that rigging, masts, spreaders, and chainplate attachments must be tremendously strong. The famous single-hander and multihull sailor, Dr. David Lewis, has written that, although the stress on a monohull's rig increases directly with the wind speed in a linear relation, "with a rigid object the stress increases as the square of the wind speed, and this applies to a cruising catamaran." Although most multihulls are extremely stiff initially, their range of stability is very small, and they can capsize easily when heeled beyond what would be considered a moderate angle of heel for a single-hulled boat. For ordinary offshore sailing this might not be considered dangerous, if the multihull is correctly handled. As for being caught offshore in the worst kind of survival storm, I for one, would rather be in a proper monohull of the type described earlier. Correct handling of a multihull at sea means that special care should be taken to reduce or take in sail before a blow commences, that automatic sheet releasing devices should be used, and that in heavy weather, most multihulls should be kept end to (preferrably stern to) the wind and seas. Sheet releasing devices and storm tactics for multihulls will be discussed in Chapter 7.

A capsizing at sea, always extremely dangerous, can be especially so in a multihull, because she may have a strong tendency to turn turtle and remain in the bottoms-up position. Of course there is some comfort in the fact that she will normally float and serve as a crude life raft, but obviously such a position involves considerable risk to the crew's welfare in a storm far offshore, especially in cold weather (means of coping with this situation will be discussed in Chapter 4 when we deal with emergencies). Most seagoing multihulls need special means to prevent their turning turtle. Such means might be ballasted keels, specially placed sponsons (floats attached to the hull), or masthead floats (see Figure 12).

Since multihulls usually depend on light displacement for their high speed, ballast keels that are especially heavy and bulky should be avoided. Thin, bolted-on, fin keels of moderate weight similar to those used on the Michael Henderson designed catamaran, *Misty Miller*, are least harmful to performance, but fins that are not integral or faired into the hull may be subject to damage in prolonged heavy weather at sea. Indeed, *Misty Miller* had to drop out of the 1964 Singlehanded Transatlantic Race because one of her keels dropped off as a result of sheered bolts. Another possible drawback of ballast keels is that they detract from the boat's floatability, and extra buoyancy in the form of air or foam-filled tanks, compartments, spaces, or possibly air bags might have to be provided to offset the weight of the ballast. In my opinion it is more important for multihulls to be buoyant than for monohulled sailboats, because the former have less reserve stability than the latter, and multihulls can normally travel at relatively high speeds, which subjects them to the possibility of more serious damage from collisions with flotsam, such as floating driftwood. Another consideration is that when ballast is added to a multihull, construction usually has to be kept extra light for the sake of keeping the displacement light. This is not necessarily bad unless, of course, strength is sacrificed.

Outriggers or sponsons in the form of outboard flotation chambers attached near the hull's rail (see Figure 12) can be very helpful in preventing a capsize or turning turtle. The unusual catamaran of the proa

*The ocean racing catamaran* Misty Miller *fitted with bolted-on fin keels and a masthead float as safety measures against capsizing. One of her keels broke loose in the 1964 Singlehanders Transatlantic Race. (Eileen Ramsay)*

# FIGURE 12: ANTI-CAPSIZING FOR MULTIHULLS

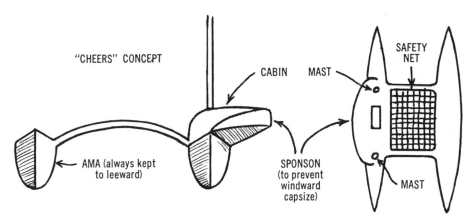

"CHEERS" CONCEPT

CABIN

MAST

SAFETY NET

AMA (always kept to leeward)

SPONSON (to prevent windward capsize)

MAST

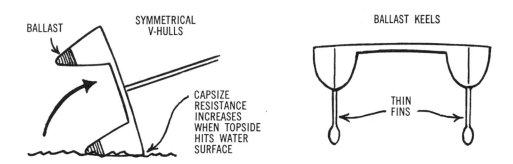

BALLAST

SYMMETRICAL V-HULLS

CAPSIZE RESISTANCE INCREASES WHEN TOPSIDE HITS WATER SURFACE

BALLAST KEELS

THIN FINS

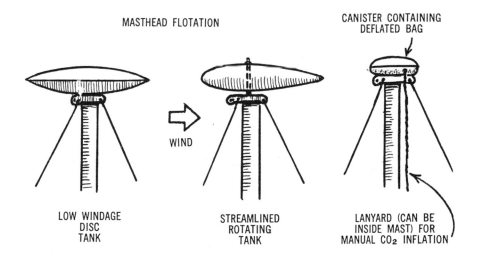

MASTHEAD FLOTATION

CANISTER CONTAINING DEFLATED BAG

WIND

LOW WINDAGE DISC TANK

STREAMLINED ROTATING TANK

LANYARD (CAN BE INSIDE MAST) FOR MANUAL $CO_2$ INFLATION

type, *Cheers,* which finished third in the 1968 Singlehanded Transatlantic Race, used a sponson to prevent capsizing to windward in case she got caught aback by a sudden wind shift or was rolled to windward by an unusual sea. Leeward knockdowns were prevented by the *ama,* or flotation hull, that was always kept to leeward. In size and shape, this hull was similar to but considerably lighter than the main hull, which carried the cabin and rig. The hulls were double-ended and booms could be swung 180 degrees in order that the boat could move "forward" or "backwards" to change tacks. The *Cheers* concept was certainly interesting and successful in many ways, but it provided very minimal accommodations, and it certainly was no guarantee against capsizing in the very worst weather.

In my opinion, most seagoing multihulls should be fitted with permanent masthead floats. These are usually lightweight, rigid tanks securely fastened to the masthead similar to those illustrated in Figure 12. Note that both types are streamlined to minimize windage, type A being a fixed circular disc, while B is teardrop-shaped and pivoted so that it always heads into the apparent wind. The function of these floats is obviously to prevent the masthead from sinking if it hits the water in the event of an extreme knockdown. Sufficient flotation will, of course, keep the boat from turning turtle, but the tanks must be strong and extremely well attached to the mast. Emergency or temporary floats will be discussed briefly in Chapter 7. Some multihull clubs require that the underside of wing decks be painted bright international rescue orange in order that a capsized craft can be spotted easily from the air. This seems a very sound idea, especially if masthead flotation is not carried.

Of course there are advantages and disadvantages in every aspect of the multihull concept, but from a safety standpoint, I think it is reasonable to say that the type is suitable for offshore work when the following conditions can be met: the boat must be of adequate size (at least twenty-five feet long approximately); she should be designed by a recognized naval architect experienced in multihull design; she should be strongly built and rigged in accordance with proven and tested methods; capsizeability should be minimized with the measures previously mentioned; she must be watertight and equipped with the customary safety devices found on monohulls (such as pumps, seacocks, life lines, rubber rafts, etc.), but in addition she should have safety nets between hulls, sheet releases, perhaps hand grips under wing decks (for use in the event of a capsizing), and a means of righting by flooding and later pumping out one hull (to be discussed in Chapter 4); she must be cautiously handled (sail reduced early, for example); and the passage should be well planned to minimize the risk of bad weather. Obviously many of these conditions apply to a monohull also, but I think they are especially important for a multihull.

As a final thought on monohulls versus multihulls for offshore work, it should be added that while there is great merit in the often-heard argument which approbates the seaworthiness of the multihull because she cannot sink, one should not be misled into thinking that all sinkable boats are dangerous. The usual ballasted monohull will sink if she is filled with water, but she will not sink, no matter what happens, if she is kept watertight. She can capsize, turn turtle, or pitchpole, but she will remain afloat so long as her openings are closed and she is not holed or punctured. Furthermore, in the bottom-up position, she is normally unstable, tending to self-right. Of course, the safest possible boat would be the ballasted, self-righting monohull fitted with enough flotation to keep her afloat even if she were filled with water. There are some boats of this type being produced today, and undoubtedly more will feature flotation in the future. In my opinion, however, it should not be necessary to buoy up a soundly designed and constructed, monohull sailing boat when her decks and cabin are watertight and all of her openings can be absolutely, quickly, and conveniently closed. More will be said about multihulls and their handling in heavy weather in Chapter 7.

Blue water cruising may offer the ideal means of escaping from increasingly constricted, overpopulated and polluted waters, but offshore ventures should never be attempted in vessels that are not entirely seaworthy. An unsuitable craft may make many successful passages, but sooner or later she will be caught out in heavy weather. In summary, I think the most important qualities of seaworthiness are: strength, watertightness, buoyancy, and ultimate stability. Any sailor who goes to sea in a vessel lacking these qualities may be deliberately thumbing his nose at Davey Jones. He won't get away with it for very long.

# 3 / PREPARATIONS FOR SEA
## AND SAFETY EQUIPMENT

After the initial purchase of a boat, the new owner must turn his attention to seeing that his craft is well found and properly equipped for safe operation. Of course, it is advisable that the owner become acquainted with his new boat gradually by taking short, shake-down cruises before embarking on any extended passage. The boat should be thoroughly tried and tested, and "bugs" should be eliminated before she ventures into exposed waters or leaves the vicinity of readily available help or repair facilities. Even if the boat is not new and the owner has used her in sheltered waters for many years, she should be tested and given a thorough inspection before being taken into unprotected waters, especially if a lengthy cruise is planned.

*Choosing a Surveyor*

As said in Chapter 1, before buying a used boat or even a new boat in many cases, it is highly advisable to have her surveyed. Also, I think it is a wise plan to have any boat, even a familiar one, inspected by a competent surveyor before she is taken offshore on an extended passage. Dependable surveyors, however, are not always easy to find. There are more than a few, who hang out a shingle or advertise in the yellow pages of the telephone directory, who are not entirely competent. I know of several boat buyers who were badly misled by poor surveys that resulted in repair costs far beyond expectations. Then again there are some quite competent and honest surveyors who may temper their reports slightly when they are hired by yacht brokers, insurance agencies, marina operators, or other professionals from whom future survey jobs are expected. There is no sure way of selecting an absolutely reliable surveyor. It may help to ask knowledgeable boating friends, especially one who has had his boat professionally inspected recently. Ask to look at his surveyor's written report, so that you may judge its thoroughness. This should provide you with a few clues of competency.

Something should be known about the surveyor's background, such as his training, his past experience with boats, whether he specializes in certain kinds of construction, if he has had experience in boat yards, training in naval architecture or marine engineering, and so forth. I don't mean that there should be a Senate investigation, but it is important to get a competent, completely candid surveyor. One suggestion that might be helpful would be to write a letter of inquiry to *The Telltale Compass*, a yachtsman's newsletter published at Lake Oswego, Oregon, which has compiled, among other collections of valuable information, a small list of reputedly reliable surveyors. Another source is the National Association of Marine Surveyors, Inc., Box 65, Peck Slip Station, New York, New York 10038, or Lloyds Register of Shipping, 17 Battery Place, New York, New York 10004. If you are located some distance from a known, capable surveyor, it is often well worth while paying extra for his transportation to your area. After all, the cost of a survey is usually a very small percentage of the total investment, and a thorough inspection may very well save money in the long run by revealing a condition that can be cured before it gets out of hand.

Some surveyors are very touchy about being disturbed, followed about, or having questions asked of them while they are actually inspecting a boat. Obviously, they should not be pestered or distracted while they are at work, but in my opinion the one who employs a surveyor has every right to quietly watch the inspection and later to ask questions. After all the employer is paying for the work. Of course, he should also ask for a full and detailed written report, preferably in a letter as well as on a standard printed form.

## The Hull

It is a wise plan for the boat owner himself to learn all he can about hull inspection in order that he can spot a problem before it becomes serious, and so that he can intelligently observe a survey inspection and ask meaningful questions of the surveyor. Also, of course, when on an extended cruise the owner often must be entirely self sufficient, especially when offshore, and he must observe his vessel with an eagle eye and make continual inspections. He should read all he can on the subject, ask questions of boat yard foremen and technicians, and ask opinions of respected "old hands." The novice should have a word of warning, however, about advice from sailors with only slightly more experience than himself. There are more than a few self-appointed experts, and free advice is sometimes worth exactly what it costs.

Before giving a new or used boat a detailed examination, the prospective buyer should give her a general, over-all, sizing-up. He should observe her lines, rig, cabin house, accommodations, cockpit, bright work, general appearance, state of upkeep, condition of equipment, and so forth. He should observe the fairness of her topsides, and look at her trim to see if she is listed or floating down by the head or stern. If she is a fairly small boat, the prospective buyer should notice how much she heels when he steps aboard at her rail, for this will give some small indication of her stability. It is a good idea to bounce up and down on one's feet while walking across the deck to test its sturdiness. Of course, all deck gear and mechanical devices should be looked over, although later all mechanical and electronic equipment should be carefully examined by a surveyor or marine technician. Particular notice should be taken of the joiner work, as this is indicative of the degree of care taken in the boat's entire construction. As designer-sailmaker Ted Hood has said, "The things you can see are an indication of the things you can't see." The mast and rigging should be very carefully examined later, but a glance up the sail track can often be revealing, when it comes to discovering an unwanted mast bend or permanent set. In short, don't discount a boat's first impression. It can tell a great deal. Needless to say, the boat's past history, designer, and builder should be known. Also, every attempt should be made to discuss the boat with the yard manager who serviced her, but don't expect him to be extremely critical if the seller is a regular customer.

As for the thorough boat examination, a few tips are as follows: Examine the bilges under the cabin sole, the floor timbers, keel, mast step, and especially the frame heels for rot, splits, corrosion, or insecurity. Look for water marks, stains, blisters, and blemishes that indicate water leaks, especially around deck beams, under the head and icebox, at the stem, in the stern lazaret (near the horn timber particularly), under the rail, and along the sheer clamp and deck shelf. Blemishes in these areas may indicate the possibility of rot in a wooden boat or corrosion in one of metal. Bulging or buckling of decks or other surfaces may indicate rust swelling on steel hulls. Look for dank-smelling, mildewed areas indicating lack of ventilation. These places are a possible source of rot in a wooden boat. Likewise, unfairness in the hull's exterior or areas of blistered, peeling paint or rust streaks could mean rot or wasted members or fastenings. These areas should be examined carefully and sounded (gently) with a small hammer. Most surveyors make maximum use of the hammer to detect wasting, rot, delamination, weak fastenings, voids, and so forth. When the hammer's tap produces a solid, hard ringing sound, this indicates a healthy condition, whereas a comparatively dull, dead thud could indicate a very unhealthy condition. Most competent surveyors prod no more than absolutely necessary with a knife or ice pick to detect soft wood, but some prodding will be needed on areas strongly suspected of rot. Sometimes, perhaps when the boat is double planked, it may be advisable for the surveyor to drill a small test hole, with the permission of the owner, in order to examine the wood chips. If they are punky, powdery, or sour smelling, rot may very well be present.

Boats should be very carefully examined for strains. Some signs of severe strain are: cracked frames; hogged sheer or sagging ends; wide seams or splits in planking; slight shifting or movement of bulkheads, straps, or chainplates; irregularities in the topsides; sinking or movement of the cabin sole; separation of joints; slight changes in the hull's shape (comparing one side with the other); sinking in or change in the crown of a cabin top, especially when the mast is deck-stepped; bent or sagging beams, posts, partners, step, and other members in way of the mast; radial cracks in a fiberglass gel coat or any crack in the laminate; and so forth. Some cracks in the structural members of wooden boats may not be indicative of strains, but simply of the wood drying out during a long period of dry storage. In many cases, the wood will swell and close the splits after the boat has been launched. Nevertheless, it is not good for a boat to leave her out of her natural element for long periods of time. Seams in the topsides should be examined carefully. Very often a sailboat that does not leak a drop at anchor will make water seriously when heeled in a breeze, because caulking has not been renewed and the topsides have dried out and opened up in the hot sun. Such topsides should generally be painted white to minimize heat absorption. Wooden boats should also be examined for evidence of worms or other borers, especially at the bottom of the keel or inside the bottom of the centerboard trunk.

Fiberglass and ferro-cement construction are far more difficult to inspect than wood, because strengths and weakness are concealed inside the material. As for ferro-cement, I would look for cracks, pin holes, leaks, rust stains, irregularities in the surface, and sound with a hammer for voids. Also, check the attachment of bulkheads, decks, and chainplates. Learn all you can about the boat's construction: where she was built, who designed her, and the exact method used in her construction. Most important, hire a surveyor who has had experience with the material.

With fiberglass, learn what you can about the method of construction (whether it is hand lay-up or chopper gun, and the molding method), the character of the laminate (the number of layers of roving, for example), the laminate thickness, the method of stiffening and reinforcing the hull and deck, and the method of joining the deck to the hull. It is a good idea for the owner of a glass boat to save any sections cut out of the hull or deck, such as those cut out when through-hull fittings or ventilators are installed, in order that laminate thickness and construction can be judged or tested. Tapping with the hammer or even a coin can reveal air pockets or delaminations; sighting along the topsides or bottom of the hull can reveal hardspots (mentioned in Chapter 1) or areas that need stiffening; and of course, applying pressure to certain areas, such as the deck, can reveal over-flexibility. Look for delaminations at any exposed edges, chips in the gel coat, and deep cracks at any sharp bends, especially at hard chines. Most cracks in the gel coat do not penetrate into the laminate, unless perhaps they are concentrated and of a radial type that indicate stress. Fatigue cracks in the gel coat, which are not serious in themselves, might warn of a condition that could later crack the laminate. Look for these cracks around engine beds, under the bows of fast, V-bottom motor boats, or around any hardspot or area that seems comparatively flexible. Such areas might need to be stiffened with structural members reinforced with extra plys of laminate, or otherwise have the stress distributed over a larger area. Other areas subject to great stress, such as at fittings or chainplates, should be strengthened with extra thick laminate in the manner suggested in the last chapter. Through bolts and rivets should be carefully checked wherever possible, especially where the deck joins the hull. Listen for any sounds of ballast shifting in the keel while the boat is rolled. Some stock boats have chunks of ballast sealed, but not always properly bedded and secured, inside a fiberglass keel.

Some surveyors may shine a strong light through the hull when pigmentation in the gel coat or interior finish allows transmission. This method of inspection can be very helpful in detecting areas that are resin-rich (with too much resin) or resin-dry (with too little resin). The former condition may result in crazing of the resin, while the latter condition may result in voids or delaminations. Laminate flaws revealed by light transmission usually show up in the form of irregular, spotty, or stained areas, but they are often difficult to interpret accurately and so should be left to the experienced eye of a competent surveyor. Minor amounts of air bubbles in the laminate and general translucency are usually not considered harmful. In fact, sunlight shining through and visible from the inside of a hull may indicate a healthy laminate rather than one of insufficient thickness, as is often supposed.

With any type of construction, of course, the condition of the fastenings is of the utmost importance, especially on boats of wood or other materials that are comparatively non-monolithic. Fastenings should be carefully inspected wherever possible by tapping them, looking for hairline cracks in paint around their plugs and cracking paint between the frames and planking, by scraping the heads of fastenings to look at their metal, and by looking for corrosion or rust stains. In suspicious areas where fastenings are concealed, wood plugs covering screws should be removed and occasionally, a few fastenings themselves might be taken out for careful examination. Most high-quality boats will have fastenings of a good quality bronze such as Everdur, copper rivets, or in some cases Monel. Be extremely wary of boats put together with uncoated ferrous fastenings or yellow brass screws. Look for erosion or deterioration of the wood surrounding a fastening. Tannic acid from improperly seasoned wood (especially oak) can attack the fastenings and cause subsequent decay in the nearby wood. Test the nuts on major bolts to see that they are not wasted, are tight, and that the threads are not stripped. Washers of ample size should be used. Suspicious looking keel bolts might have to be removed for examination especially when a long, offshore passage is planned. A new method of inspecting keel bolts is with the use of a portable x-ray machine. This method is said to be practical and reasonable in price. An article on this procedure was published in *Rudder* (September, 1969).

## Electrolytic Corrosion

A very important consideration is compatibility of the metal fastenings, hull straps, chainplates, and particularly underwater fittings such as struts, propellers, etc. on boats used on salt water. As mentioned in the last chapter, the use of dissimilar metals can lead to electrolytic corrosion. Boats with metal hulls are especially vulnerable. Figure 13 shows the galvanic series, a scale of metals listed in the order of their electrolytic corrosion resistance. Fastenings and underwater metals should, if possible, be close together on the galvanic scale to minimize corrosion. For instance, copper, bronze, and Monel are close together on the list, but bronze and ferrous metals or bronze and aluminum are far apart, and so the latter combinations may very well cause serious problems in salt water.

Electrolytic corrosion may show up in two related but slightly different forms: galvanic action, and stray current corrosion (commonly referred to as electrolysis). Both of these types of corrosion result when two metals are immersed in, or even subjected to moisture from, an electrolyte solution (sea water) and an electrical current passes from one metal to the other via the solution. However, the principal difference lies in the fact that with galvanic action, a spontaneous, low-tension current is generated by the metallic connection of dissimilar metals in the solution, while with the electrolysis, the current is supplied by an outside source, such as the boat's battery.

Galvanic corrosion may be prevented or minimized as follows: by using high-quality noble metals that are close together in the galvanic series for fastenings or underwater appendages; by isolating or insulating the metals whenever possible so that no current can flow through the metallic contact side of the circuit; by using zinc sacrificial protectors; or by using an impressed cathode control system. The latter method is a means of impressing a small electrical current into the water from a control anode (a positive electrode) which converts the boat's metal appendages into cathodes (negative electrodes) that won't corrode, because current only erodes at the anode. The installation of sacrificial zincs is usually a simpler if somewhat less effective method of controlling galvanic corrosion. In this case, zinc plates, especially designed for the purpose, are secured to any appendages that can corrode, and the zinc, which is almost the least noble metal in the galvanic scale, corrodes instead of the appendage. Of course, the zinc protectors have to be replaced periodically when they deteriorate. Common mistakes in the installation of sacrificial protectors are: using zincs that are too small or insufficient in number, not electrically connecting zincs to the appendages they are to protect, and painting the protectors. Incidentally, great care must be taken to use bottom paints whose metallic contents are compatible with the metals on the boat's bottom. Beware of using mercury antifouling paints especially. Figure 13 shows the simple principle of galvanic action.

Electrolysis results from stray current or cross-grounding. The fundamental principle in avoiding electrolysis is to keep the current inside all wires. If the wires or electrical connections should leak current, or cross grounding should allow a flow of current through the water from a ground plate to an appendage, for instance, then serious corrosion might occur. Particular care should be taken with the installation of radio telephones, when these have their own ground plates, for, if the current is not properly confined in a two-wire system, the flow might run underwater between the radio's plate and the boat's battery ground, which is often by way of the propeller, shaft, and engine. Be sure that a well qualified marine electrician has installed or inspected the radio and the entire wiring system. Another source of serious corrosion, and perhaps serious shock to a swimmer coming in contact with certain underwater metal appendages, is the possibility of cross-grounding with shore current at some marinas. At certain dockside installations, incorrect positioning of the electric plug in its receptacle might cause a current flow from the hot side of the shore line through the boat's ground system, through the water, and back to the shore. One means of avoiding cross-grounding is by using an isolation transformer capable of handling all current needs, or sometimes a polarity indicator that has a warning light or buzzer may be used.

FIGURE 13: PRINCIPLE OF THE GALVANIC CIRCUIT

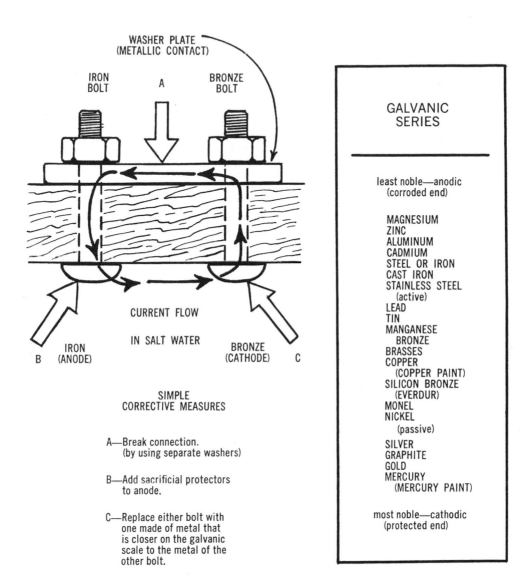

WASHER PLATE
(METALLIC CONTACT)

IRON
BOLT

A

BRONZE
BOLT

CURRENT FLOW

IN SALT WATER

IRON
B    (ANODE)

BRONZE
(CATHODE)    C

SIMPLE
CORRECTIVE MEASURES

A—Break connection.
(by using separate washers)

B—Add sacrificial protectors
to anode.

C—Replace either bolt with
one made of metal that
is closer on the galvanic
scale to the metal of the
other bolt.

GALVANIC
SERIES

least noble—anodic
(corroded end)

MAGNESIUM
ZINC
ALUMINUM
CADMIUM
STEEL OR IRON
CAST IRON
STAINLESS STEEL
(active)
LEAD
TIN
MANGANESE
BRONZE
BRASSES
COPPER
(COPPER PAINT)
SILICON BRONZE
(EVERDUR)
MONEL
NICKEL
(passive)
SILVER
GRAPHITE
GOLD
MERCURY
(MERCURY PAINT)

most noble—cathodic
(protected end)

## Wiring and Piping

Faulty wiring can also result in electrolysis when wiring leaks current as a result of inadequate insulation or wet wires; or in some cases, when the current strays through damp wood. It is a good practice to install very heavy wiring between battery terminals and a radio telephone, including the ground plate wiring, to eliminate electrolysis between the ground plate and propeller caused by voltage drop through the wiring.

Some important points for safe and efficient wiring are: the use of high-grade, standard, copper wire of ample size, protected by an impervious insulating cover, installed high out of the bilge, and secured with insulated clips; the electrical system protected by fuses or circuit breakers installed on the hot (ungrounded) side of the system; terminal connections secured so that they cannot work loose from vibration; a master cut-off switch installed on the ungrounded conductor as close as possible to the battery and accessible outside the engine compartment; and wiring installed so as to cause minimal compass deviation. The storage batteries should be installed in a well-ventilated area, preferably away from the engine and gas tanks, in a well-secured, lead-lined box protected by a non-conductive cover, so that metal objects cannot fall on the terminals and cause sparks or a short circuit. Details for sound wiring are set forth by the National Fire Protection Association (60 Batterymarch Street, Boston, Massachusetts) in the booklet No. 302 entitled *Fire Protection Standards for Motor Craft.* Another good guide is *Safety Standards for Small Craft* published by the ABYC, which was mentioned in the first chapter.

A proper bonding and grounding system not only can help alleviate electrolysis (and radio noise too, incidentally), but also afford protection against fire or damage from static electricity or lightning. More will be said about this in Chapter 4 when we discuss fire prevention and lightning protection.

Properly installed and carefully inspected piping is no less important than proper wiring, because it is obvious that a broken pipe can result in foundering. As mentioned in the last chapter, all through-hull pipes should be fitted with readily accessible valves, and these should be inspected periodically, lubricated, and kept in good operating condition. It is preferable that all shut-off valves be of the seacock type, barrel-plug valves, that operate with lever handles. Many modern boats use plastic hoses instead of metal pipes. Good grade plastic or non-collapsible rubber hoses are resistant to fatigue, which is sometimes caused by engine vibration, but they should be *securely* attached to the through-hull fitting with proper stainless steel hose clamps. Beware of plastic through-hull fittings; some types have been known to break, and hoses can slip off plastic nipples quite easily. Such casualties have resulted in the sinking of several boats.

An important point with low fixtures such as pumps and the head is that the installation should never allow back-syphoning, because in this case a faulty or stuck check valve could allow the boat to flood and possibly sink. To assure against back-syphoning, the discharge hose should be looped and vented as shown in Figure 14. Even if the head bowl is above

## FIGURE 14: SOME PLUMBING SUGGESTIONS

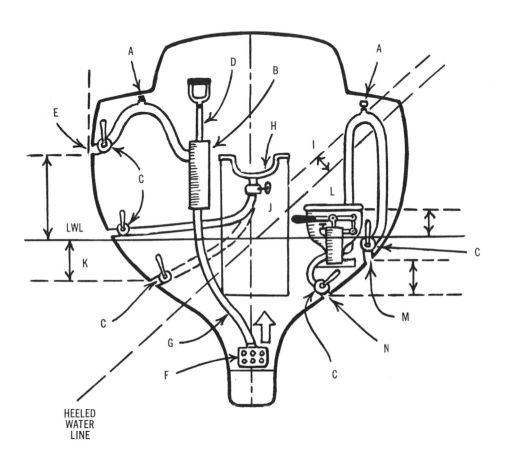

A—anti-syphon vents. B—bilge pump installed in cockpit (not in seat locker). C—plug-type seacocks. D—sturdy, unbendable rod. E—pump discharge as high as possible, but below tumblehome to avoid staining topsides (may be in transom if discharge is not excessively long or crooked). F—strainer attached to end of intake hose. G—hose flexible to allow lifting to clear strainer. H—sink as close as possible to centerline. I—looped lines and sinks above highest normal angle of heel. J—easily accessible shut-off valve if sink is not on the centerline. K—sink discharge above LWL or at least one foot below LWL to avoid freezing. L—head W.C. above LWL. M—head outlet below LWL but abaft and higher than intake N.

the waterline, as it should be, a sailboat's discharge hose should have a high loop to avoid possible back-syphoning at large angles of heel. Beware of weak holding tanks and self-contained chemical toilets, because a recent heavy weather race demonstrated their vulnerability to falling crew or gear and even to flexing hulls. Sinks are usually higher above the waterline, but they can run water into a sailboat when she is heeled; thus they should be located as close as possible to the boat's centerline, and of course, their discharge lines must have a readily accessible shut-off valve. Some of these details are shown in Figure 14. Water tanks should be well secured and baffled to prevent violent sloshing in a seaway. A seagoing boat should have her water supply divided between several tanks in case one tank leaks or the water in it goes bad.

Piping around the engine should be carefully inspected to see that there are no fatigue cracks or leaks from vibration. Metal pipes subject to severe vibration should be fitted with short lengths of hose at connections to tanks, engines, etc. Of course, the propeller shaft should be carefully inspected for correct alignment, because serious vibration and other troubles can result when the shaft and engine are out of line. Copper lines should be connected to the engine with flexible tubing, but where vibration is minimal, a slow bending, circular loop in the line may suffice. If the engine is flexible-mounted to reduce noise or vibration, all connections between the hull and engine must also be fully flexible. A careful inspection should be made around the stern tube (where the shaft penetrates the hull), as this area can be damaged by poor shaft alignment, or possibly by a broken, unbalanced propeller, or by one blade that fails to open on a folding propeller, which will cause violent vibration. It is a wise plan to release the shaft at the engine coupling and pull it out just enough to check for wear or shaft scoring at the bearings. Also, be sure the wheel is securely attached to the shaft.

The exhaust installation should be carefully inspected to see that water, either sea water or condensation, cannot run back into the engine manifold. There should be a condensation trap at the low point in the line, and the exhaust pipe should run uphill from the transom to a high loop or stand-up muffler. As said earlier, the exhaust should be fitted with a seacock as a safeguard against following seas entering the pipe. Actual inspection of the engine itself should be made by a qualified mechanic, who will check the compression, check for worn bearings, valve seatings, and so forth. Obviously, a trial run can tell a great deal. Easy starting, quietness, smoothness and lack of vibration even at high RPMs, ability to idle down, sufficient oil pressure, smoke-free exhaust, etc. are, of course, favorable indications. Proper fuel tank installation, as well as engine room ventilation, will be discussed in Chapter 4 when we deal with fire.

*Steering Gear and Centerboard*

Another important area of boat inspection is that having to do with steering. Cables, sheaves, worm gears, the rudder head fitting, quadrant, etc. should get a careful going over, but even more important is the examination of the rudder. The inspector should look for excessive play or looseness at the pintles and heel; for signs of fatigue at the fastenings of the heel fitting and the bushing; for binding at the rudder stock or jamming in the hard over position; and warping, corrosion, delamination or chafe of the rudder blade. Also the rudder drift bolts, straps, gudgeons on the keel or skeg, and of course the tiller or wheel itself should be examined. One can't be too careful in checking the steering gear, because rudder losses and other steering failures at sea are all too frequent. Centerboard boats need periodical, thorough inspection of the pivot pin, pendant, cable sheaves, and all parts of the lifting mechanism. Look for signs of corrosion, wear, chafe, or fishhooks (wire snags) in the pendant, and see that all parts are well lubricated.

An obviously essential area for meticulous inspection is all parts of the rig, especially when the boat is to venture offshore. This will be discussed in some detail in Chapter 6.

*Equipment*

In equipping a boat for safe operation on any waters, the first consideration should be legal requirements. These are presently set forth in the Motorboat Act, but new regulations are being prepared by the Coast Guard under authorization of the Federal Boat Safety Act of 1971. Legal requirements include such items as life preservers, engine ventilation, backfire flame arrestors for carburetor, fire extinguishers, bells, whistles, and navigation lights (required by the Rules of the Road).

Appendix A contains equipment and standards recommended by the Coast Guard Auxiliary. More comprehensive equipment lists have been compiled by yacht racing organizations. Standard requirements for races are set forth by the North American Yacht Racing Association (NAYRU) in its Offshore Equipment Lists, reproduced in Appendix B. These lists, which are revised and updated periodically, vary in requirements according to how a race is classified as to length and exposure. Although all the equipment and standards suggested by the NAYRU are obviously not required of cruising boats (or racers not racing), the lists form a good basis for equipping any boat.

It is very important to bear in mind that listed equipment requirements are the *minimum* of what should be carried on a vessel. Even lists as comprehensive as the NAYRU's do not include items that many experienced sailors would consider valuable or even essential. In the following paragraphs we will elaborate on some of the more important equipment recommended by the NAYRU, and then we will suggest a few additional items that don't appear on current NAYRU lists.

One of the most important pieces of equipment is the bilge pump. It is surprising to see the number of new boats that have either no permanent bilge pump or a faulty or inadequate installation. Pumps are not merely conveniences. In the event of a collision, grounding, knockdown, broken pipe, working of the hull in a seaway, or related emergencies, a means of clearing the bilge quickly could mean the difference between reaching port or foundering. Pumps should have ample capacity; *at least* seven gallons per minute for small cruisers. Many boats are fitted with small, cheap, plastic pumps of the plunger type, but most of these are unreliable in heavy weather partly because their flimsy plunger rods can easily become broken or bent or their cylinders cracked with rough use. Large-capacity, Navy-type, plunger pumps of brass are generally considered reliable, but even more highly recommended are the diaphragm bilge pumps, such as those made by the Edson Corporation or by the English designer-yachtsman, Michael Henderson (no relation to the author). Small hand pumps of this type can be obtained with double action, meaning that water is pumped when the handle moves in each direction, and their capacity can be more than 20 gallons per minute with a hose of 1.5-inch diameter. Electric pumps are a great convenience, but they are not always dependable, especially in heavy weather or emergency conditions when they are most apt to be needed.

It is not unusual to see a permanent bilge pump's discharge line connected to a cockpit scupper outlet below the water line. This practice could be dangerous, because check valves are not always reliable. A pump's discharge outlet should be as far as possible above the waterline to prevent the possibility of back-syphoning, and on a sailboat that can submerge the outlet while heeling, the line should be looped and vented. Hoses should be of large diameter and non-collapsible, and the intake at the low point in the bilge should be fitted with an *accessible* strainer. It is surprising how often pumps become clogged with chips or dirt that always seem to accumulate in the bilge. Another source of pump clogging is paper labels that peel off canned goods. If cans are kept in or near the bilge, their labels should be removed.

The recommended location for a permanent bilge pump is in or near the cockpit, but not inside a seat locker unless the locker is an integral part of the watertight cockpit. If it is necessary to open the lid of a seat locker that can allow flooding of the bilge when the pump must be used during a knockdown or when decks are awash, then the open locker might admit more water than the pump can remove. It is also a wise plan to have another pump (not necessarily built-in) below in the cabin in case it becomes necessary to pump without going on deck or to supplement the deck pump. Needless to say, a few buckets should be carried for a real bailing emergency. I know of an ocean racer that nearly sank at sea as a result of a broken discharge pipe when the bilge pump clogged and no bucket could be found on board. The crew was forced to bail with a suitcase.

Lifelines and pulpits should be considered essential on any vessel that ever ventures into unprotected waters. Although the latest NAYRU equipment lists and the ABYC standards specify that the top rail or wire of a life line or rail be at least 24 inches above the deck, some experienced seamen feel that the minimum height above deck should be 27 inches. The point is that the upper lifeline should always be considerably higher than knee level, because otherwise the wire or rail would tend to trip a person, and thus it might be more of a hazard than a help.

Details of lifeline installations are given in the NAYRU lists in the appendix. It should be emphasized that stanchions must be through-bolted, and the entire installation should be strong enough to withstand the weight of a heavy man being thrown hard against the assembly. The ABYC suggests that the installation be capable of withstanding a "static" force of approximately 600 pounds. Sailboats often have a special problem where lifelines attach to a bow pulpit, because the foot of a lowcut jib will chafe on the upper lifeline or pulpit rail. The most practical solution to this problem with a minimal sacrifice to safety seems to be the installation of forward stanchions set slightly inboard of the pulpit in order to provide a narrow gateway for the passage of the jib's foot. Racing sailors concerned with the greatest possible aerodynamic efficiency will prefer the low-footed "decksweeper" jibs, but cruising sailors will normally carry a jib with its foot sufficiently high to clear the lifelines, and such a sail will also afford much better visibility for the helmsman and catch less water.

No piece of permanent equipment is more important than an accurate, easy-to-read compass. Of course, the main steering compass should be mounted directly forward of the helmsman on the boat's centerline, at a comfortable reading distance below his eye level, but in a spot that is out of the way as much as possible so that the instrument will not be hit, stepped on, or bumped into. Small cabin sailboats should usually have their compasses mounted behind small windows or domes in the bridge deck or after end of the cabin trunk. Larger sailers with wheel steering will normally have their compasses mounted in binnacles atop a sturdy pedestal just forward of the helm. These pedestals cannot be made too strong, because heavy crew members often grab them for support or are sometimes thrown against them in a seaway. Not long ago it was reported that such a pedestal was torn from the cockpit sole of a well known ocean racer when it became entangled by the mainsheet during an all-standing jibe. A curved pipe rail over the binnacle might be installed so as to afford a convenient hand grip and also to guard against fouling of the mainsheet.

Great care must be taken to place the compass where deviation is minimal. Not only should the placement be away from ferrous metals, but also as far as possible (at least three feet is the rule of thumb) from electronic equipment. Electric wires should be as far as possible from the compass, but where they must be close, the wires should be run in twisted pairs (one lead twisted about the other) in order to help cancel out their magnetic fields. Great care should be taken to keep portable gear that is electrical or of ferrous metal away from the compass. The well-known yacht *Fiddler's Green,* owned by Dr. Edmund B. Kelly, was lost on a lee shore at night, because someone inadvertently put down a photographic light meter too close to the binnacle. Remember that even a beer can placed next to the compass may cause some deviation.

Compass errors from deviation can be minimized by adjustment with correcting magnets. These are often built into the compass and they can be moved with adjusting screws. In most cases, for greatest accuracy, the compass should be corrected by a professional compass adjuster unless the skipper is experienced with such matters. But even though the compass is adjusted by a professional, all errors can seldom be completely eliminated because of the sizeable masses of iron (the engine or keel for example) or electronic gear near the cockpit on most boats. Thus, most craft should carry "deviation cards" to record the compass errors on the various headings. All compasses should be gimballed, but sailboats require special gimballing that allows the card to remain horizontal and swing freely at large angles of heel. Don't use a powerboat compass on a monohull sailboat.

Navigation light requirements are specified in the Rules of the Road under which the vessel operates. International Rule lighting is required on the high seas and this same lighting is permissible on U. S. inland waters. In the interest of simplicity and uniformity it seems highly desirable that boats be equipped with International lighting (except in the rare instance where a state law might prohibit this). Sailboat lights are often obstructed by sails; therefore, it is advisable to carry the optional lights described in Rule 5 (b). This rule allows a vessel under sail to carry, in addition to her normal red and green side lights and stern light, a 20-point red light over a 20-point green light at the masthead, sufficiently separated so as to be clearly distinguished, and visible for two miles. Obviously, in steamer lanes at night, it is also prudent to carry a powerful flashlight that can be shown on the sails when converging with a ship. The owner of a new boat, either sail or power, should be sure his boat's lighting meets legal requirements, because surprisingly, some stock boats are fitted with improper lights.

The NAYRU equipment lists require a marine radio receiver and transmitter of at least 25 watts for sailboats racing long distances in unprotected waters. Having such a means of sending distress signals during a serious emergency is a wise precaution for any vessel going offshore. Radio signals can have a good range, and they are of great assistance to the Coast Guard or other rescue boats or aircraft in conditions of poor visibility. The distress signal, the spoken word "Mayday," or a two-tone warbling alarm is given over the radio-telephone emergency frequency, 2182 kHz (or SOS over the ship-telegraph frequency, 500 kHz). The United States national distress frequency for VHF-FM is channel 16, 156.8 mHz. Until quite recently it was common practice to use the backstay of a sailboat for the antenna, but several dismastings pointed up the fact that when the antenna supporting mast is lost, the radio is put out of action, often at the very time when transmission is most desperately needed. It is now customary to carry a whip antenna that is independent of the rigging. With radio telephones, there is the risk that the vessel's batteries might be low or drowned out during an emergency, thus it is a wise plan to carry at least one but preferably two emergency locator beacons. These are small, lightweight waterproof transmitters that are quite reasonably priced (in the neighborhood of $100 apiece). They operate automatically, sending out warbling distress signals usually on the emergency frequencies of 121.5 mHz and 243 mHz, which are monitored by aircraft and the Coast Guard. Some of these beacons are fitted with high intensity strobe lights to assist in locating victims visually.

So far our equipment discussion has been related mostly to permanent installations, but, of course, portable type safety equipment is no less important. The first consideration of this latter type should be for life saving devices which are required by law. Federal regulations (under the Federal Boat Safety Act of 1971) now require that one U. S. Coast Guard approved life saving device for each person be on board every boat. Of course, this does not preclude the use of any buoyancy or flotation equipment not approved by the Coast Guard so long as the approved equipment is aboard. For instance, there are some good flotation jackets on the market (some are foreign) that are waterproof, light-weight, and non-restrictive to body movement, but which are not approved. Such jackets may not be suitable for real emergencies, but they might be ideal on certain occasions when, for example, it is wet and cold, but visibility is good and the weather does not warrant the wearing of standard, bulky life jackets. There are small, handy but unapproved rescue packs that can be carried in one's pocket and can be inflated instantly with $CO_2$ in an emergency. To qualify for an approved life saving device, a cushion, vest, ring buoy, or life preserver must be in good condition and must bear Coast Guard approval markings, which means that the equipment has been inspected and its construction and performance judged satisfactory.

A few thoughts on life preservers are: Buoyant cushions currently may legally be used on boats under 40 feet long provided they meet certain requirements as to size, construction, and have their buoyancy material (kapok, for instance) sealed inside a vinyl bag. Even though such cushions meet Coast Guard requirements, however, they are inferior for life saving purposes as compared with life preservers that are designed for no other purpose. Nevertheless, cushions are usually handy, and when they are sufficiently long (at least 22 inches with handles at least 20 inches), they can be worn similarly to a life vest by inserting a leg through one handle strap and the opposite arm and shoulder or neck through the other with the cushion covering the chest so that wearer is floated face up (never wear a cushion on your back). Be sure the handles are securely attached. Life preservers must be readily accessible with jackets or vests distributed throughout the boat (accessible from the bow as well as the stern) and with a ring buoy or two near the helmsman. Ring buoys should never be lashed in their holders, nor should they be attached to standing rigging that can make the buoys inaccessible in the event of a dismasting. At night, water lights should be attached to ring buoys and at sea, eight-foot (above the water) man-overboard poles, as described in the NAYRU lists, should be attached to the buoys. Horseshoe-shaped buoys are usually preferable to closed rings, and they should be equipped with whistles, dye markers, and drogues or small sea anchors to lessen drift. In shark-infested waters, repellent is often recommended, but a more modern and effective means of protection is with the use of the Johnson shark screen, a durable black plastic bag, with buoyancy rings, that can be unfolded from a small package to house and hide a man overboard. Water lights should be high-intensity, preferably the Xenon strobe types, and sufficiently bright to be seen in fog or broad daylight. Life jackets or buoyancy belts should always be worn by non-swimmers, by young children, by water skiers, and by adult swimmers in heavy weather or in other potentially hazardous conditions. Life preservers, jackets, and even cushions that will be used for life preservers should be bright yellow or international orange for maximum visibility. Even brilliantly white preservers or life buoys can be difficult to see amidst white horses or breaking seas. All life saving devices that are stowed in

*A canopy will greatly increase the odds for survival in a liferaft in heavy weather at sea, especially in cold waters. Note the boarding ladders on both rubber rafts. (U.S. Coast Guard)*

closed areas should be removed periodically for airing and inspection.

The necessity for life rafts will depend to a large extent on how the boat will be used, on the boat's condition and design, and on the characteristics of her environs. Well-found boats provided with flotation that stay close to shore in protected waters normally will not need a life raft, but sinkable boats that sail at night and venture offshore or sail in foggy waters near rocky shoals or dangerous lee shores obviously should carry a raft (or rafts) capable of taking off the entire crew. Of course, racing sailboats must meet the NAYRU raft requirements (Appendix B). The modern inflatable rubber raft of proper design is considered far more suitable for the purpose of life saving than conventional dinghies or even rubber boats. Non-inflatable life rafts of balsa or other light-weight, rigid materials are satisfactory when they have watertight bottoms and canopies to reduce the hazards of exposure, but they lack the buoyancy of gas-filled rubber rafts, and the deck space they require for stowage makes them impractical for most small craft. Dinghies can serve as lifeboats in some emergencies, such as in the case of an uncontrollable fire in fair weather, but in heavy weather they are subject to serious damage and swamping. On the other hand, inflatable life rafts provide: great resistance to damage (except from the blow of a sharp object), tremendous buoyancy, great resistance to capsizing, easy motion in seas, a large load capacity (yet requiring little space for stowage), and good protection for occupants when equipped with a canopy. Inflatable life rafts should be compartmented with at least two separate air chambers, and they should automatically inflate and eject from their cases. It is important that rafts are periodically inspected by the manufacturer or other competent authority. The NAYRU suggests inspection every three years, but the Cruising Club of America (CCA) recommends that this be done every two years when the boat is used seasonally.

Stowage of inflatable rafts often presents a problem, because they must be instantly available and yet strongly secured and protected against sun, extremely prolonged water soakage, and physical damage. Ordinarily, stowage should be on deck near the cockpit. The CCA suggests that an ocean racing sailboat keep her raft in a well secured pen-box (a square, topless container with low sides as shown in Figure 15) located just forward of the companionway hatch. The bottom of the pen-box should be open and slightly raised off the deck with a slatted grating to support the raft so that water collecting in the box will drain out promptly. Rafts may be covered with a loose white fabric or packed in fiberglass cannisters, but it is not advisable to use an inverted dinghy as a cover. A simple means of securing a raft is with rope lashings that may be cut easily with a knife or released with pelican hooks. A raft inflated on deck can very easily be blown or washed away in heavy weather, so it is recommended that the stowed, deflated raft have its painter well secured to the boat. When at sea, emergency equipment to be packed in the raft will include: a sea anchor, a hand inflating pump, flares, dye marker, a bailer, repair kit, fishing kit, screw type wooden plugs for punctures, perhaps a spare cylinder of $CO_2$ for inflation, a knife, rescue quoit with line, a strobe or flash light, a first aid kit with sunburn lotion, antibiotic, and pain killer in addition to standard items, dye marker, signal mirrors, two paddles, a locator beacon, emergency drinking water, and a few cans of food (pemmican is recommended).

Safety belts are considered essential on a seagoing sailboat, and at certain times, they could be just as valuable on an offshore powerboat. These belts are equipped with stout lanyards and heavy snap hooks, which allow the wearer to attach himself to a handrail, life line, or some part of the rigging so that he is able to work with both hands. In other words, when secured with a proper belt, the crew member can temporarily disregard the old adage, "one hand for the ship and one hand for yourself." It is generally agreed that the best safety belts are the harness type with shoulder straps. Offshore sailors should occasionally practice using these belts in

## FIGURE 15: SAFETY EQUIPMENT

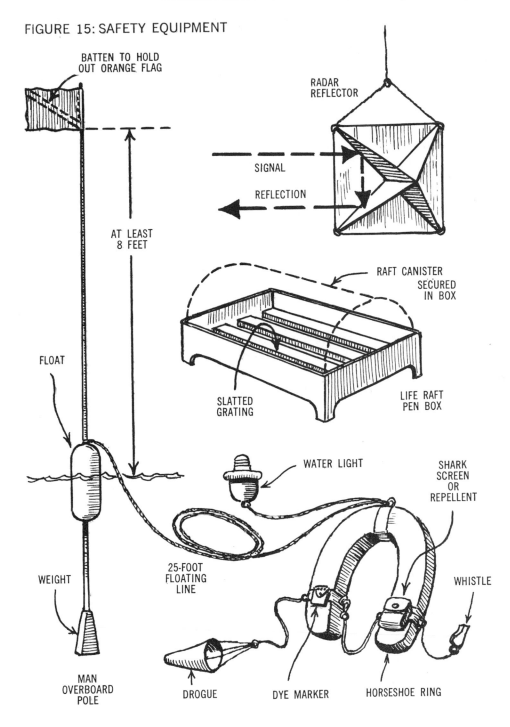

BATTEN TO HOLD
OUT ORANGE FLAG

RADAR
REFLECTOR

SIGNAL

REFLECTION

AT LEAST
8 FEET

RAFT CANISTER
SECURED
IN BOX

FLOAT

SLATTED
GRATING

LIFE RAFT
PEN BOX

WATER LIGHT

SHARK
SCREEN
OR
REPELLENT

WEIGHT

25-FOOT
FLOATING
LINE

WHISTLE

MAN
OVERBOARD
POLE

DROGUE

DYE MARKER

HORSESHOE RING

daylight and fair weather so that their proper use will be instinctive under adverse conditions. A friend of mine, who is a good sailor, hooked his safety belt's lanyard to a shroud while preparing to lower a sail at night. The lanyard was shorter than he realized, and when he moved away from the shroud, the line took up abruptly and jerked him off balance so that he fell to the deck. This kind of accident, which might seem amusing but could be serious, is best avoided with practice and thorough familiarization with the equipment.

A radar reflector hoisted aloft greatly improves the chance that a boat will be spotted by radar-equipped ships in conditions of poor visibility. However, skippers should not be overconfident that they will be seen merely because their vessel carries a reflector. Visual and radar watches are somewhat lax on some merchant ships, and heavy rain, or high swells, or rough seas can hamper or obscure the signal reflected by a boat. Reflectors should be carried at night and in foggy weather, especially in steamer lanes, but even with a reflector, it is the safest policy for the small boat skipper to assume that his reflection is not seen and to give ships a wide berth whenever possible. Radar reflectors are generally most effective: when they are prevented from swinging excessively, when they are hoisted as high as possible, and when they are as large as is practical. Many makeshift reflectors, such as crumpled sheets of aluminum foil are nearly worthless, but homemade reflectors can be effective when made in conformance with standard models. The surfaces should be smooth metal or wire mesh and meet each other at exact right angles to form corners so that if the radar signal is not reflected directly back to its source, it will return indirectly, no matter what the direction of the source, after bouncing from one surface of the reflector to another or others (see Figure 15). Suspending the reflector from two (or possibly three) points, as illustrated, will improve the chances of presenting a corner to the transmitting ship for maximum opportunity of causing a reflection. It has been suggested that offshore sailboats in steamer lanes might improve their visibility on radar screens with large swatches of aluminized tape or cloth sewn into reinforced areas of the sails. To a large extent, however, the effectiveness of such an arrangement would depend on the angle of the sails to the direction of the radar signal. Flat sided metal masts can be helpful in reflecting a signal, but in most cases only when the boat is not heeling.

Another aid to collision avoidance is the use of extremely bright Xenon strobe lights that can be mounted on the masthead or some other high point. These lights can be seen in fog, smoke, or haze, and they are allowed under the Rules of the Road as "flare-up lights" to attract attention.

Distress signals are included in the Rules of the Road (see Appendix C). Equipment needed for International distress signals consists of: a

Very pistol with parachute flares; radio transmitter (already mentioned); International code flags N and C; a square flag of International orange that may be waved from side to side or hoisted over or under a ball; the Canadian "Surface-to-Air" signal, consisting of a four-by-six-foot red-orange cloth with an 18-inch black square and an 18-inch black circle 18 inches apart on the longitudinal axis of the flag; a gun or firecrackers; and a loud, dependable horn. Freon horns are loud but not always dependable, because they may leak gas. It is advisable to carry such a horn with spare cans of freon, but only to supplement a loud mouth horn or hand-pumped, bellows-type, fog horn. Although it is not mentioned in the Rules of the Road, remember that the national ensign flown upside down is a commonly recognized distress signal. Incidentally, a knotted flag is an ancient means of signifying distress.

In addition to having equipment specifically designed for safety purposes, offshore craft should carry essential tools, repair kits, and spare parts. A suitable wrench or a spare tiller in certain emergencies might become as vital to the crew's welfare as the boat's lifelines, for example. Basic tools for a seagoing boat would include: several sizes of screw drivers, including one that could be used with a brace; brace and bits; hand drill with bits; adjustable, non-adjustable, and needle nose pliers; an assortment of wrenches (monkey, Stillson, crescent, end, socket, spark plug, etc.); hammer and hatchet; hacksaw and small wood saw; chisels; marlinespike; crow bar; tin snips; files; sandpaper; a small wood plane; a sheath knife; clamps; vise; a wire cutter; bolt cutter; and a hand clamping tool for installing compression sleeves on wire cables.

Repair kits should include: a complete sewing kit with assorted needles, thread, twine, beeswax, tape, cloth patches, etc. for the purpose of mending sails, whipping lines, and for chafe prevention; an electrical kit with spare batteries, bulbs, fuses, electric tape, copper wire, etc.; a fiberglass kit (resin, catalyst, fiberglass cloth, tape, and roving); engine spare parts kit (gas engine: points, condenser, rotor, water pump seal, impeller with pin, distributor cap, ignition spray, generator belt, fuel pump diaphragm kit, coil, spark plugs, and ample lube oil; diesel engine: two or more injectors, starting motor solenoid, primary fuel pump, fuel filters, injector feed lines, water pump impeller, belts, lube oil, hydraulic clutch fluid and an aerosol can of starting fluid [containing ether], a slight amount of which can be squirted into the air intake to help starting in cold weather); a plumbing kit with spare parts for the head, extra hoses, hose clamps, a syphon hose, gaskets, nipples, packing, and soft, wood, tapered plugs that may be driven into any through-hull fitting's orifice; leak repair kit (caulking cotton, bedding and seam compound, foam rubber, waterproof adhesives including underwater epoxy and thiokol or silicone rubber, cup grease, putty, small sheets of plywood and soft metal); and a rigging repair kit (extra turnbuckles, toggles, clevis pins, cotter pins, sail slides, hanks, grommets, shackles, a coil of flexible wire as long as the longest stay to replace broken rigging, binding wire, wire clamps, chain or metal straps for rigging extensions, and the hand clamping tool mentioned earlier).

Other spares for extended cruising would include: an extra or emergency tiller, an extra rudder head fitting, a spare spreader, spare battens, spare handles for winches, roller reefing, etc., blocks, sail stops, lines of every size, an extra heavy anchor (perhaps a disassembled type for easy stowing), and plenty of extra sails, especially storm sails. Of course the spares should also include an assortment of nuts, bolts, screws, tacks, nails, and miscellaneous boat hardware that has not yet been mentioned, such as: eye bolts, eye straps, extra cleats, extra sheet track slides, tangs, and so forth. On sailboats, ample chafe preventers, such as baggy wrinkle, split rubber hoses, etc. should be carried. Spare parts for the stove might be considered more closely related to convenience than safety, but obviously these should be carried too when it is necessary for the vessel to be self-sufficient for considerable periods of time.

Other safety-related items not mentioned in the present NAYRU equipment lists but which many experienced sailors consider important are: a bosun's chair for making inspections or repairs aloft; a face mask for making underwater inspections or repairs; a barometer; safety nets, especially at the bow to provide extra protection for the crew and prevent sails from washing overboard; a collision mat (to be described in Chapter 4); a sea anchor, useful especially to slow drift when near a lee shore; an easily accessible marine-type fuel line filter, or preferably twin filters, installed in such a way that one can be removed without shutting off the engine; jack wires running from the cockpit to the foredeck for the purpose of allowing a safety belt hook to slide forward or aft without the wearer having to unsnap his hook during transit; a jury rudder or emergency means of steering if the main rudder becomes damaged; weather cloths secured to the life lines aft to help keep water out of the cockpit; a strong dodger to keep water out of the companionway especially when the after end of the cabin house is raked forward; and binoculars for spotting distant channel marks and increasing visibility, especially at night. Although the NAYRU allows the option of either bolt or rigging cutters, heavy duty wire cutters or a hacksaw will probably be the more effective means of cutting through stainless steel rigging.

In this chapter we have not discussed the important matter of first aid supplies, but a thorough coverage of first aid is beyond the scope of this book, and the author is not a doctor. It is strongly recommended that every offshore boat without a doctor on board carry a complete and detailed first aid manual and the medical supplies suggested by the manual. Perhaps the best such book is Dr. Peter F. Eastman's *Advanced First Aid Afloat*, whose author has seagoing, as well as medical, experience. A second highly regarded book is *First Aid Afloat*, written by Paul B. Sheldon, who is also a seaman as well as a doctor. Another good manual is *Handy Medical Guide for Seafarers* by Dr. R. W. Scott, written especially for commercial fishermen.

There is much wisdom in the saying, "Be ready for the worst, and the best will take care of itself." This is a good slogan to keep firmly in mind when preparing for sea.

# 4 / HANDLING EMERGENCIES

The well-known multihull sailor-designer, James Wharram, has written, "Sailing the sea is like playing a continuous game of chess, and the only way to be safe is to be several moves ahead." This simile is particularly apt for a discussion of emergencies afloat, for the odds definitely favor the sailor who anticipates a crisis and plans well in advance how to cope with it. Of course forethought should not only be given to rectification of possible emergencies, but also to preventive measures that will minimize the possibility of their occurrence.

## Capsizing

On small, properly buoyant boats in warm, protected waters, capsizings are seldom dangerous; but in cold, rough waters, offshore or away from help, such an accident might very well be a serious emergency. Obviously, extra precautions to assure against capsizing should be taken when the boat lacks proper flotation, has a known tendency to turn turtle, is in unprotected or cold waters far away from rescuers, is manned by an inexperienced crew, or when visibility is poor. Precautions would include: keeping bilges dry; being very careful not to overload (especially small, open boats); paying careful attention to weight distribution (for example, keeping a heavy crew off the foredeck of a speed boat in steep head seas, or not allowing the stern to squat excessively on small outboard motorboats); shortening sail on capsizable or swampable sailboats; adding flotation (temporarily at least) to any sinkable boat; and adding masthead floats to any craft such as a multihull that can turn turtle. Incidentally, on a sailboat having a non-ballasted centerboard, it may be helpful to stability when reaching or maneuvering in a strong breeze to keep the board about halfway up in order to reduce the length of the heeling arm (see Figure 4), and help avoid tripping on the board. Needless to say, non-swimmers should don life vests or flotation jackets, especially in strong winds or rough seas that could break aboard and fill a boat that lacks a self-draining cockpit.

A brief review of elementary, last-minute actions to avoid capsizing are: to slack sheets on sailboats (offshore multihulls should have automatic sheet releases); to luff up when sailing closehauled, but to bear off when the apparent wind is definitely abaft the beam; to shift all crew weight to the high side; to keep small power craft with open cockpits stern to or bow to dangerous seas, and to slow down in rough seas. It is very important to avoid shipping water or allowing heavy seas to break aboard because of the free surface effect, i.e., the water rushing to leeward and seriously endangering stability. A surprising number of small sailboats are not fitted with reefing gear, but it is highly desirable that there is a handy means of reducing the mainsail with such arrangements as roller reefing, reef points, or lacing lines.

General rules for conduct after capsizing on a small sailboat are as follows: (1) Climb over the windward side and station at least one crew member on the centerboard to prevent the boat from turning turtle. (2) Check the crew to see that none are injured, missing, trapped under the sails, or tangled in a line. (3) Don life jackets if they are not already on. (4) Secure a float such as life preservers or an empty plastic jug to the masthead to help prevent the boat from turning turtle. Some boats with metal masts may have a strong tendency to turn bottom side up when their masts become filled with water and therefore require either permanent or temporary masthead floats. In attaching a temporary float, secure it to the halyard in such a way that it can be pulled down after the boat has been righted. (5) Retrieve any loose gear that may be floating out of the cockpit and lash it to the boat. Locate and secure the bailing bucket and pump. (6) Lower sails, stop them to the booms or deck, and secure the outboard end of the boom to the boat near her centerline. (7) If the boat is drifting towards a lee shore or in rough seas and strong winds try to anchor. (8) Put an extra crew member (if he is available) on the centerboard and have the crew lean back (outboard) while holding onto the rail or a short line attached to the rail in order to right the boat. (9) Climb aboard over the stern or one side while a crew member counterbalances the boat and squat in the center of the cockpit after the boat has been righted. (10) Bail as rapidly as possible with a large bucket until boat is sufficiently empty for the crew members to climb aboard and assist in bailing and general clean up. Under ideal conditions in a very small boat with abundant flotation (suitably placed) when the weather is not too heavy, righting can very often be accomplished quickly without even lowering sails; but on the other hand, in severe weather, in a fairly large boat, the careful righting procedure just listed may not always work. In this case, the capsized victims must simply wait for outside assistance or wait for conditions to moderate to the point where self rescue is possible. An extremely important rule that should be emphasized is to *stay with the boat*. If the boat will float, she will afford support, and the victims will be more easily spotted by rescuers when they are with the boat. Victims are often drowned when tempted to swim for a "nearby" shore.

Overly zealous rescuers in boats under power are sometimes more harmful than helpful. Common mistakes are for the rescue boat to approach the capsized craft too soon, too closely, with too much speed, and from the wrong side. Normally the rescue boat should standby well clear to leeward because a high sided powerboat to windward will drift down on and possibly damage the capsized boat or injure her crew. Unless the skipper of the capsized craft is a novice, is incapacitated, or asks for instructions, he should be in charge of the operation and give instructions to the rescue boat. If any crew member in the water is injured, fatigued, or seriously chilled, he must be rescued immediately, and possibly this could justify a downwind approach. Ordinarily, however, when there is no immediate urgency, the capsized boat should be approached cautiously from leeward, well to the side of any floating gear or lines, with the rescue boat's bow angled to the wind. A line can be thrown to the capsized crew and the rescue boat can be held or even pulled to windward when she is a small boat or the capsize victims can be pulled to the rescue craft. At this point, the rescuer must see to it that his propeller is not turning (so those in the water will not be cut) by putting the gear in neutral or perhaps by cutting power. Care should be taken to keep crew members away from the prop and from where they could be crushed between the boats. The rescue crew should fend off and be careful not to damage the sails or mast of the capsized boat, and it is very important to see that floating lines do not foul the prop. Although it is usually better to approach a capsized boat from leeward, an individual man in the water should nearly always be approached from the windward side. The specific problem of rescuing a man overboard will be discussed later in this chapter.

If all the crew of the capsized craft are fit, and the situation is well in hand, then it is usually best that the righting take place before the rescue boat comes alongside. After the capsized boat is upright, she can be partially cleared of water by lifting her bow from aboard the rescue craft to let water flow out of the cockpit and over her stern. Further clearing can be done with buckets or pumps, of course, or the swamped boat can be gently towed a short distance which will make the water rush aft and flow over her transom or through transom bailers if she has them. A boat should never be towed in the capsized position, as this will almost certainly cause damage. Unless there is a substantial bitt on the bow of the capsized boat, the towline should be made fast around her mast and led through a chock near her stem. At least one person should remain aboard the towed boat to steer her.

The most difficult boat to right is the multihull that has turned turtle. Due to her extreme beam and the fact that she normally lacks ballast, a multihull usually has far greater stability upside down than right side up. When outside assistance is available, the righting problem is often solved with a tow boat pulling laterally, at right angles to the multihull's longitudinal axis. The tow line is attached to the rail of the further hull, the line is run over the bottoms of the upside-down hulls, and then, of course, it is made fast to the stern bitt or cleat on the centerline of the tow boat. When the towing operation begins, the hulls will start to move sidewise, but the mast and sails, sticking downward in the water, will resist the movement. The rig's resistance, combined with the pull on the far hull will create a powerful turning moment that should soon right the boat. The tow boat's pull may be most effective if a stationary gin pole can be used to raise the tow line as shown in Figure 16. If the multihull and her rig simply move sidewise without turning right side up, an anchor might be dropped and its line made fast to the outboard rail of the near hull. The operation is illustrated in Figure 16. Towing should be done slowly, and it may be necessary to put some crew weight on (or flood) the near hull during the initial stages of the operation.

The real difficulty in righting an upside-down multihull comes when it is necessary to self-rescue. In fact, righting may be impossible without outside assistance unless the boat has special provisions for flooding and pumping her hulls. As said previously, it is sound practice for an offshore multihull to be fitted with a permanent masthead float to lessen the likelihood of turning turtle. However, it is a fact that a great many boats that sail in unsheltered waters and can turn bottomside up do not carry masthead floats, and furthermore such flotation can break off. This happened to the catamaran, *Apache Sundancer*, when she capsized in the 1970 "Round Britain" Race. Figure 17 shows a possible solution for righting an upside-down multihull. Notice that the system requires specially installed hoses, valves, and a sizeable pump. For such a system to be effective, it is important for the boat to have at least some positive stability (tendency to right) at a 90-degree angle of heel. Positive stability for most multihulls ends (begins to become negative) between the heeling angles of 80 and 105 degrees approximately, with the lower angles generally applying to unballasted catamarans. Obviously, any shifting of ballast or heavy gear during a capsizing could seriously hamper a righting operation. It is extremely important that all boats, multihulls especially, have their ballast and heavy equipment secured to withstand a 180-degree turnover.

An explanation of the self-rescue system shown in Figure 17 is as follows: After the multihull turns bottomside up, Valve A is opened in order to flood Hull 1. Then Plug B is pulled from the end of the vent line leading from that hull, because water will not fill it unless the air is allowed to escape. The flooding of Hull 1 will cause it to sink and the boat to turn on its side so that the mast is approximately horizontal and on or close to the water's surface. This position of the boat will allow accessibility to a life raft or float which may be hauled with a halyard or floated to the masthead to protect against turning turtle again. The next step is to convert the air vent line into an intake hose for the powerful hand pump secured to the side of the deck house. This is accomplished by shutting Valve C, which may be reached through a hatch in the deck of Hull 2. Of course, the hose which allowed the flooding of Hull 1 now becomes a vent pipe to let air into the hull as the water is pumped out. As the hull is pumped clear of water, the boat with positive stability to at least a ninety-degree angle of heel should right herself, though it might be necessary to put some crew weight on the keel or centerboard of Hull 2. Also, sails should be lowered. If the hulls are made of wood and do not have enough weight of equipment to sink when flooded, then just enough ballast should be secured in the bilges to permit sinking after flooding. However, to assure that the entire boat will not sink, it is a wise plan to add a sufficient amount of flotation amidships (in the main hull of a trimaran or in the wing deck and deck house of a catamaran) to counteract the added ballast. Of course, it is very improbable that the righting could be accomplished during a storm. The crew must try to hang on to the multihull's bottom and survive until the wind and seas abate. If the boat is fitted with a permanent masthead float that prevents her from turning turtle, additional temporary flotation such as a rubber raft should be attached to the masthead immediately after capsizing as a precaution against the permanent float breaking off, which is a distinct possibility in rough seas.

*Running Aground*

Along with capsizings, groundings are probably the most commonly encountered type of emergency. Running aground in sheltered waters on a soft bottom at a slow speed is seldom a serious accident, but grounding on rock, coral, or even hard sand or shell at any speed or on soft bottom at high speed can be very serious, especially in rough water or ground swells. Because of their comparatively deep draft, sailboats are subject to ground-

FIGURE 16: RIGHTING A CAPSIZED MULTIHULL

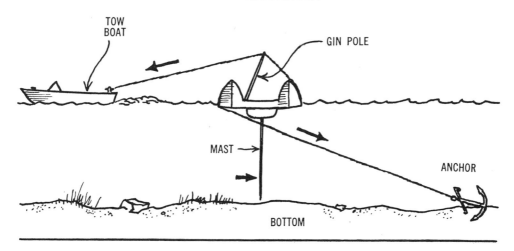

FIGURE 17: MULTIHULL SELF-RESCUE PRINCIPLE

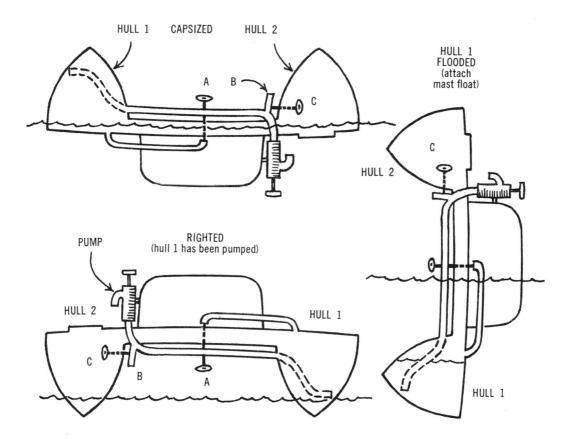

ing more often than power craft, but the latter are more often vulnerable to rudder or propeller damage when contact with the bottom is made. Needless to say, such accidents are best avoided by paying close attention to navigation. Not only must buoys and channel markers be respected, but charts should be carefully studied, even in "familiar" waters, and in most localities it is important to observe the state of the tide and consult the tide tables.

As with any emergency afloat, rules cannot be given to cover every situation, but some general suggestions for action after grounding follow.

When under sail, try to come about at once. If the helmsman reacts instantly when he first feels contact with the bottom, he may be able to tack with the help of a backed jib. Tacking will usually head the boat towards deeper water and permit heeling, which will decrease draft and allow the boat, in most cases, to be blown away from the shoal. If the boat cannot be tacked immediately, lower all sail promptly. One of the commonest mistakes in a sailboat grounding is failure to lower sail at once when the boat cannot be headed for deeper water. When sail is left hoisted, the boat is generally driven further and further ashore.

When sail is lowered or if the boat was run aground under power, try backing off following a reciprocal course backwards under power or by kedging with an anchor when the boat has no engine. Kedging requires setting an anchor far astern (or ahead when trying to move forward) and then pulling the boat towards it. Backing by any means, however, should usually not be attempted unless the rudder and propeller are free. When the keel has considerable drag (is deep aft), it will pay to put crew weight on the bow. Of course, every skipper should be thoroughly familiar with the underwater shape of his boat. If the boat does not back off immediately, study charts and/or sound from the dinghy or dive under water with a face mask to determine exactly where the deep water is and what is the best direction for the boat to be headed so that she can be most easily freed. While this study is being made, it may be necessary to anchor in order that the boat not be driven harder aground. If the grounding was on rocks or a hard bottom, inspect for damage. Think twice about getting free if the hull is holed, because the boat might sink into deep water after she is extricated. When the boat is lodged in a soft bottom she might be pivoted so that she can be pulled off in the direction of least resistance toward the closest deep water. In the absence of a tow boat, the grounded vessel will probably be pivoted most easily by kedging off the bow (or stern in some instances) with an anchor layed out abeam. Anchors may be carried out in the dinghy, raft, or by wading in some cases.

Heeling the grounded boat is advantageous for two reasons. First, it is obvious that draft will be greatest when the keel is vertical, but the second reason, not so obvious, is that the hull lifts slightly when it is heeled. This is explained in Figure 18. If we assume that in the fore-and-aft view of a heeled hull the heeled waterline passes through the intersection of the centerline and the upright load waterline, then it can be seen that the immersed area, called the "in wedge," exceeds the volume of the emersed area, the "out wedge." In actuality, however, if there is no change in the boat's displacement, there must be equality between the in and out wedges; therefore the boat lifts or "rolls out" to create this equality.

Heeling may be done with sails when the boat is positioned in such a way that she will blow away from, rather than towards, the shoal, or booms with weights at their ends might be swung out abeam to produce moderate heel. A dinghy filled with ballast, heavy gear, or even water, hoisted to the end of the main boom with a tackle or the main sheet can be effective. Of course, the dinghy might also be lifted by securing it to the boom end and then topping up the boom. For extreme heeling or careening it is usually necessary to set out abeam a large, heavy anchor to which a masthead halyard is attached for the purpose of hauling the masthead down towards the anchor. Be careful about using the main halyard for this purpose, because it is usually not designed to take a lateral strain and the halyard could become jammed or break its sheave. If the anchor cannot be made to hold due to the upward strain, very shoal water might permit the use of mooring pickets. These are twisted metal rods, illustrated in Figure 19, that may be screwed into a soft bottom. Perhaps an anchor and a picket (or another anchor) spread far apart may be used as shown in the illustration. If the boat is heeling toward the shoal, it may very well be necessary to set out, in the direction away from the shoal, another anchor that will oppose the pull of the careening anchor or pickets in order to prevent the boat from being pulled further aground after her keel breaks free. This is also illustrated in the diagram. Notice that the anchors are not set directly abeam but they lead somewhat forward of the beam so that the boat can be pulled ahead. Of course, the forward pulling force is supplied by the kedge, a towboat, or perhaps by the grounded vessel's own power. As the vessel is moved ahead, slack must be taken in on the careening halyard and opposing anchor line, and then anchors will have to be reset further ahead if she is still not off.

When the boat is grounded in calm water on a soft mud or clay bottom, very often she is held fast by the suction of her embedded keel. Frequently, this suction can be broken by rolling the boat. She might be sallied (rolled from side to side by shifting crew weight), or perhaps a rescue boat could be persuaded to power back and forth nearby to create waves.

If the grounded vessel is towed off, care must be taken to see that securing bitts or cleats are substantial and securely bolted. Some authorities recommend jerking the grounded vessel free with the tow boat taking a slight running start. This method can be effective, but it can also be *extremely dangerous*. Towlines are often springy or somewhat elastic, especially those of nylon, and if they break under great strain, they can whiplash and seriously injure a man. In one case, a man was killed when the heavy towline cleat pulled off the deck and was catapulted by the springy line against the man's head. Everyone should stand well clear of a line under severe strain. It is usually safer to secure a towline around the base of a mast, but the lead chocks must be well fastened. In some cases it may be advisable to secure the towline to a bridle which passes entirely around the hull. Before being towed off, be sure to check the vessel's bilges to see that she is not badly holed. If she is impaled on a sharp rock or coral, planking might be ripped off the bottom, and of course, if she is badly holed she might sink into deep water when she is pulled free. Obviously, there should be a clear understanding of exactly how the towing operation will be carried out by those on both the towed and the towing boats. It is often preferable that both ends of the towline are secured with turns around the bitt or cleat in order that the line can be eased out or cast off at any given moment from either end.

With a vessel grounded on sand (or other bottoms of loose consistency) care must be taken, when she uses her own power, to see that quantities of sediment are not sucked into the engine's water intake. Then too, when the boat is heeled down, be sure that the intake is submerged or the engine will overheat. Of course it is also important to see that the propeller is free to avoid damaging the blades.

Centerboard boats may enjoy a great advantage in avoiding running hard aground since the board hitting bottom provides a forceful, automatic warning, but it is often risky to sail in shoal waters with the board fully down, because, in this position, it can be damaged or perhaps bent during a hard grounding when the boat is heeled. Dagger boards are, of course, far more susceptible to this kind of damage than are pivoted boards. In my opinion, it is generally the safest policy to sail with the board partly housed when there is any possibility of grounding. This is especially true with most metal or high-aspect-ratio centerboards.

Obviously, tide is a very important consideration when a vessel is grounded. In many cases it may pay to wait until the water rises before attempting to free her unless the grounding took place at the very highest tide. In areas of extreme tides an important factor to consider is whether or not a keel boat will fall over on her side when the water recedes. Unless she can be shored up securely, it is usually best to let the boat heel progressively further as the tide drops until she rests on the turn of her bilge.

FIGURE 18: RISE OF HULL & DRAFT WHEN HEELED

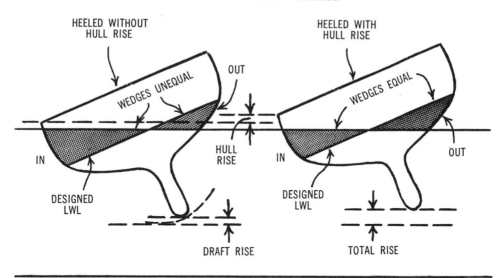

HEELED WITHOUT HULL RISE

HEELED WITH HULL RISE

WEDGES UNEQUAL

WEDGES EQUAL

OUT

IN

IN

OUT

DESIGNED LWL

DESIGNED LWL

HULL RISE

DRAFT RISE

TOTAL RISE

FIGURE 19: KEDGING OFF

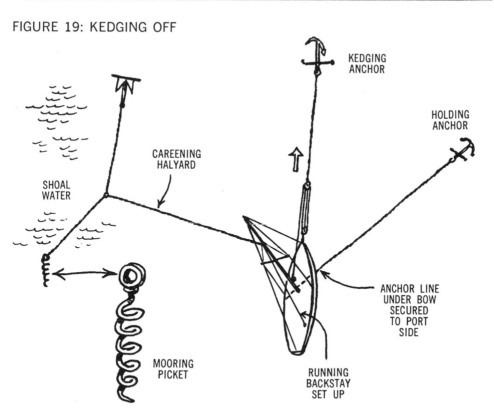

SHOAL WATER

CAREENING HALYARD

KEDGING ANCHOR

HOLDING ANCHOR

MOORING PICKET

RUNNING BACKSTAY SET UP

ANCHOR LINE UNDER BOW SECURED TO PORT SIDE

*Coast Guard statistics show that most accidents and personal injuries result from collisions—with failure to keep a forward lookout being the major cause.*

Padding in the form of cushions, coils of rope, and fenders under the bilge can afford protection against a hard bottom. If the boat is induced to remain upright, balanced on her keel, she could fall over and be seriously damaged. In some cases, however, the boat might be properly shored up, or a masthead halyard might be attached to an anchor, picket, or even a tree on a nearby shore to hold her upright.

## Collisions

With today's waterways becoming increasingly crowded, collisions are becoming one of the most frequent forms of marine accidents. Then, too, small boat collisions are becoming more serious in the extent of damage and personal injury, because powerboats are becoming faster, and they are being operated by an increasing number of novices. The two principal causes of collisions are: failure to keep a lookout; and failure to obey the Rules of the Road. The importance of keeping a good lookout cannot be overemphasized. The latter is the greatest single cause according to the

*With the increasing traffic on today's waterways, it is vital that we have clearly written and uniform Rules of the Road that can be understood by all boatmen. (Lee Troutner)*

U.S. Coast Guard. Rules of the Road are seldom disobeyed deliberately but usually through ignorance. It is becoming more and more apparent that a shockingly large number of boat operators are not thoroughly familiar with the Rules of the Road. In many areas of this country, mere children without full knowledge of the Rules or skill and judgment in boat handling are careening about at lethal speeds in high-powered motorboats. Furthermore, many motor manufacturers seem to be bent on increasing the horsepower of their products. Few sailors want legislation enacted that would require the licensing of boat operators, but unless the collision rate decreases and novice boatmen are made aware of their responsibilities as operators, we may soon see the day when licenses are mandatory for boat operators just as they are for automobile drivers.

Lack of knowledge of the Rules is not always due to irresponsibility or apathy on the part of operators, for, in many instances, boatmen are simply confused by the Rules. This is largely due to the fact that currently there are so many different sets of Rules in use. United States waters are governed by three separate sets of Rules (Western Rivers, Great Lakes, and the Inland Rules), while racing sailboats use a different set, the Yacht Racing Rules of the International Yacht Racing Union, as adopted by the North American Yacht Racing Union (commonly called the NAYRU Rules). Then, of course, there are the International Rules of the Road for use on the high seas. In a very general way, the various Rules agree, but on certain specific points there are differences.

A point that frequently leads to confusion is the one involving the right of way between two sailboats on different points of sailing. Under the International Rules and the NAYRU Rules, a sailboat on the starboard tack running free has the right of way over a port-tack boat that is close-hauled, but under the Inland Rules, the close-hauled boat has the right of way over the boat running free regardless of which tack the boats are on.

A common misconception is that sailboats always have the right of way over power craft. Of course this is not so, for a sailboat has no right of way when she overtakes a powerboat, she is not allowed to hamper a large vessel under power in a narrow channel, and she must keep clear of vessels fishing. The latter point, by the way, is a real source of confusion. Although the International Rules briefly define "engaged in fishing" as fishing with nets, lines, or trawls, but not fishing with trolling lines, the Inland Rules simply say that sailing vessels underway shall keep out of the way of boats fishing with nets, lines, or trawls, and there is no further definition of the term fishing. It seems that in the Coast Guard's opinion, the intent of both Rules in regard to fishing vessels is the same, but the Coast Guard also feels the differences in wording are unfortunate, and the converging of a sailing and trolling vessel on Inland waters might lead to a right of way problem that could only be resolved in court.

Since 1964, an effort has been made to consolidate the three United States Rules of the Road into one uniform set that would basically agree with the International Rules. In fact, there was recently a bill before Congress "to unify and consolidate" the rules under a version known as the "United States Nautical Rules." Such a set of uniform rules should be a great help in clearing up some of the right-of-way confusion, but when such rules will become effective is anyone's guess. This bill has now been shelved temporarily until after an international conference on the Rules of the Road to be held in London in late 1972, and changes to the Rules, of course, must be ratified by the nations using them; thus it may be quite a few years before uniform rules become effective. Until then, it certainly seems advisable to give way on any point of ambiguity. In regards to the trolling-vs.-sailing-boat dilemma on Inland waters, it is prudent for the sailboat to keep clear of a trolling boat and vice versa. When the latter has the fishing signal displayed, i.e. a basket in the daytime, the sailboat is obliged to honor the signal and keep clear. Fishing boats, however, must never obstruct a fairway.

Another source of confusion in most densely populated boating areas is the use of whistle signals. Of course the various Rules of the Road specify these signals, and they can be very necessary in converging situations to signify intent or agreement. The fact is, however, that most small boat operators seldom use sound signals, and some boatmen never carry the horn where it is available for instant use, usually close to the helm. Of course the horn should be readily available and whistle signals should always be answered, but there are some good arguments for using restraint in initiating whistle signals in certain situations. Take the case of a popular, narrow fairway which, on a typical Sunday in midsummer, is crowded with every variety of small craft coming and going. If all the boats were to blow their horns at the same time, the result might be chaotic. Furthermore, it is unfortunate but true that many novices might become confused and make an unpredictable and possibly dangerous change of course. This problem was discussed by Jim Martenhoff in an interesting article, "What's Wrong with Whistle Signals," appearing in *Rudder* magazine (January 1969). According to the author, even Coast Guard vessels at certain times decline to initiate whistle signals to small boats for fear of causing confusion. A common sense approach to the problem seems to be to refrain from sounding the horn every time another boat heaves into view, and to limit use of whistle signals to: responding to another boat that has initiated signals; occasions when it seems advisable to let another boat know your intentions; occasions when another boat's intentions are not obvious or are questionable; and of course, any situation where there is a definite risk of collision. The dilemma is that care must be taken not to let failure to sound the proper signal contribute to causing a collision. An invaluable principle is: when approaching another craft, it is advisable, whenever possible, to alter course early so that your intentions will be clear even without sound signals long before you come close to the other vessel.

In recent years, a surprising number of small craft have been run down or nearly run down by steamers in certain areas where ship traffic is concentrated, such as in the English Channel. The reason for this is often the overconfidence of boat operators that they can be seen and easily avoided by large ships. During many close calls and sometimes when collisions occur, the small boat involved is not seen at all, or else she is seen too late for evasive action by the large vessel. Remember that large ships moving at high speeds are very slow to turn or slow down. The boatman should bear in mind that small craft are often hard to see from ships even in fair weather, that lookouts and radar watches are sometimes lax on

merchantmen, (especially, perhaps, on automated ships that carry a reduced crew), that small craft navigation lights are difficult to see (or impossible to see when blocked by sails), and that radar signals, even those
returned by a lofty radar reflector, are often difficult to see or interpret
in heavy weather. It is always the safest policy for the boatman to assume
that he is not seen by a larger vessel and keep well clear. At night or
when visibility is poor, it is important to keep the radar reflector hoisted;
and a loud horn, bright spot light, and flares should be readily available
to the helmsman. Converging steamers should be checked constantly with
bearings and their courses estimated by noting the position of range and
other navigation lights. When close to a ship at night it is a wise plan
to shine repeatedly a powerful light on one's sails (or deck house on a
power boat) and also to aim the light beam directly, but briefly, at the
ship's bridge deck and pilot house windows.

Another reason for keeping well clear of a large ship is to avoid close
contact with the wave system of her wake. Even when a boat is so far
from a ship that there is little concern over the possibility of collision, the
wave' train of a large vessel moving at high speed can combine with the
wind waves to produce steep and perhaps dangerous seas. The Tumlare-
type, double-ended sloop *Cohoe* was pooped in 1950 by a sea which, in the
opinion of her skipper, Adlard Coles, was made to break aboard by the
wash of a passing ocean liner. Recently, a man was washed overboard
(but later was recovered) from the deck of the schooner *America* (replica
of the famous *America*) when she nosed into the wash of a large passenger
ship making eighteen knots during a moderately calm day on the Chesa-
peake Bay.

Small craft often collide with each other or heavy flotsam such as
floating timber through negligence in keeping a constant lookout. Motorboat operators must be sure that they have good visibility over the bow at
planing speeds (see Chapter 1), and there must be at least two people
aboard a boat towing water skiers so that the helmsman is free to look
ahead continually. On sailboats there is often a problem of good visibility
over a high cabin top. In my opinion, it is not sufficient that the helmsman
merely has clear visibility forward when he is standing; his seat should be
sufficiently high so that his view is unobstructed when he is sitting.
Low-cut sails present a serious obstruction to the helmsman, especially the
deck-sweeping Genoa jibs seen on most modern racing boats. Some of
these sails have plastic windows, but these can seldom be made large
enough to eliminate dangerous blind spots. I would like to see racing
organizations ban decksweepers, because their slightly superior aerodynamic efficiency hardly seems worth the risk of collision. A jib cut a foot
or more above the deck can make a world of difference to good visibility,
and this can have a great bearing on safe sailing in crowded waters.

*Emergency Repairs*

It is highly advisable for any skipper taking his boat offshore or away from readily available assistance and repair facilities to put considerable thought on the subject of emergency repairs. For maximum self-sufficiency, the vessel should be well equipped with tools, spare parts, and repair kits. These were discussed in Chapter 3. Some of the more common accidents that require emergency repairs are: rigging failures, hull damage that results in serious leaks, and rudder or steering gear failure.

Perhaps the most frequent failures offshore occur in the rigging of sailboats. The principle cause of rig failure is from breakage due to flaws, fatigue stress, or wear of metal linkage fittings. The reasons for such failures, as well as other aspects of rigging, will be discussed in Chapter 6. The discussion here will deal with emergency action and repair after the damage occurs.

The importance of continuous rigging inspections, especially at sea, cannot be overemphasized, because the failure of a single linkage fitting could allow the whole rig to go by the board. A watchful eye should be kept open for: worn threads on screw fittings; hairline cracks in turnbuckles, toggles, or swaged end terminals; loose locknuts; missing or worn cotter pins; broken strands on standing rigging; and any bent or worn fitting that helps support the mast. Of course any fitting that shows signs of weakness should be replaced or reinforced at once.

When a rigging weakness is spotted on one side or at one end of the vessel, she should immediately be put on the tack or point of sailing that minimizes stress on the weakened area until repairs can be made. For instance, if a crack appears in a starboard shroud turnbuckle, the vessel should be put on the port tack. Spares may not always be available, so improvisions may be necessary. Quite often a weak fitting can be reinforced with shackles or a short length of chain and shackles, or a stay with a broken strand may be strengthened by clamping a short length of wire beside the stay's weak area with clamps or compression sleeves installed with a hand clamping tool, such as a Nico press (see Chapter 3). Beware of using small screw shackles, however, because they are weak at the threads, and if cotter keys are used with shackles, be sure that the keys as well as the shackles are strong. Don't use compression sleeves on wire rope that has a hollow or crushable fiber core.

If a headstay or forestay should break, it is important to head off onto a dead run immediately to make the wind pressure act in a forward direction. If a headsail is still standing, delay lowering it until one or more halyards can be secured to the stem head, bowsprit, or bitts or windlass (if far enough forward) in order that the mast can be held forward. To direct as much pull forward as possible, it is advantageous to rig both ends of a halyard forward (as shown in Figure 20), and then lead the hauling part aft to the halyard's winch mounted on the mast. If a backstay breaks, the boat should be luffed up head to wind while the mainsheet is strapped in tight to hold the mast back. It is usually a good idea to start the engine to hold the boat into the wind. When the boat is equipped with runners, these should be set up tight, of course. The mainsail may be lowered if there is a stout topping lift which the mainsheet can pull against to exert a force aft. Later the main halyard can be shackled to the end of the boom to reinforce the topping lift (see Figure 20).

When a windward spreader or shroud breaks while the boat is heeled to a fresh breeze, it is very doubtful that the mast can be saved, but this might be possible if the helmsman can tack immediately. It is prudent to develop the seamanlike habit of glancing at the leeward rigging and spreaders immediately before tacking to see that the shrouds or fittings are not hanging loosely. As said in Chapter 3, a spare of the longest stay should be carried on an extensive passage offshore. This spare should be flexible 7 x 19 or 7 x 7 wire, so that it may be cut to any required length and eyes can be formed easily with clamps or sleeves to replace any broken shroud or stay. In the event that the entire stay or shroud cannot be replaced, however, a short piece of wire rope can be clamped beside the break, provided there are sufficient clamps or compression sleeves (perhaps two or three) on both sides of the break. Broken spreaders may be fished together with splints and binding wire if there are no spares. Quite often the sea will be too rough to allow working aloft. In this case, a boom or spinnaker pole may be used temporarily as a long spreader close to the deck (see Figure 20). It really doesn't matter, from the standpoint of mast support, whether the spreader is short and high or long and low, if the angle between the mast and shroud remains about the same. The long spreader should be secured with guys so that it doesn't swing forward or aft, and, if possible, the inboard end of the pole should be secured against the mast (not merely hooked to the spinnaker pole track, which might be pushed off the mast by the strong lateral force). The outboard end of the pole should be securely lashed to the shroud and the inboard end will have to be somewhat higher than the outboard end, so that the angles between the pole and shroud above and below the pole are equalized. Of course, the shroud will have to be lengthened to accommodate the long spreader. This might be done with a short length of chain as shown in Figure 20.

Unfortunately, dismastings are not uncommon. Although such accidents are usually frightening, they are seldom extremely dangerous. Crew members are seldom injured, because the rig normally falls overboard to leeward. Of course, the first action to take after a dismasting is to be sure

FIGURE 20: JURY RIGGING

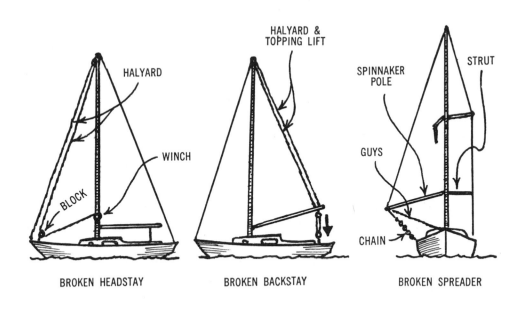

HALYARD

WINCH

BLOCK

BROKEN HEADSTAY

HALYARD & TOPPING LIFT

BROKEN BACKSTAY

SPINNAKER POLE

STRUT

GUYS

CHAIN

BROKEN SPREADER

FIGURE 21: RIG RECOVERY

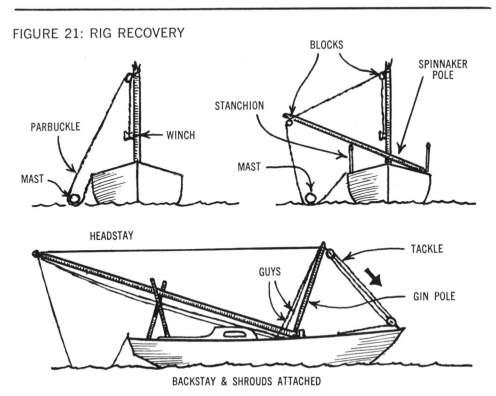

PARBUCKLE

WINCH

MAST

BLOCKS

SPINNAKER POLE

STANCHION

MAST

HEADSTAY

TACKLE

GUYS

GIN POLE

BACKSTAY & SHROUDS ATTACHED

that no one is injured or pinned under the fallen rig. Then the mast must be brought on board before it can puncture or otherwise damage the hull. If the mast cannot be lifted aboard and heavy seas are causing it to pound against the hull, the spar should be cut away before the boat is holed. A metal mast cut loose will generally sink, but it may be possible to tow one of wood on a very long line so that the spar cannot be thrown against the hull by the sea. Spars are most easily cut loose with heavy wire cutters, or even a hacksaw. An acquaintance of Jean Gau told me that after the *Atom* was dismasted off the coast of South Africa in February 1966, singlehander Gau lost his wire cutters overboard, but was able to cut away the masts with a hacksaw blade held between his fingers. It is usually easier to cut through bronze turnbuckles than stainless steel rigging. Bolt cutters will not cut cleanly but will merely crush heavy 1 x 19 stainless steel wire, but some fittings such as pins or open-barrel turnbuckles might be broken with heavy bolt cutters. In many cases, of course, it will be easiest to remove the rigging pins. Bringing the broken mast aboard will be quite a chore, but using parbuckles fore and aft on the spar will facilitate the lifting operation. A parbuckle (rope lifting sling) is rigged by attaching one end of a line to the rail, passing the line under the spar, and bringing it back to the rail where it may be hauled on to raise the spar (see Figure 21). The hauling end of the line might be led through a block attached as high as possible on the stump of the broken mast, or to another mast on a two-master, to facilitate lifting (see Figure 21). If friction of the mast against the hull prevents hoisting, then perhaps the parbuckle might be led outboard through a block at the end of a pole or boom suspended over the lifelines as shown in the illustration.

After a dismasting, help may be summoned with distress signals, usually with flares or a radio (if the antenna was not a part of the rigging), or the victims will have to proceed under power or devise a jury rig. When the weather moderates, the broken spar on deck (or the towed spar) may have to be used for a jury mast. It might be possible to lash the broken spar to the stump of the mast which still remains stepped and in the vertical position, but more than likely a short stump will have to be unstepped and the longest section of the fallen mast will have to be stepped. This will require squaring off a ragged break and shortening the stays. Of course when the break occurs far aloft, it is often only necessary to remove the broken top or lash it securely to the standing part of the mast. In some cases, however, stays and shrouds will have to be attached to the mast just below the break. Even with only a short section of spar standing, a surprisingly efficient jury sail plan can sometimes be improvised. Very often small heavy weather sails can be used on the shortened spars, or even large sails can be hoisted by their tacks or clews in lieu of their heads.

*A 35-foot Ohlson yawl successfully jury-rigged with only a mizzen mast.*

There is usually no problem in securing new fittings to a wooden jury mast, but fastening to an aluminum spar may be a little more difficult. The simplest means will probably be the use of stainless steel self-tapping screws.

Raising a jury mast requires some ingenuity and reasonably calm weather. A tall mast section is often stepped most easily with the use of a gin pole as illustrated in Figure 21. A strong halyard or stay from the masthead is attached to the top of the gin pole on its after side, while a tackle used for hauling the mast up is attached to the top, forward side of the gin pole. Shrouds and guys must be rigged to prevent the pole and mast from swinging and falling over to one side. Strong heel ropes must be used to keep the heel of the mast from slipping forward. Before strain is taken on the tackle, the top of the mast should be lifted by hand (or with sheer legs) as high as possible so that the force applied will largely lift the mast rather than slide it forward.

Less frequent but often far more serious than dismastings are hull punctures or major leaks. Hulls can be stove in from collisions with other vessels, grounding on rocks, or striking at high speed heavy flotsam such as driftwood; while serious leaks can be caused by: broken through-hull fittings or their pipes and hoses, seams that open up, stress cracks, broken fastenings, spewed caulking, and so forth. The first action to take after discovering that water is rapidly rising in the bilge is to slow down; on a sailboat, sail should be reduced quickly. Have crewmen start pumping and/or bailing immediately, and try to discover the source of the leak. Check the head and all through-hull fittings, and if a pipe or hose has broken or become detached from its nipple, shut off the seacocks at once. If there is no seacock, tape the hose or remove it and drive a soft wood tapered plug into the orifice that penetrates the hull. When there is nothing wrong with the through-hull fittings, a careful search must be made for holes, cracks, or open seams. Of course, check to see that the water didn't come through an open hatch or porthole. Provided that no one heard a loud thump from striking a floating or submerged object and the seas are rough, it might be assumed that the boat has started her caulking, opened some seams, or possibly developed some cracks from being hard driven. Minor leaks may be in way of the chainplates, around the mast partners, through the deck or through the stuffing box. In any case, slowing the boat and easing the strain on her will help alleviate most of these leaks. Places to check for open seams or cracks are: at the bow along the stem; at and below the chines forward; under transverse bulkheads, especially those forward; along the garboards, especially in way of the mast step; the counter, transom, and stern tube; in the keel; and at the hull-deck connection. Cracks or seams can be plugged with caulking cotton and seam compound, or with large seams, even rags covered with cup grease can be effective. I once kept afloat an ancient wooden boat with wide open seams by smearing them with a mixture of cup grease and soft putty.

As said previously, leaks are far more easy to locate and deal with when they are accessible. If possible see that sections of the boat's ceiling can be removed and that lockers, all parts of the bilge, and closed spaces can be reached. A leak near the waterline on one side might be raised out of water by heeling or listing the boat, while a leak at the bow or stern might be minimized by changing the trim of the vessel.

Obviously, it is important to empty the bilge as soon as possible. When this cannot be done with the pumps, there is a neat trick that has been used successfully on several occasions. The engine's water intake line is removed from its through-hull fitting (after its seacock has been closed, of course) and the hose is placed in the bilge so that it will suck up the bilge water and remove it through the exhaust. Care must be taken, however, to be sure that the bilge is free of any floating matter that could clog up the engine's water pump. It might be prudent to cover the end of the intake hose with a screen or fine net that would act as a filter. After the bilge is empty, of course, the engine must be stopped or the intake hose reconnected to its fitting to avoid overheating the engine.

Large holes through a hull below the waterline are very difficult to plug. Sometimes all that can be done is to delay sinking until help can be summoned or until the boat can be run into shallow water, when she is close to shore. If the hull is holed from grounding, don't be too hasty about freeing the boat, for she could later sink in deep water. When the bottom or topsides are stove in (i.e. the planking is pushed inward) and the hole is not too large, a temporary repair might be made from the inside by covering the fracture with grease and putty-covered rags, followed by a kapok cushion, and followed by a small sheet of plywood all of which is pressed tightly against the hole with a shoring piece. The shore may be a pole or plank, one end of which is forced against the plywood patch while the other end is wedged against a vertical surface on the opposite side of the boat. After the patch is forced tightly against the hole, a stringer can be nailed over the patch to ribs on either side of the hole. The cushion, which is used to fill in the hollow or curve of the bilge may not be needed if the hole occurs at a flat section of the hull, and in some cases the plywood or possibly a sheet of lead or copper might be nailed directly to the planking. In addition to the repair inside the hull, the hole might be covered from the outside with a collision mat. This is a rectangular or triangular piece of soft canvas (sometimes weighted with lead) with lines attached to the corners so that the mat can be held in position over the hole with at least one line (a hogging line) passing under the hull. Water pressure will tend to force the mat against and into the hole. If possible, when the hole is partially above or near the water line, wood battens might be nailed over the canvas to help hold it in place.

Holes in metal or fiberglass hulls present a problem in that patches cannot be nailed on. Planks or pieces of plywood might be screwed with self-tapping screws to fiberglass or metal boats in some cases, while wood wedges or plugs wrapped in rags smeared with grease or tallow might be driven into small holes in a metal hull. Before a patch is applied, its underside should be thickly covered with soft putty and grease or bedding compound, and the patch will have to be held or wedged in place with shores while the screw holes are drilled. Of course, a collision mat or even a piece of soft blanket perhaps smeared with grease, covering the hole from the outside will be most helpful. Cracks or seams might be filled underwater with the flexible compounds used to caulk swimming pools, such as Permanent Sealer or Hypalon. Some holes might be plugged with underwater epoxy, or even concrete, preferably applied from outside the hull. Underwater epoxies such as the product made by Permalite Plastics Corporation of Costa Mesa, California, or "Sea Go-in" Poxy Putty (obtainable from Lands' End Yacht Stores in Chicago) will harden when totally or partially immersed in water, and these are said to adhere to fiberglass, wood, steel, or concrete. An authority on boat salvage, Captain C. M. Crichton, has written that concrete prepared with soda can be used successfully to plug holes. For the fastest setting, Captain Crichton recommends a mixture of half cement and half soda, which he says will harden underwater in half a minute. He warns, however, that the mixture will not be very strong. A crude device that might be used to plug temporarily a small hole or split from the outside while repairs are made inside the hull is to hang a bag of sawdust over the leak. A bag made from coarse cloth such as burlap will emit the grains of sawdust which will be sucked into the hole or crack and hopefully clog it. The sawdust will be encouraged to escape through the burlap if the bag is prodded with a boat hook.

Of course, holes or damage above the waterline, to the hull, deck, or cabin trunk will be much easier to repair, but ample tools and patching materials should be carried. As said previously, emergency equipment should include a few sheets of plywood, lead and copper. Perhaps they could be stowed out of the way under the bunks. Emergency planking, splints, or shores might be obtained from doors, tables, bunk boards, boom crutches, spinnaker poles, oars, dinghy seats, and so forth. Obviously, sails and awnings will make good emergency patches for holes in the deck or cabin trunk, but a large cloth patch should be braced with a wood framework and battens should be nailed over the cloth to hold it in place. Recommended tools were listed in Chapter 3.

Small holes or cracks in piping may be temporarily plugged with stick-type caulking compounds such as "Krakstik," which is designed to stop water leaks in pipes and tanks, or "Oyltite-Stik," intended for oil and gasoline leaks. These sticks are made of waxy substances that may be rubbed or wiped into a crack even when liquid is running out with considerable force. Of course, waterproof tapes can also be used to great advantage on pipes or hoses.

Let us now turn to steering casualties. The rigors of distance sailing and especially racing offshore impose tremendous strains on the entire steering mechanism of a sailboat. As suggested earlier, an extra tiller and rudder head fitting should be carried, and in some cases, on an extended passage, it is a wise plan to carry some sort of preassembled jury rudder. An emergency outboard rudder might be hung quite easily on gudgeons pre-mounted on the transom of a boat having a plumb stern. Some other kinds of jury rudders are suggested in Figure 22.

System A depends on the shifting of a drag, towed astern, from one side of the boat to the other with the use of a steering bridle attached with rolling hitches to the tow line. The further to one side or the other the drag can be moved, the more effective it will be; hence it will help to lead each end of the bridle through blocks at the ends of a spar lashed across the stern and extending outboard on each side as illustrated. The drag must be capable of exerting considerable force or else the system will not

# FIGURE 22: JURY STEERING

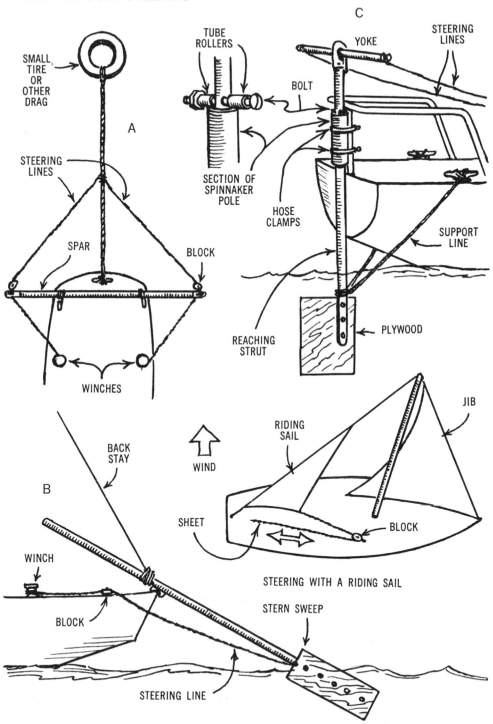

SMALL TIRE OR OTHER DRAG

STEERING LINES

A

SPAR

BLOCK

WINCHES

TUBE ROLLERS

SECTION OF SPINNAKER POLE

BOLT

HOSE CLAMPS

REACHING STRUT

C

YOKE

STEERING LINES

SUPPORT LINE

PLYWOOD

BACK STAY

WIND

B

WINCH

BLOCK

STEERING LINE

STERN SWEEP

RIDING SAIL

SHEET

JIB

BLOCK

STEERING WITH A RIDING SAIL

be effective. Perhaps a small motor scooter tire or a very small sea anchor would supply about the right amount of drag for an easily-turned, medium-sized boat.

System B is a simple stern sweep, which is nothing more than a crude steering oar. Although steering might be accomplished by pushing from side to side the inboard end of the sweep, it is doubtful that there would be sufficient leverage to turn a vessel of any size; thus steering lines attached near the blade will undoubtedly have to be rigged. These lines may be led to each quarter and then to sheet winches on either side of the boat. The sweep might be attached to the boat with shackles or stout lashings around the permanent backstay fitting as illustrated, or a better system would be to attach the sweep's end to a spinnaker pole fitting secured to the stern rail. This was the system used aboard Clayton Ewing's yawl *Dyna* when she sailed 980 miles without a rudder during the Transatlantic Race in 1963. *Dyna's* stern sweep was attached to her boomkin with a bell fitting.

The third jury rudder illustrated is similar to the one used by Wallace Stenhouse's sloop *Aura II*, when she sailed 1,800 miles without the use of her rudder during the 1968 Transatlantic Race. This rig consists of a vertical rudder stock (made from a spinnaker guy reaching strut in *Aura's* case) that turns inside a section cut from a hollow aluminum spinnaker pole, which is secured to the stern pulpit with steel hose clamps. The rudder is turned with steering lines attached to a yoke at the top of the rudder stock. In *Aura's* case, the yoke was a boathook run through the strut's inboard end fitting where it was secured with bolts. The illustration suggests a method of preventing the stock from dropping through its casing (the hollow pole section), which consists of inserting a bolt through the stock just above the casing. Both ends of the bolt are allowed to protrude slightly and they are covered with short sections of metal tubing that are allowed to roll against the top of the casing, thereby minimizing friction of the bolt ends bearing down on the casing.

The least effective emergency rudder rig illustrated is steering with a drag, but few jury steering rigs of any kind are really efficient, so it is extremely important that the crippled boat be well balanced under a suitable combination of sails. In many cases sail boats, especially those with divided rigs, can be steered with sails alone, simply by trimming and slacking sheets. Twin head-sails boomed out on each side are often effective when running. Sometimes a jib boomed out to windward can be carried with the reefed mainsail when well off the wind. When reaching, a stay-sail trimmed in flat (but sheeted to weather) will help hold the bow off when the boat tends to round up into the wind. It is difficult to steer a reaching sloop with her sails alone, but one possible method is suggested in Figure 22. A large jib is carried to supply the power and hold the bow off, while a small riding sail is set on the backstay to be used as a steering sail. Trimming the sheet of the riding sail will cause the boat to luff while slacking the sheet will let her fall off, provided the boat has a lee helm under jib alone. If the boat has insufficient lee helm, a non-overlapping jib could be used, or perhaps a drag could be rigged to leeward. There are all kinds of alternatives and the best method of emergency steering can only be found with extensive experimentation. Such experimentation is well worth the effort before a steering casualty occurs.

The jury rudder systems illustrated in Figure 22 may also be used on many single-screw powerboats. With small planing boats particular attention must be paid to distribution of crew weight. At slow speed, many planing boats with fine bows need weight aft to keep the bow high for the best steering control. With twin-screw boats, steering nearly always can be controlled with the throttles. When a turn to starboard is required, the port screw is given more speed than the starboard screw and vice versa.

When steering with a jury system, vessels nearby should be warned of your lack of maneuverability. Generally, the International Code flag D (Delta) will be hoisted, which signifies: "Keep clear of me; I am maneuvering with difficulty."

### Man Overboard

When proper precautions are taken, there is not a great deal of risk that a man will fall overboard, but nevertheless, complacency and overconfidence in one's surefootedness can lead to carelessness that might result in such an accident. Typical causes of a man falling overboard are: failure to abide by the nautical dictum, "one hand for the ship and one for yourself;" failure to use a safety harness; failure to kneel while working on the foredeck in a seaway; lack of caution when moving along the side deck in heavy weather; failure to watch ones feet to avoid tripping over fittings or slipping on loose sails or wet brightwork; and the use of unnecessary acrobatics (when handling racing sails or furling the mizzen on a yawl, for example). It might also be added that a boat owner's failure to install pulpits and lifelines of adequate height (above knee level) has contributed to some falls over the side. As said earlier, lifelines must be at least 24 inches, but preferably 27 inches or higher, above the deck. Also, there should be ample grab rails along the cabin house and in some cases, usually on the larger offshore boats, curved pipe rails should be installed near the main mast and the helm, just forward of the binnacle perhaps. It should be kept in mind that a boat's motion in a seaway can be extremely irregular, and even the wake of a powerboat passing close aboard can cause a man to lose his balance.

When a man is seen falling overboard, action should be taken as follows: the observer shouts, "Man overboard to port (or starboard)" as loud as he can to alert the rest of the crew, while simultaneously, he reaches for the nearest life preserver to throw near and, if possible, to windward of the victim. The nearest man to a ring buoy with drogue and a man-overboard pole should immediately throw these in the water, and another crew member, often the one who first observes the accident, should keep his eyes on the victim or man overboard pole (when the victim is not visible) or waterlight at night. It is extremely important that one man devote his undivided attention to keeping track of the location of the man. He should rivet his gaze on the man, or on the equipment near him, or on the spot where he was last seen before disappearing behind the wave tops. In the confusion of rapid maneuvering, it is all too easy to lose track of the exact direction in which the man lies, and in rough water it is surprisingly difficult to spot the man again, even when he is not very far away.

When the vessel is under power, the helmsman puts the gear into neutral and turns the stern away from the victim to avoid cutting him with the propeller, and then maneuvers into a recovery position. When under sail, the standard recovery procedure is to jibe, because this normally brings the boat alongside the victim in the quickest possible time (see Figure 23). However, there are several probable exceptions to the jibing rule, such as in very heavy weather or when certain light sails (the mizzen staysail, for example) are carried. Another possible exception might be when a man falls overboard and leaves only an inexperienced wife and/or a child aboard. Furthermore, when running dead before the wind there would be an option of jibing or tacking, because neither maneuver would shorten the distance to the victim, and tacking might be the safer method of turning. Still another exception is in a strong breeze and rough sea, when care must be taken that the boat does not get too far to leeward of the man. In other words, the rule for jibing should not be a hard and fast dictum, but it should be used with common sense and in accordance with the particular set of circumstances.

If the man should fall overboard at night, in fog, or in other conditions of poor visibility, the helmsman should note his compass course and the time of the accident, because it may be necessary to calculate a return course to the victim. While the boat is being readied to tack or jibe, the helmsman should hold a steady course to most easily keep track of the victim's location. It is important that one capable crew member be assigned the job of navigation. He must keep track of the time, speed of the boat, leeway, and the various course changes.

FIGURE 23: MAN OVERBOARD

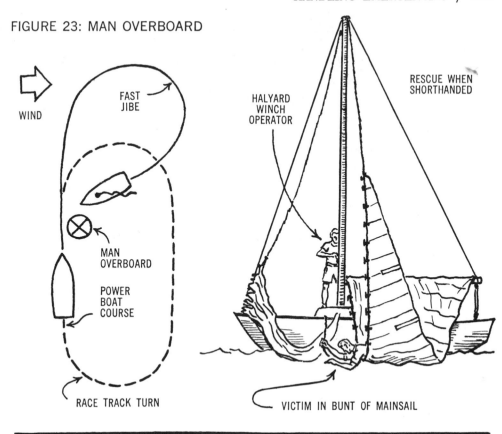

WIND

FAST
JIBE

MAN
OVERBOARD

POWER
BOAT
COURSE

RACE TRACK TURN

RESCUE WHEN
SHORTHANDED

HALYARD
WINCH
OPERATOR

VICTIM IN BUNT OF MAINSAIL

FIGURE 24: SEARCH PATTERNS (IN POOR VISIBILITY)

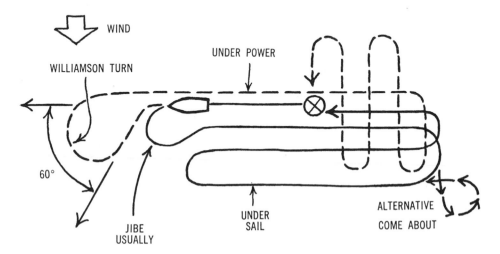

WIND

WILLIAMSON TURN

UNDER POWER

60°

JIBE
USUALLY

UNDER
SAIL

ALTERNATIVE
COME ABOUT

If the victim has not been spotted by the time the boat returns to the estimated position at which the accident occurred, the boat should continue sailing or motoring past that location on a course reciprocal to the heading at the time of the accident until there is not the slightest possibility that the locaton has not yet been reached. If the boat must beat back to the victim she should beat to a location about dead to windward of his estimated position. A boat with auxiliary power may save time and minimize navigational errors by using her motor to return on a direct reciprocal course. When the skipper and navigator agree that they have gone past the victim on the return course, the vessel should then work back towards the victim in a back-and-forth parallel search pattern. The parallel courses should extend about equal distances on either side of the victim's estimated position, and the tracks should be no further apart than double the range at which the man could be spotted, taking into account visibility and wave height. Search patterns are illustrated in Figure 24 with sailboat courses shown by solid lines and powerboat courses shown with dashed lines. Notice that a sailboat must reach back and forth when searching. Obviously she does not enjoy the advantage of a boat under power in being able to head directly into the wind. The sailboat may go well to windward of the victim's estimated position and then search down wind, but that would entail jibing many times; thus it might be better to start the search pattern well to leeward of the victim's estimated position in moderate weather and work to windward, tacking at each turn, as shown in the illustration, provided the boat can be tacked easily. Another advantage in searching to leeward of the victim is that his shouts will be more easily heard. In maneuvering relative to the man's position in very heavy weather, it must be remembered that it may be difficult or impossible to work the vessel to windward.

When the man overboard is spotted, the boat should come alongside him slowly and to windward. A powerboat is taken dead to windward of the man, fairly close aboard, beam to the seas, and her power is cut off or at least the gear is put in neutral so that there is no possibility of the victim being cut by the propeller. A sailboat is brought up to windward on a close reach with her sheets started and sails luffing. The speed of the sailboat can be controlled by alternately trimming or slacking sheets. Although a leading insurance company advises bringing the recovery boat to leeward of the man overboard just before hauling him aboard, experienced seamen agree that in almost every case, the boat should be to windward of the man in order that a lee is created, so that the boat will drift down on him, and so he may be hauled aboard over the low side, rather than the high side. When approaching the victim, lines or ladders should be hung over the side, and a crew member should stand by with a boathook while another throws the man a heaving line. Headway must be almost entirely stopped. There should be no trouble in bringing the victim aboard when there is ample crew, but a heavy man, exhausted or injured, will be extremely difficult to lift over the side when shorthanded. In this case, an effective means is to launch the rubber raft, not entirely inflated, and let the victim crawl or be hauled into it. From the raft, he can more easily be helped over the side. Another means of pulling the man aboard is with the use of parbuckles (described earlier) or with the use of the main halyard on its winch or with the halyard supporting a tackle. If the victim is injured, a swimmer in a lifejacket attached to a line may have to go over the side to assist in the operation.

An interesting article on rescuing a man overboard when shorthanded or with an inexperienced crew appeared in the British publication, *Yachting Monthly* (November, 1970). The editor of the magazine performed experiments to determine the best method for a wife with moderate sailing experience to recover her husband who had fallen from a small sailing cruiser. One conclusion was that the wife should not immediately throw a life preserver to her husband, because it was assumed that she could not throw it soon enough or close enough for the man to reach without an exhausting swim. The article suggested that the wife should come about, sail back to her husband without attempting to kill headway to any great extent, and then drop him a buoy. With the man safely in his buoy, the wife could sail past him, come about again, and return for his pick up. She should maneuver so as to approach him close-hauled (preferably on a close reach) aiming slightly to windward of him, and just before reaching him, let the sheets fly to kill speed. This method seems very practical in general, but I don't like the delay in throwing the life buoy. When the husband finds it necessary to go forward in heavy weather and leave his wife at the helm, of course he should take every precaution, don a life jacket, and wear a safety harness; but in addition, I think, the wife should have a life buoy by her side so that she can throw it instantly if her husband goes over the side. There is a self-inflating life buoy on the market, called "Sav-a-life Rescue Ball," that is enclosed in a container the size and shape of a soft baseball for easy and accurate throwing. Inflation is automatic after the ball hits the water. Furthermore, it might be prudent to tow a stout line with a rescue quoit or even a buoy at its end. After falling overboard several men saved themselves by grabbing lines (even the taffrail log line on at least one occasion) towed far astern. Obviously any man who sails with an inexperienced wife only should make a special effort to teach her basic seamanship and boathandling in case he goes overboard or is incapacitated.

The *Yachting Monthly* article suggested a method that proved quite effective for bringing the exhausted man aboard. A parbuckle is made out of the mainsail by letting its luff slides run off their track and letting the bunt of the sail hang over the side, the victim crawls into the bunt, and then he may be lifted aboard by winching or swigging up on the halyard. Similarly, a jib might be used to assist in reboarding. A long tailed jib is simply lowered and hung over the side without being unhanked. In this case, the victim might be helped aboard by hauling in or up on the sheet. These methods are illustrated in Figure 23.

On a very maneuverable power boat in clear weather, a simple rudder-hard-over turn is the quickest way to return to a man overboard. As said before, the boat should be turned towards the side from which the man fell to swing the propeller away from him, and, on a single-screw boat, the propeller should be stopped temporarily. On a twin screw boat, the engine nearest the side from which the man fell is stopped, and when clear of the man, the other engine is given full (or almost full) power to turn the boat in the quickest possible time. After about half or more of the turn has been completed, the engine nearest the center of the turning circle might be reversed to tighten the turn if this seems advisable. When fairly close to the victim, to windward of him, the engines should momentarily be backed to kill headway and then stopped. A line is thrown to the victim while the boat drifts down to him. A slower but more sure recovery method is the "racetrack" turn, which consists of an initial 180-degree turn towards the side from which the man fell, followed by a short run on a straight course that is reciprocal to the original course, followed by another 180-degree turn, and another straight course on the same heading as the original course until the victim is reached. The advantages of this maneuver, which makes a course configuration similar to a race track (see Figure 23), are that it assures that the man will be outside the boat's turning circle and allows a straight final approach to the victim.

A recommended powerboat return in poor visibility is the maneuver that the Navy calls a Williamson turn (see Figure 24). The turn is also used if it is not known exactly when the man fell overboard. As can be seen by the dashed line course, the vessel is turned towards the side from which the man fell (or probably fell )until she is approximately 60 degrees from her original heading, and then the rudder is shifted so that the vessel turns the opposite way and continues turning until she is back on her original track headed in a direction that is reciprocal to the orginal course. Although the method does not allow a very quick recovery, it is advantageous in limited visibility, because it brings the vessel back on her original track; and immediately after the turn has been completed, the skipper can be assured that the victim will be somewhere ahead (not astern). The 60-degree initial turn previously mentioned is by no means a hard and fast rule. For a small maneuverable boat, the angle might be considerably less. The turning characteristics of the boat should have been determined through commonly used maneuvers or prior experimentation.

It should be kept in mind that the victim will drift a considerable distance to leeward if the vessel is slow to return, but this drift will almost always be less than the leeway of most searching craft, such as small cruising sailboats being luffed along slowly, or high-sided, shoal-draft powerboats with wind and sea on the beam. In the case when the boat is returning to the man's position over some distance at a normal speed, the net difference between the man's drift and the boat's leeway may be very little, but in many cases a boat that makes significant leeway will end up to leeward of the victim when the return is a reciprocal course on the original track with the wind and sea abeam. Current will not affect the situation, unless, of course, the victim and boat are in different conditions of direction or velocity of flow.

Large ships losing a man overboard will generally use backing maneuvers when well clear of the victim, and, when way is lost, lower a small boat. Usually vessels in the immediate vicinity should be notified by radio or signals that a man is overboard if the victim cannot be found immediately. The International Code signal for "man overboard" is the letter O (Oscar), which may be made with the O flag or any other method of signaling.

From time to time, recovery of an object thrown overboard should be practiced in order that the skipper can become thoroughly familiar with the turning and drift characteristics of his boat under a variety of conditions and so the regular crew can learn man overboard procedures.

## Shipboard Accidents

Whenever boarding a boat, it is worth mentally noting the obvious, that one is entering a relatively accident-prone environment and that medical facilities will be unavailable. It is beyond the scope of this book to deal with medical treatment and first aid, but obviously a complete medical kit should be on board, and it is important to carry a detailed first aid manual written by a doctor, preferably one who is an experienced boatman (two manuals were suggested in Chapter 3). This section, therefore, will be limited to a list of causes and suggestions for prevention of some common shipboard accidents that can result in personal injury. It should be mentioned with respect to shipboard accidents generally that green hands should always be warned of possible hazards they might not foresee.

*Falls.* Most of the common causes of falls on deck were discussed in the previous, man overboard section. However, it is worth repeating here that slippery surfaces should be kept to an absolute minimum. It is inadvisable to use varnish where a person will walk. An unavoidable slippery surface should have strips of abrasive cloth glued to it; decks must be made skid-proof with molded-in rough patterns, abrasive paint, or the use of raw teak; and, as said earlier, there should be ample hand rails both in the cabin and topside. Beware of leaving tangles of lines or loose sails lying on deck. Synthetic sails are especially slippery, and so they should be bunched together and tightly stopped when it is necessary to leave them lying on the foredeck. When moving along the deck of a heeled sailboat, it is usually safer to use the windward side. In heavy weather, never work with both hands simultaneously unless you are secured to the boat with a line or safety harness. Companionway ladders are often a cause of serious falls. It is essential that ladders or steps are skid-proofed, are provided with hand grips, and are well secured. A person should nearly always be facing a ladder when using it. Descending into a cabin with one's back towards the steps can be a dangerous practice when there is any motion.

*Burns.* A major source of burns on a boat is the galley stove. Cooking in a seaway, especially when the boat is heeled, should be done with caution. For heavy weather cooking, it is essential that the stove have gimbals (with the turning axis running fore-and-aft) and an adequately high rail to prevent pots from sliding off. Pots should be deep and have wide, flat bottoms; they should fit the stove properly, have clamps to hold them securely in heavy weather; and they should never be over-filled. The cabin sole in way of the galley must be skid-proof, and it is important that the cook be provided with a safety harness to allow working with both hands. Incidentally, the small bulkhead-mounted, single burner Sterno stove, which is gimballed both fore-and-aft and athwartships, is very handy and relatively safe in rough weather. It is also desirable, whenever possible, for the dining table to be gimballed, but at least it should be provided with fiddles. In fact, all counters or working surfaces in the galley should have fiddles.

A frequent cause of burns and also falls below deck is the wakes of speeding powerboats that pass close aboard. It is almost criminal the way some powerboat operators fail to consider the effect of their wakes on other craft, especially on those at anchor that cannot maneuver to meet the waves bow or stern on. Waves caused by a speeding boat, especially one of heavy displacement, can be more dangerous than the seas normally encountered offshore, because people on a craft being rolled by a wake are often caught unawares. A wave-making boat should give any vulnerable

*As well he should, this midshipman looks apprehensively at the block that, in the event of failure, could injure his leg. He should be abaft the winch and facing forward where he can watch the jib and where his leg will not be in the bight of the sheet. (U.S. Navy)*

craft a reasonably wide berth and slow down. The helmsman of the boat about to be rolled, or anyone on deck, should warn everyone on board, especially those below and the cook, that waves are coming. In some cases, when a planing boat will make less waves by going fast, and when there is no speed limit or risk in going fast, it may be advisable for the wave-maker to speed up. After all, the important consideration is to minimize the size of the wake.

*Winch injuries.* A number of serious accidents have resulted from sheet or halyard winch failures or improper handling of winches. Although the design and construction of winches have been greatly improved in the last years, there are still failures in brake mechanisms, pawls, and springs, especially in some of the cheaper makes. Such failures can allow a winch under strain to "runaway," or spin inadvertently. The principle danger of a run-away winch is that its handle can strike someone on the head, arms, or elsewhere. In some cases, usually on halyard winches without handle locks or with defective locks, handles can actually be thrown for a considerable distance. Another potential danger in handling winches is catching one's fingers under the turns of line or wire on the winch. Allowing the rope to slip off the winch may also cause injuries, if, for example, the mishap allows a boom to drop on someone's head.

Some safety suggestions for handling winches are as follows: keep your head well clear of a winch handle; grip the handle firmly when operating a winch; whenever possible, use winch handles that lock in place; remove winch handles when they are not in use; consider the use of winch wheels (special wheel handles) instead of conventional handles on reel halyard winches; don't oil the brake band of a reel winch; consider the use of an adjustable, toggle-and-screw-pin brake (such as the kind made by Barient) so that the load on a winch can be eased gradually; keep your fingers away from the "swallow" of a winch (the point where the line feeds onto the winch) when cranking in and especially when slacking off a line; keep tension on the fall (end) of the line when taking a turn of line off a winch if the line's standing part is under great strain; be careful (on halyard winches especially) to keep the fall of the line nearly at a right angle to the winch axis or slant it toward the base of the winch, in order that the line cannot slip off the end of the winch; be careful when clearing an override or line tangled on a winch by seeing that the strain on the standing part is taken by another line while the tangle is being cleared; and be extremely cautious in handling winches with gloves on (or don't wear gloves), as a glove can become pinched between the turns of line on a winch and perhaps draw a finger under a turn.

*Sailhandling injuries.* In heavy weather, sails are often difficult to manage, and poor handling can result in minor or sometimes serious injuries. The spinnaker frequently causes trouble in a fresh breeze. Failure to keep a turn of halyard or sheet on a winch when hoisting or lowering the sail can cause bad rope burns on the hands. Spinnakers should be handed by one leech only in order that they will spill their wind. When hauled in by both leeches simultaneously, the sail will fill and take charge, possibly causing falls, rope burns, or other injuries. Crew members working on the foredeck should avoid standing under the spinnaker pole while it is being raised or lowered, and the man tending the topping lift must be careful to see that no one is under the pole. More than a few foredeck men have been "beaned" with spinnaker poles. A more serious injury can result from being hit on the head with the main boom during a jibe. It is essential that the helmsman give all crew members ample warning of an imminent jibe in order that they may duck their heads and brace themselves when the boom swings over. Sailing by the lee should be avoided, but if it is necessary, a preventer should be rigged from the boom's end to some point forward to guard against an inadvertent, all-standing jibe. When handing flogging sails, care must be taken to avoid being hit by fittings such as hanks or shackles. The flapping sail should be muzzled and stopped immediately as it is being lowered in a strong breeze. It is usually a good idea to tie the working jib or staysail sheets to their clews with bowlines in order to eliminate hard, heavy shackles that could hit crew members in the head. Whenever possible, lower or hoist a sail in the lee of a sail that is already hoisted. On cruising boats, it is often a good idea to carry permanently rigged lazy jacks to minimize possible risks of injury or falling overboard when taking in sail during a blow, since the lazy jacks will keep the sail under better control. A short strop attached to the backstay for the purpose of supporting a boom is no substitute for a proper boom topping lift. It is far handier and safer to have a strong lift running from the boom's end to the masthead and then to a cleat at the base of the mast. Such a rig will permit lowering sail with the boom broad off in an emergency.

*Injuries from lines.* There is tremendous energy locked inside a line under great strain, and this energy can suddenly escape with dangerous consequences if the line slips, breaks, or pulls its fitting loose. As said earlier, no one should stand directly behind a towline under strain, especially one made of a semi-elastic material such as nylon, because its parting could cause a dangerous whiplash. Also, it can be dangerous to snub abruptly a line under great strain. Snubbing should usually be done by surging the line with a turn or two around the cleat or bitt so that strain is put on the line gradually to minimize shock loading. Of course lines must be properly coiled to prevent kinking, which will weaken them. Some injuries occur when trying to clear snarls, jammed knots, or jams on cleats, when the line is under strain. Strain should be taken off the fouled line, (usually with another line), and only proven, accepted knots, such as the bowline, square knot, half hitches, sheet bend, rolling hitch, and towboat hitch should be used. Halyards of slippery synthetic rope should usually be hitched on their cleats to assure that they will stay cleated. Be wary, however, of hitching a line made of vegetable fiber when speed of release is important, because the line may swell and jam when it gets wet. Never stand in a coil or in the bight of a line when it is under strain. When a fitting is under stress from the pull of a line, always consider the direction in which the fitting will travel if it should let go, and stay well clear of its predicted path. As mentioned before, rope burns on the hands can be avoided by handling a line under strain with a turn around a cleat or winch. Be especially careful with braided lines, because they are relatively smooth and the smaller sizes are often difficult to grip firmly with the hands.

*Mooring and anchoring injuries.* Poor landings at slips, docks, or alongside other boats are an occasional source of injuries. Hernias or crushed feet or hands can result from trying to fend off a heavy vessel that is moving too fast. Risk of these accidents can be minimized with practice in boat handling, by carrying an adequate crew, and by judicious use of fenders. As previously stated, inexperienced crew members should always be well instructed with regard to possible dangers they might not foresee. Backs are sometimes injured when heavy anchors are weighed. Even a light anchor can be very difficult to break out when it is deeply buried in the bottom. When the anchor line is at a short stay, nearly straight up and down, the vessel should be propelled with power or sail to break the anchor loose in order to spare the human back. If the anchor is very heavy, it can be brought on board with a windlass and tackle. Light anchors can be hauled up by hand, but there is a proper technique for minimizing strain on the back. Instead of keeping the legs straight and bending the back when hauling in or up on the rode, a man weighing the anchor should alternately bend and straighten his legs and keep his back straight. In other words, lifting should be done, as much as possible, with the legs instead of the back. In letting out scope, care must be taken not to let the anchor line or chain run away by keeping adequate turns on the bitt or Sampson post. Never grab a runaway line, or especially chain, close to the chock, hawse hole, or bitt, because your hand could be mangled. The bitter end of the rode should always be made fast to avoid the possibility of losing the anchor in the event of a runaway.

*Working aloft.* Although one seldom hears of a man falling from a mast, this kind of accident does happen on rare occasions. In fact, I once saw a man fall from aloft and hit the deck. Such a sight is not easy to forget. It is hardly ever prudent to climb a mast, hand-over-hand, while the vessel is underway. Unless the mast is equipped with a ladder or the shrouds have ratlines, a man should nearly always be hauled aloft in a proper bosun's chair. People who have never been aloft in a seaway seldom realize how much a boat's motion is magnified at the masthead. Hanging on when aloft can be difficult even when the boat's rolling seems mild at the deck level. It is important, therefore, that a man in a bosun's chair is secured to the mast to keep him from swinging, and he should be lashed into the chair so that he cannot fall out, even if unconscious. While being hauled aloft in a seaway, of course, he must grip the rigging tightly, but in addition, there should be a downhaul line made fast to the chair's bottom, which is tended by a man on deck who prevents the chair from swinging by keeping the line taut. Normally, there are two men working the winch that pulls the chair aloft, and they must follow the orders of either the man in the chair or the downhaul tender, who should be looking up the mast continuously. Once the man in the chair is where he wants to be, the brake must be fastened in such a way that it cannot be tripped accidentally or the halyard must be hitched securely on a substantial cleat. No one should stand under a man who is working aloft in case a tool is dropped accidentally. The lowering operation must be done slowly and smoothly with a turn or two of the halyard around the winch, or with two people *firmly* holding the handle of a reel winch. Before going aloft in the bosun's chair, be sure that the halyard and its block and shackle are adequately strong. It is advisable that boats with seven-eighths or three-quarter rigs have an extra masthead halyard or a strong topping lift capable of supporting a man in a chair in the event that the main halyard cannot be used.

*Carbon Monoxide.* Asphyxiation from carbon monoxide occurs on boats more often than most people would suppose. As most automobile drivers know, carbon monoxide is a colorless, almost entirely odorless (unless mixed with exhaust fumes) gas emitted from gasoline and diesel engines. Death can be caused by breathing heavy concentrations of the gas. Dangerous concentrations are usually caused by a leaking exhaust system inside an enclosed space, such as a cabin or engine compartment that lacks adequate ventilation. Safeguards against asphyxiation are to check the exhaust line carefully for broken gaskets, holes from rust, etc. and to ventilate the cabin as much as possible (without jeopardy to safety in heavy weather) when the engine is running.

## Fire and Lightning

Coast Guard statistics on boating accidents show that almost every year fires and explosions are the leading cause of property damage and are second only to collision in causing personal injuries afloat. Improper installation, inadequate ventilation, and carelessness in the handling of gasoline engines and liquified petroleum (LP) gas stoves and their fuel systems account for most of the accidents. At the time of this writing, Federal requirements for prevention of fires and explosions (specifically: ventilation, backfire flame control, and fire extinguishers) are very minimal and inadequate under the Motorboat Act of 1940, but in the near future broader and more comprehensive standards will be drawn up by the Coast Guard under the authorization of the Federal Boat Safety Act of 1971. It is expected that eventually the new requirements will more closely follow many of the recommendations published by the American Boat and Yacht Council in the book *Safety Standards for Small Craft* and the National Fire Protection Association in the booklet *Fire Protection Standards for Motor Craft* (No. 302), but it should be kept in mind that these new requirements will still be minimum standards and that they will not necessarily assure maximum protection in all cases. The best protection is afforded by having a boat inspected or surveyed to see that she conforms in every way to the highest standards of the Coast Guard, the ABYC, or the NFPA on volatile fuel systems, electric wiring, and fire fighting equipment, and also, of course, the boat owner should learn all he can about the causes of fires and explosions.

Many boatmen seem insufficiently impressed with the potential shipboard hazards of gasoline. Perhaps this results from the casual way the fuel is handled on shore, around filling stations and automobiles. It should be remembered, however, that gasoline on a boat presents an entirely different safety problem, not only because self sufficiency is a vital factor when afloat, but because the hull of a decked boat is a natural catchment for gas fumes. As nearly everyone knows, it is the fumes and not the gasoline itself that are explosive, and since fumes are heavier than air, they will sink to the bottom of any closed receptacle, such as a hull. Authorities tell us that one cup of gasoline can produce enough fumes to equal the explosive force of fifteen sticks of dynamite. Thus the message seems clear: first, don't let any fumes escape inside a boat, and secondly, if they do escape, remove them as quickly as possible with a good ventilating system. In addition, of course, all measures should be taken to prevent ignition of possible fumes with safe electric wiring and the careful use of matches or lighters.

In regard to preventing fumes from escaping inside the hull, the essential consideration is the resistance to leakage and the reliability of the tanks and fuel lines. In fact, the entire fuel system must be tight from the top of the fill pipe to the engine carburetor. Approved practices and standards for the fuel system in brief form are as follows:

• The tops of all fill pipes should be securely attached to deck plates which are located outboard of cockpit coamings at a point where any fumes or spillage of gas will go overboard.

• Fill pipes should, if possible, be straight, and if there is any flexibility in the hull (there usually is), which allows a slight movement between the deck plate and tank, a section of flexible, strong, rubber hose should be used near the top of the fill pipe. This section must be securely fastened to the fill pipe with non-corrosive, screw-type clamps at least ½ inch wide, and the hose should be located where it can be easily inspected. The Coast Guard recommends that a fill pipe extend to the bottom of its

## FIGURE 25: FUEL TANK AND VENTILATION

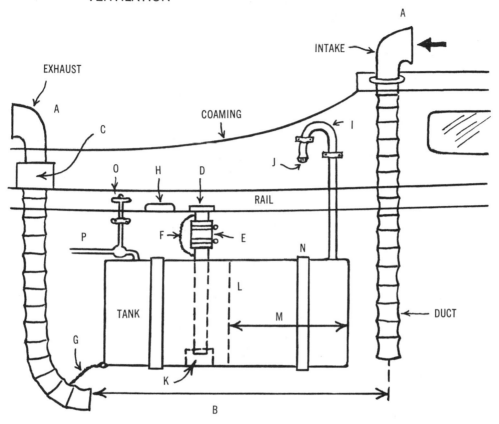

A—cowl ventilators, intake higher. B—ducts sufficiently far apart for thorough purging. C—blower location. D—fill pipe connected to deck plate. E—flexible hose with stainless steel clamps. F—jumper wire for grounding. G—tank grounded. H—deck scupper at low point to discharge fumes or spilled gas. I—air vent outside coaming securely attached and protected and with swan neck facing aft (powerboat vent may go through upper topsides if there is a high loop in the line). J—removable flame screen. K—Coast Guard recommends fill pipe extend to bottom of tank in well to form liquid seal. L— tank baffle. M—baffle's distance to end of tank not over 30 inches. N—secure holding straps insulated from tank. O—shut-off valve. P—fuel line at top of tank. (A pick-up tube, not shown, extends from the fuel line at the tank's top to a strainer at the tank's bottom.)

tank where it will terminate inside a well to form a liquid seal so that the tank cannot be exploded from an ignited fill pipe (see Figure 25).

• Fuel tank vents should also be outboard of the cockpit coamings where fumes can escape into the open air. A vent anywhere inside the hull is extremely dangerous. The ABYC and NFPA recommend a vent pipe with a minimum inside diameter of 9/16 inch and that vent outlets be fitted with removable flame screens as protection against flash-back from an outside source of ignition. The top of a vent pipe should have a swan neck bent aft in such a way that it cannot admit rain or sea water.

• Fuel tanks must be securely fastened to withstand continuous motion and a beam-ends knockdown, or even a capsizing. NFPA and ABYC standards recommend that the tanks have no openings or fittings in the bottom, sides, or ends, and that they have permanent labels giving manufacturer's name, date of manufacture, capacity, construction material and thickness, intended fuel, and maximum test pressure. A tank must be capable of withstanding a pressure of at least three pounds per square inch without leaking. Recommended tank materials are Monel (nickel-copper), copper (internally tin coated), Everdur, and galvanized iron or steel (but not internally galvanized when the fuel is diesel oil). Rounded tanks are preferable, and they should have a reasonable amount of air circulation on all exterior surfaces. Baffles are extremely important to give strength and to restrict the surging of fuel inside the tank. The NFPA allows brazed construction, but be wary of low-heat solders. I have vivid memories of a tank's soldered seam bursting open and spilling gas in the bilge while I was sailing a small yawl during a rough night offshore. As a result of the experience, I lean towards welded construction, but, whatever the method, of course, the work should be done only by craftsmen who are thoroughly experienced in making fuel tanks. It would be a good idea for the tank label to state whether the tank is made in accordance with NFPA or ABYC standards. Some fuel tank installation and ventilation details are shown in Figure 25.

• Fuel distribution metal tubing for gasoline engines should be seamless copper, nickel copper, or copper nickel with a minimum wall thickness of .032 inch, according to recommendations of the ABYC. The tubing must be well supported and protected as much as possible against vibration. Securing clips or straps should be resistant to corrosion and of a design that cannot cut or abrade the fuel line. ABYC standards recommend that the line run at or above the level of the tank top to a point close to the engine connection. Flexible tubing should separate a fuel line secured to the hull from that part of the line secured to the engine, but the flexible tubing should be the heavy-duty, aircraft type or types approved for marine fuel system use.

• A fuel line shut-off valve should be installed very close to the tank, and another should be located near the engine. They must be firmly secured and supported independent of the tubing. The tank valve should be operable from outside of the engine compartment, with a reach rod perhaps. Packless valves should be used, and shut and open positions must be plainly marked or else have positive stops at both positions.

• Gas line filters must be readily accessible and independently supported. As with any component of the fuel system, filters should be made and approved for marine use. It can be dangerous to use an automobile-type filter on a boat. The bowl should be of non-corrosive metal and large enough to trap at least a pint of water. For maximum safety, glass bowl strainers are generally not recommended. Marine filters should be designed for top servicing, because drains at the bottom could leak.

• The carburetor must be fitted with a backfire flame arrestor secured to the air intake in accordance with Federal requirements. In addition, the NFPA specifies that carburetors have drip collectors of adequate capacity, which return all drips and overflow to the engine intake manifold.

• Electrical grounding of the fuel system is extremely important to prevent a build-up of static electricity that could cause a spark. Any non-metalic flexible hoses in the line must be bridged with a heavy (at least No. 8) copper wire. Sparks due to static electricity can result from a number of activities, such as the filling of a gasoline tank, friction caused by a boat working in a seaway, or even the running of water through a hose. Thus it is advisable to bond and ground all metal fittings that could produce a spark anywhere that fumes could accumulate. Some essential safety points in connection with electric wiring and the battery were discussed in Chapter 3, but it is well emphasized: that all electrical devices should be approved for motor craft use; wiring should be well insulated and of adequate size to prevent voltage drops and overheating; each circuit should be fused or fitted with non-self-resetting circuit breakers; and only spark-proof switches located as high as possible above the bilge should be used (don't use a knife-type switch in a low position or anywhere fumes could possibly accumulate). Electrical components of the engine should be as spark-proof as possible. Spark plugs, for example, need caps or shields to prevent arcing.

Batteries have an explosive potential of their own when they lack ventilation. In fact, I was once aboard a boat whose batteries blew up. A tightly covered battery box can trap hydrogen gas generated by a lead-acid battery, which could be detonated by a spark. Of course, battery boxes must be covered to prevent the accidental dropping of tools on the terminals, but the lid should have air holes and the entire battery compartment should be reasonably ventilated. Details for safe electrical systems can be obtained from the two booklets previously mentioned that are published by the NFPA and ABYC.

• Engine and fuel tank compartment ventilation is set forth in Coast Guard Pamphlet No. 395. Some general rules on the subject are as follows: There should be one or more intake ventilator ducts with cowls (or the equivalent) bringing air into the engine compartment and one or more

*Coast Guard statistics on boating accidents consistently show that the greatest property damage comes from fire and explosions. Improper fueling is a major cause.*

exhaust ducts and cowls. The NFPA recommends two intake and two exhaust ventilators with ducts. The exhaust ducts must lead from the lower portion of the bilge and the intake ducts lead at least midway to the bilge below the carburetor intake. Ducts are generally made of non-collapsible, flexible hose, and they must be routed clear of and protected from contact with hot engine surfaces. The NFPA recommends a minimum duct sectional area of one square inch for each foot of beam. Although not required legally at the present time for pleasure craft, a bilge blower is highly recommended, but it should be a spark-proof marine type located as high as possible above the bilge in an exhaust duct. It is essential that the bottom of an exhaust duct go to the lowest point in the bilge, but it must be kept above the normal level of bilge water, and ducts should be installed without dips that could catch rain water that might blow into the cowls. Although the forward cowls usually face forward and are the intake vents, in some cases (if both ducts are sufficiently low in the bilge), when a boat is at anchor, the circulation of air below might be improved by turning the forward vents aft and the aft vents forward, so that air below will flow from aft forward. On sailboats in rough weather when the engine is not running, ventilators should be removed and their openings closed for the sake of watertightness, but every effort should be made to keep air circulating below as well as possible. In the final analysis of course, watertight integrity is more vital than ventilation. Thus it is important, especially in power boats, that engine room vents be positioned where they will be protected from water coming aboard in rough weather.

Carelessness in fueling is probably the greatest cause of explosion and fire. A list of precautions is as follows: take on fuel during daylight whenever possible; be sure the boat is securely made fast; find out how much fuel is needed and check condition of the vent line (see that it is not loose or clogged); close openings into the cabin through which fumes might enter; when the gas tanks are aft, it is usually advisable to take on fuel with the bow headed into the wind, so that fumes are blown away from the cabin; turn off switches and stop motors, engines, or any devices that could cause sparks; don't smoke, strike matches, or light stoves while fueling; keep the fuel hose nozzle firmly in contact with the fill pipe to avoid the possibility of a spark from static electricity; do not run fuel into a tank so fast that it spills or overflows; after fueling, wipe up all spills; if the fill pipe is in the bottom of the cockpit (it shouldn't be), fan out the fumes before opening the companionway slide and see that cockpit scuppers are clear of the water so that fumes can escape; open all hatches and ports and let the boat air out for at least five minutes before starting the engine, turning on switches, or striking matches; and run the blower and sniff the bilge for fumes, being sure that all gasoline odors have disappeared, before starting the engine.

A few final thoughts relating to engines and fires are: be sure there is ample insulation between a hot exhaust pipe and any wooden member of the hull; be sure that exhaust system supporting straps are resistant to heat; see that the drip pan under the engine is of ample size to catch any drips and that it is deep enough not to overflow on a heeled sailboat; keep the bilges and engine compartment clean and free of oil or grease.

Many people do not realize that, although the explosive hazards of oils are much less than those of gasoline, diesel fuel can be explosive under certain conditions of fume concentration, and of course, risk of fire is present whenever flammable fuels are carried. Almost the same precautions should be taken with diesel engines as with those using gasoline.

The greatest source of boat fires, other than the engine and its fuel system, is the galley stove. It is generally agreed that the safest proper cooking stove (with fully adjustable heat) is the kind that burns vaporized alcohol, but even this stove has caused fires through careless handling or improper design or installation. The safety advantages of alcohol as a fuel are that it will not explode, and its flame can be extinguished with water. Although the use of water on alcohol fires is recommended by the ABYC and NFPA, my own experiments have shown that a small amount of water that is insufficient to extinguish the fire completely could float the fire to a potentially dangerous location, such as to an oily bilge, where ignition could take place after a brief period of smoldering. My feeling is that unless a considerable quantity of water is used, an alcohol fire should be smothered with dry chemical, carbon dioxide, or perhaps with a towel. Soda or flour can smother such a fire effectively, but great care must be taken when using any dry powder not to splash the flaming liquid.

Fires from alcohol stoves are generally caused by flare-ups, by spillage of fuel, leaks in the fuel line, failure to watch a stove after it is lighted, and improper location of the fuel tank's shut-off valve. To avoid these possible dangers, it is necessary to have a basic understanding of how the stove works. In simplified form, the principle is: that alcohol is fed from its storage tank by gravity or air pressure to a "primed" or pre-heated section of tubing, where it is vaporized by the heat. The vapor then passes through perforations at the burner where it is ignited to give a hot, almost colorless and odorless flame. Flare-ups are usually caused by incomplete priming or failure to heat adequately the tubing near the burner where vaporization takes place, so that raw alcohol passes into the burner and bursts into a high flame when it is ignited with a match or lighter. Actually, these flare-ups need not be dangerous if the burner's valve is shut immediately, if the stove operator keeps clear, and if there are no hanging towels or curtains over the stove that can catch on fire. With the valve shut, the blaze should soon die down. If not, let the pressure off the fuel tank, or, if the feed is by gravity, shut the fuel line shut-off valve. Remember that water will extinguish an alcohol fire, but a considerable quantity should be used. It is always advisable to have a large pot or bucket of water handy when lighting the stove in case a flare-up should get out of hand.

Other sources of stove fires are carelessness in spilling fuel when filling the tank and overflowing the priming cups. The latter must be sufficiently deep to hold enough alcohol for adequate heating of vaporization chambers without danger of overflow even in rough weather. Also, there must be a large, deep, removable metal drip pan under the stove to catch any spilled alcohol. This pan should be thoroughly clean and dry of fuel before the priming cup is lighted. Be sure that there are no leaks in the fuel line. Tighten all threaded connections, and see that the line is properly gasketed.

Once the stove is burning, it should be continually watched to see that all flames are burning properly. If an unwatched burner flame should happen to go out, due to temporary clogging of the burner by sediment, a sudden draft, a pot boiling over, or some other cause, then raw alcohol could accumulate where it might cause a flare-up. The raw alcohol could be ignited by the hot burner. When a burner goes out, it might be relighted immediately (while there is sufficient heat for vaporization), but if it cannot be relighted at once, the burner should be turned off, and then it will be necessary to reprime.

More than one boat has caught on fire because a stove flare-up made the fuel tank shut-off valve inaccessible. Despite contrary recommendations by the ABYC, many boats are equipped with shut-off valves that can only be operated by reaching across the stove. This means that if the stove blazes out of control, the valve cannot be turned at the very time when it is imperative to shut off the fuel supply. Valves should not only be accessible, but they should be capable of being closed with one turn, and the open and shut positions should be clearly marked.

Kerosene stoves, which are similar to the alcohol type we have been discussing, are also quite safe, but they require a fire extinguisher (rather than merely water) to put out a flare-up that is out of control. Regardless of the fuel, however, a fire extinguisher should always be mounted in or near the galley. The ABYC does not recommend wick-type burners, because their performance may be adversely affected by the boat's motion. All accepted standards warn against the use of gasoline for stove fuel aboard boats. With any kind of stove, the woodwork around it, especially overhead, should be well protected with asbestos and sheet metal. Also, it is important to keep all stoves clean, because accumulations of grease from cooking can be highly flammable.

Many boats are fitted with liquified petroleum (LP) gas stoves (or other appliances) because of their convenience in not needing to be primed. These appliances can be extremely dangerous if they are not properly installed and carefully handled. They should be given the same respect as a gasoline engine and its fuel system, because LP gas and gasoline vapors have the same dangerous characteristics; both are heavier than air, and both are potentially explosive. In some respects, LP gas, which includes propane and butane, may be even more hazardous than gasoline, because it is easily diffused and is difficult to dispel by overhead ventilation, and, furthermore, it is relatively odorless. In fact, the ABYC and NFPA recommend the odorizing of LP gas used on boats. It is therefore important that LP gas cylinders be carried on deck or in a ventilated deck box fitted with a drain at the bottom which leads overboard. Thus any possible leakage of gas will escape well clear of the boat's interior. LP gas systems should have a pressure gauge to allow a periodic (at least biweekly) convenient means of checking for leaks. The pressure should be read with the main cut-off valve and the cylinder valve open, while the appliance valves are shut. If the pressure remains constant for ten minutes after the cylinder valve is shut, this indicates there are no leaks. Of course a drop in pressure would indicate a leak. The application of soapy water to all connections is an effective means of locating the leak.

A few rules for safe operation of LP gas stoves (or other gas appliances) are as follows:

• Always keep the cylinder valve shut unless the appliance is actually in use. Be sure that the valve is shut in any emergency.

• See that the appliance valves are shut before the cylinder valve is turned on.

• When lighting the stove, apply the lighted match (or lighter) to the burner *before* its valve is opened.

• Watch the stove while it is being used to see that the flame does not go out. If it should go out (from a sudden draft, a pot boiling over, etc.), shut the valve immediately.

• In order to ensure that minimal gas will remain in the fuel line, shut the cylinder valve first and allow the fuel to burn out of the line before shutting the appliance valves.

• Test for leaks in the system, in the manner previously described, at least every two weeks.

• See that the entire system is installed in accordance with NFPA standards (set forth in Booklet No. 302).

• Never use a flame to look for leaks.

Other main causes of fires on boats are from solid fuel heaters, overheated electric wiring, spontaneous combustion, and smoking in bunks. As for the latter cause, it should never be permitted. Heaters burning wood, coal, or charcoal must be surrounded by insulation. They should preferably be on hollow tile bases or legs and have a proper stack to prevent spark emission and back draft. Careful measures should be taken to see that the fuel cannot spill out in a seaway, and the heater should never be left for long periods unwatched. Open fireplaces need screens to assure that sparks will not be emitted. Electric wiring has already been discussed. As said earlier, major safety considerations are proper fusing, wire size, and insulation. Spontaneous combustion can result when oily rags are stowed in an air-tight space, perhaps in a paint locker, or, in the old days, an oilskin locker. Do not stow foul weather suits in air-tight spaces if they are genuine oilskins. Be sure that all lockers are ventilated, and do not keep old paint rags.

There are three elements necessary to support a fire: high temperature, oxygen, and fuel. Fire fighting techniques are concerned with eliminating one or more of these elements. The temperature can be lowered with water or other cooling agents; the oxygen can be removed or partially eliminated by smothering with a blanket, salt, soda, foam, by keeping hatches closed, etc.; and the fuel can be cut off by shutting fuel tank valves or cutting away the burning material. Fires are generally classified into three different categories according to the material afire and the recommended method of containing and extinguishing them. Class A fires are those in ordinary, solid combustible materials, such as wood, cloth, paper, and so forth. Extinguishing is usually accomplished most easily by cooling (or quenching) with water or solutions containing large amounts of water. Class B fires are those in flammable oils, grease, petroleum products, etc., and extinguishing should be accomplished by some form of smothering and shutting off the fuel supply when this is possible. Using water on this type of fire might tend to spread it, because burning gasoline and oils float. Class C fires are those in electrical equipment. Water should not be used to fight Class C fires because of the danger of shock or even electrocution where high voltages are involved. This type of fire is best fought with a nonconductive, extinguishing medium that smothers the flames. It is important to cut off electrical switches and de-energize the affected circuit during a Class C fire.

Extinguishers approved by the Coast Guard are: foam, carbon dioxide ($CO_2$), dry chemical, and Freon. These are B type extinguishers (mainly for class B fires), and size requirements are presently specified in the Motorboat Act. Dry chemical extinguishers use a powder, contained under pressure, such as sodium bicarbonate (baking soda) or potassium bicarbonate ("purple K") combined with certain additives. Approved extinguishers of this type have a gauge to indicate whether or not the unit has adequate pressure for effective operation. Dry chemicals smother flames and will extinguish any of the three classes of fires, but water or foam are usually much more effective against class A fires of considerable size. Foam consists mainly of water, therefore it should not be used on Class C fires, but it is effective against Class A as well as B fires even on vertical and overhead surfaces. $CO_2$ obviously contains oxygen, but it is actually an oxygen-depriving, smothering gas. Indeed, humans should not breathe it more than momentarily in tightly enclosed spaces. $CO_2$ is especially effective against low fires, in the bilge for example, because the gas is heavier than air, and it will sink down and blanket the fire. The ABYC recommends that a portable $CO_2$ extinguisher be used in the vicinity of the galley. Large boats often have built-in $CO_2$ systems that are automatic and/or manually operable from the bridge or helmsman's position. As a matter of fact, permanent $CO_2$ systems are a very good idea on some small boats with inaccessible engine compartments. A relatively new and very effective extinguisher is Freon gas, which works almost instantaneously by smothering, cooling, and breaking down the chain reaction that keeps a fire going. Automatic systems using flame detectors that are activated by infrared-sensitive photocells are said to be highly effective. It is prudent, however, to avoid prolonged exposure in a closed compartment to a large

*The Coast Guard subduing the fire on a blazing derelict. In such a circumstance, it is obviously wise to approach the flaming vessel from the windward side.*

quantity of Freon applied to extremely hot metals (copper or brass, especially), as a poisonous gas could be generated. The DuPont Company recommends type FE 1301 Freon for use in fire extinguishers.

Be sure to keep extinguishers where they will be readily available and most likely needed, in or near such areas as the galley, the engine compartment, and the steering position. Extinguishers should be inspected periodically to see that they are in top working order, but do not test by opening the extinguisher's valve, because this might partially deplete the contents or allow pressure to leak out. Checks can be made by examining the pressure gauge, looking at safety pins and wires, or weighing the extinguishers. Follow maintenance instructions on the extinguishers, or have them checked by qualified authorities such as a competent chandler, the manufacturer, or Coast Guard. Do not use extinguishers that are not recommended, such as carbon tetrachloride or chlorobromomethane (CBM), because they can give off a poisonous gas that could be lethal under certain conditions.

Some general rules for fighting fires are as follows:
• With an LP gas fire, shut cylinder valves immediately.
• With Class B fires, shut fuel supply valves at once.
• With Class C fires, turn off electrical switches to de-energize the affected system.
• With Class A and alcohol fires, use water. A draw bucket can be a most effective fire fighting tool.

• When underway, reduce speed of boat, and turn her so that the wind blows the fire in the direction of least flammability or vulnerability. If the fire were in the bow, for example, the boat should be headed off with her stern to the wind. Obviously, the boat should be headed so that flames are blown away from fuel tanks or other vulnerable areas.

• With any fire, keep calm but act at once. The longer a fire is allowed to blaze, the more the temperature will increase and the more difficult the extinguishing operation will be. Bring all available extinguishers to bear immediately.

• Small fires might be smothered before they get started with anything available, such as a cushion, dish towel, blanket, salt, soda, etc.

• Consider the possibility of throwing the blazing object overboard. In some cases, this might involve chopping away the burning material; thus an ax or hatchet can be valuable.

• An asbestos glove could be handy not only for gripping hot pots in the galley, but for throwing a flaming object overboard, beating out small fires, or shutting hot valves that are surrounded by flames.

• Remember that even though water should not be used on Class B and C fires, it might be used effectively to cool adjacent areas to help prevent the fire from spreading. Also electrical equipment can be wet down when it is de-energized. Then too, shock hazards are minimal from the twelve-volt systems of most small pleasure craft.

• Make every attempt to reduce drafts. They fan the flames and supply oxygen. Whenever possible, shut doors, vents, portholes, and hatches. An open hatch directly above a fire can be particularly harmful, because it will act like a chimney.

• Learn how to remove and operate a fire extinguisher before facing a fire. In most cases, direct the extinguishing agent at the base of the flame in a back-and-forth sweeping motion.

• Do not remain in a closed compartment where $CO_2$ has been squirted. Although this extinguisher is not toxic, it is suffocating.

Lightning is not only a fire and explosion hazard, but it can cause lethal injury and can puncture or otherwise damage the hull. It is true that boats are not struck very often, but the danger exists, and some form of protection is needed except perhaps in certain cases when the boat has a metal hull. The main principle behind lightning protection is the provision of a low resistance path from the point where the lightning bolt strikes to the ground. In addition, grounding helps prevent a build-up of static electricity in vulnerable parts of a boat, which might possibly encourage a lightning strike. In most cases, a bolt will strike the boat's highest point, the masthead on a sailboat or the top of a tall antenna on a radio-telephone-equipped powerboat. For adequate protection of a non-metal boat, the high point must be connected with a reasonably straight, low-resistance conductor to a ground plate or perhaps a metal keel. The grounded mast or antenna will nearly always divert to itself direct lightning strikes that might otherwise fall within a cone-shaped area (called the protective cone), the apex of which is the top of the conductor and the base of which is a circle on the water having a radius of about twice the conductor's height (see Figure 26). For maximum safety, the conductor's top (masthead or antenna tip) must be sufficiently high that every part of the boat lies within the protective cone.

Details for lightning protection systems are given by the ABYC and NFPA, and some of the main points are as follows: the entire conducting circuit, from high point to ground, should be the equivalent in conductivity to No. 8 or larger copper cable running as straight as possible. Large metal objects anywhere near the conductor should be bonded to it to prevent side flashes. The top of the conductor should terminate in a point and protrude at least six inches above the mast. This is especially important when there is an electronic wind indicator or anemometer at the masthead. A powerboat with a radio telephone can be protected if the antenna is not spirally wrapped and is provided with a transmitting lightning arrester or a means of direct grounding with a switch arrangement prior to an electrical storm. There is at least one switch made for this purpose that operates automatically, with the antenna being connected indirectly to ground when the radio-telephone is turned off. Antennas with loading coils need a bypass gap or shunt (jumper) in order that the entire aerial height can be utilized for lightning protection, otherwise the apex of the protective cone should be considered as being located just below the coil (see Figure 26).

Although many boats are grounded to through-hull fittings, the ABYC recommends that the ground plate for lightning protection be no less than one foot square. A boat with a metal hull is already grounded, but care should be taken to see that wire standing rigging and metal masts (or the track on a wooden mast) are well bonded to the hull. On non-metal sailboats with external ballast keels, the conductor can be run from the base of the mast (or sail track) to the nearest keel bolt under the mast step (see Figure 26). Stays and especially upper shrouds should be grounded and also any large metal objects that protrude above the deckhouse. In the absence of a proper lightning ground system, some protection is afforded by dropping overboard a heavy copper cable clamped to a masthead stay or shroud. A screen or large copper plate attached to the underwater end of the cable should increase its effectiveness. This temporary rig should prove most efficacious when it is connected to a leeward upper shroud, since a lightning bolt will tend to take the most direct, straight-line route.

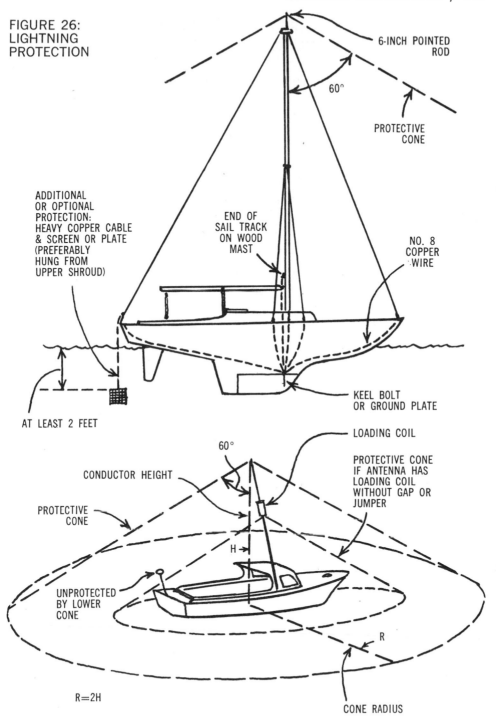

FIGURE 26:
LIGHTNING
PROTECTION

6-INCH POINTED
ROD

60°

PROTECTIVE
CONE

ADDITIONAL
OR OPTIONAL
PROTECTION:
HEAVY COPPER CABLE
& SCREEN OR PLATE
(PREFERABLY
HUNG FROM
UPPER SHROUD)

END OF
SAIL TRACK
ON WOOD
MAST

NO. 8
COPPER
WIRE

KEEL BOLT
OR GROUND PLATE

AT LEAST 2 FEET

60°

LOADING COIL

CONDUCTOR HEIGHT

PROTECTIVE CONE
IF ANTENNA HAS
LOADING COIL
WITHOUT GAP OR
JUMPER

PROTECTIVE
CONE

H

UNPROTECTED
BY LOWER
CONE

R

R=2H

CONE RADIUS

During a thunderstorm, the crew should go below if possible, and they should avoid contact with the rigging or any large metal objects. Great care must be taken to avoid touching and especially bridging objects connected to the conductive system or other metal fittings that might be struck by lightning. For instance, the helmsman exposes himself to possible danger when he grips a stanchion and a metal wheel simultaneously.

Seamanship is a broad, rather nebulous term, but its essence is the ability to anticipate and thus avoid trouble. A thoroughly competent seaman should not have a great deal to fear from emergencies, because not only does he plan how to cope with them, he takes all possible measures to assure that they will never happen in the first place.

# 5 / WEATHER, WAVES, AND
##    GENERAL STORM STRATEGY

With today's advanced weather technology and the availability of accurate forecasts, the modern seaman has a great advantage over his counterpart of the past, yet there are still numerous small craft caught unexpectedly in heavy weather each year in all parts of the world. Exposure to adverse weather remains a major threat to the safety of boatmen and their craft. Avoidance or minimization of such exposure in open waters can best be accomplished when sailors avail themselves of official forecasts and learn the basics of weather behavior. This knowledge forms the basis of judgments in deciding such important matters as: when to leave port, when to return, the best course to avoid heavy weather, the proper route and time of year for a safe passage, when to prepare for a blow, and to a large extent, how to handle the vessel during a storm.

## The Basis of Weather

A detailed study of weather is beyond the scope of this book, but statements of the basic principles of weather behavior in a non-technical manner should be helpful to those readers who wish to gain greater familiarity with the subject.

The general wind circulation of the earth consists of polar easterlies at the top and bottom of the globe, westerlies in the middle latitudes (between 30 and 60 degrees, approximately) and easterly trade winds on either side of the Equator (northeast trades north of the Equator and southeast trades to the south). In between the westerlies and the trade winds there are calm belts called the horse latitudes, and another calm belt called the doldrums divides the north and south trade wind systems at the equator. The over-all wind system of the earth results from temperature differences and the earth's rotation. Referring to the northern hemisphere, hot air at the equator rises and flows northward. Some of this air cools and sinks at the horse latitudes where a mound of high pressure girdles the earth (see Figure 27). It might be said that the sinking air splits as it descends over the high pressure mound with part of the air sliding southward back towards the equator to form the northeast trade winds and part flowing north to form the prevailing westerlies. Air that does not sink at the horse latitudes moves on at high altitudes to the poles where it sinks and then moves southwestward in the form of the polar easterlies. The wind systems of both hemispheres are given their east and west directions by the Coriolis effect, the deflection of a moving body to the right in the northern hemisphere and to the left in the southern hemisphere due to the earth's rotation on its axis. Weather tends to move in the same direction as the global wind systems. Thus, very generally speaking, storms in the middle latitudes come from the west, and tropical storms such as hurricanes or typhoons (originating in the low latitudes) travel along trade wind routes until they move northward into the prevailing westerlies, at which time, they generally curve to the eastward.

Of course the preceding description of the global winds is simplified and generalized. In actuality, there is a complex, irregular pattern of swirling winds around high and low pressure areas scattered throughout the globe, resulting principally from seasonal temperature changes and differences in heating between the oceans and land masses. High pressure cells, called anticyclones or simply highs, are mounds of concentrated air, while low pressure cells, called cyclones, lows, or depressions (by the British), are troughs or hollows in the atmosphere. Winds flow out of a high towards and into the center of a low, and the Coriolis force turns the wind so that it swirls in a clockwise direction around a high but counterclockwise around a low in the northern hemisphere. Swirling occurs in the opposite direction in the southern hemisphere. As nearly everyone knows, good weather is associated with highs and stormy weather with lows.

When air masses of different temperatures (and moisture content) collide and do not readily mix, a weather front is formed as follows: a cold front, when the cold mass advances and pushes back the warm air; or a warm front, when the warm air advances and overrides the cold mass. Bad weather is usually associated with all fronts, but cold fronts may bring violent (although relatively brief) storms with strong winds as the cold mass plows under the warm air and throws it abruptly aloft. A low is often formed along the front between two adjacent air masses when their motions are opposed and friction causes a wave or bending of the frontal line into a V shape (see Figure 28). This wave moves in an easterly or northeasterly

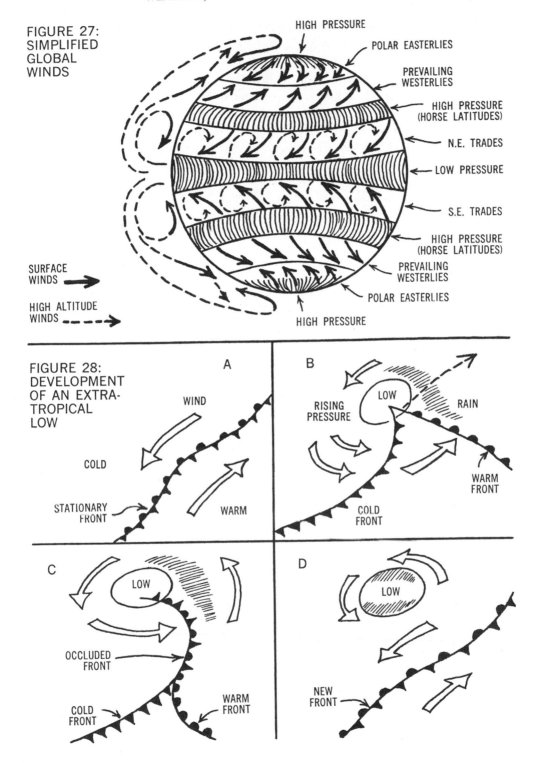

FIGURE 27: SIMPLIFIED GLOBAL WINDS

HIGH PRESSURE
POLAR EASTERLIES
PREVAILING WESTERLIES
HIGH PRESSURE (HORSE LATITUDES)
N.E. TRADES
LOW PRESSURE
S.E. TRADES
HIGH PRESSURE (HORSE LATITUDES)
PREVAILING WESTERLIES
POLAR EASTERLIES
HIGH PRESSURE

SURFACE WINDS ➜

HIGH ALTITUDE WINDS ---➤

FIGURE 28: DEVELOPMENT OF AN EXTRA-TROPICAL LOW

A
WIND
COLD
STATIONARY FRONT
WARM

B
RISING PRESSURE
LOW
RAIN
WARM FRONT
COLD FRONT

C
LOW
OCCLUDED FRONT
COLD FRONT
WARM FRONT

D
LOW
NEW FRONT

direction in the region of prevailing westerlies, and the low forms at or just ahead of the crest with a warm front to the east and a cold front to the west. Cold air to the north of the low swings around the wave crest in a counterclockwise direction and pushes the cold front around so that it chases the warm front. The faster moving cold front eventually overtakes the warm front to form an occlusion, at which time the cool air ahead of the warm front and the cold air behind the cold front meet and force the warm air upwards. This briefly describes the birth and action of the typical extra-tropical cyclone found in the middle latitudes. The sequence is illustrated in Figure 28.

*Storms and General Strategy*

High pressure cells can occasionally generate storm-force winds, but storms are normally associated with depressions and their cyclonic winds. In general, it might be said that there are four kinds of storms: thunderstorms, tornadoes, extra-tropical cyclones, and tropical cyclones.

Although there are usually turbulent vortices inside a thunderstorm, the principal internal wind forces are violent vertical currents. There are two types of thunderstorms: air-mass and frontal. The latter type is normally the most violent, especially when a fast-moving cold front meets an extremely warm, moist air mass. Thunderstorms may occur at intervals along the entire front and form what is called a squall line. Cold air burrowing low and throwing the warm air aloft will cause towering, ominous-looking cumulo-nimbus clouds (see Figure 29). Passage of the front will normally produce strong veering winds (shifting clockwise, perhaps from Southwest to Northwest). Some particularly violent squall lines are preceded by long, dark, low "roll clouds" caused by air ahead of the front being sucked up into the storm's center. Following this initial breeze towards the storm, there will be a strong outflow of cold air that can cause severe knockdowns, blow out sails, and cause other damage when a boat is caught unprepared. An air-mass thunderstorm is generally less violent. Although it also develops the cumulo-nimbus cloud, it is not associated with a front, but originates from an isolated thermal or updraft of hot air that rises into relatively cold air aloft. This type of storm may be gusty and produce lightning, rain, and possibly even hail, but it is usually short-lived, and weather conditions will probably return to those that existed before the storm.

Sailors are warned of thunderstorms principally by the appearance of the sky (and also by static on the radio). When cumulus clouds in the west show marked vertical development during the afternoon of a hot,

## FIGURE 29: CLOUDS (HENRY REGNERY CO.)

CIRRUS "mares' tails" (over 25,000 ft.)
if thick often advanced forerunners
(24 hours or more) ahead of a front

CIRROCUMULUS "mackerel sky"
(over 20,000 ft.) can predict approach
of warm front in unstable air

CIRROSTRATUS (over 20,000 ft.) whitish sheet
often causing halo around sun—can warn of
approaching warm front

ALTOSTRATUS (about 19,000 ft.) gray sheet
often warns of approaching warm front

ALTOCUMULUS (over 12,000 ft.) like sheep—
can warn of cold front in unstable air

CUMULONIMBUS "thunderhead" (thunderstorm
cloud)—can reach height of cirrus

STRATOCUMULUS (about 8,000 ft.) dark globular rolls

CUMULUS (over 4,000 ft.) fair
weather unless extreme towering up

NIMBOSTRATUS
(about 3,000 ft.)
dark rain cloud

STRATUS (about 1,500 ft.) gray sheet

*A typical cumulo-nimbus, thunderstorm cloud. (U.S. Navy)*

muggy day, the boatman should be especially watchful for thunderheads (cumulo-nimbus clouds). When a towering cumulus turns dark at the base and flares out in an anvil shape at the top, it is a mature thunderstorm. Meteorologist Alan Watts warns us, however, not to put too much stock in the anvil top, as this might occur when the storm cell is past its prime and is in a milder stage of dissipation. Of course, the close-to-shore sailor can be forewarned of frontal storms by studying late weather maps when they are available and by listening to radio weather reports. Numerous stations along the United States seaboard transmit continuous weather bureau forecasts (updated every two hours) over VHF/FM 162.55 mHz.

Tornadoes are concentrated whirlpools of air that twist around a very low pressure center. Normally cyclonic, these violent storms are extremely dangerous ashore not only because of their high winds that often exceed 300 miles per hour, but because their low pressure, which is almost a vacuum, can cause buildings to explode. Fortunately for the sailor, however, tornadoes are rare and are usually not as dangerous at sea. When one of these storms moves over the water, it will very likely turn into a waterspout, and mitigated temperature contrasts will tend to mollify the wind's intensity. Tornadoes are normally a product of extremely unstable cold front activities, and they are often found in America's mid-west, especially the Mississippi Valley. When the weather bureau considers that conditions are suited to the formation of tornadoes, warnings are usually broadcast. In the rare case of a boat encountering a waterspout at sea, evasive action can usually avoid direct contact. Due to the fact that the spout funnel can be seen a long way off, that its forward speed is relatively slow, and its destructive force is concentrated into a small area, a boat with power stands a good chance of being able to move to the side of the spout's track. Of course normal heavy weather preparations should be made, but particular attention should be paid to stopping sails thoroughly, and lashing loose gear to the deck or cabin top because of the violent updraft within the storm's vortex. There are many mysteries and superstitions connected with water spouts. One myth is that firing a gun at a spout will break it up. Perhaps there is some scientific basis that a large gun's concussion will break the partial vacuum and cause the column of water to collapse, but the efficacy of such a method seems very doubtful. At any rate it is of some comfort to know that the greatest part of a typical spout is not composed of solid water but of spray and mist. According to meteorologist George H. T. Kimble, solid water at the spout's base is seldom much higher than ten feet.

Extra-tropical cyclones were described earlier, but it should be added here that low pressure (a falling barometer) will probably precede the depression and warm front. After passage of this front but before occlusion, there should be a brief period of fair weather with higher pressure, but the fast-moving, more violent cold front will not be far behind. Thus the sailor should look for even heavier weather after passage of the first front. Winds will veer as each front passes over. Advanced warning of the approaching warm front may come from clouds in the form of high-altitude, whispy "mares' tails" (cirrus), which gradually thicken to partially fill the sky. As the front approaches, the sky may become covered with cirro-stratus, which give it a white hazy look and sometimes cause a halo around the sun. The next clouds filling in from the west could be fibrous gray alto-stratus if the air aloft is vertically stable (with little vertical movement), followed by low, dark, nimbo-stratus rain clouds. In vertically unstable air, cirro-cumulus, the small fish-scale clouds of the "mackerel sky," may make an early appearance, and they may be followed by bands of alto-cumulus (small puffy clouds looking like herds of sheep) and still later by strato-cumulus (darker, globular clouds). Rain and squalls may come from low nimbo-stratus or, in very unstable conditions, thunderstorms from cumulo-nimbus. Clouds in advance of the cold front will probably be bands of alto-cumulus, and soon afterwards towering thunderheads will make their appearance. The prudent skipper will either seek shelter, normally behind a west or northwest shore, and anchor, or else head offshore to get all possible sea room. Of course sail should be shortened or furled, and other heavy weather preparations should be made. Bad weather from the cold front should not last long, no more than a few hours normally. With passage of the front, the barometer should rise rapidly, and on many occasions the wind will blow harder for a short while even though the sky is clearing. An old weather adage warns, "Quick rise after low portends a stronger blow."

Extra-tropical cyclones frequently form in the fall when cold fronts from the north push south and meet moist, warm air over the ocean. A particularly dangerous spot, as mentioned earlier, is eastward of Cape Hatteras where warm water is pushed northward close to shore by the Gulf Stream; but this "Devil's Elbow" is only part of a much wider area of potentially dangerous weather known as the "Deadly Triangle," the boundaries of which roughly run from New York to Bermuda, to the Virgin Islands, and to the tip of Florida (see Figure 30). This general area, which is often the meeting place of tropic and arctic air masses, can very quickly generate storms that might escape the immediate notice of weathermen ashore who are paying closer attention to approaching weather from the west. The Deadly Triangle is not only subject to sudden gales in the fall and winter but to hurricanes in the summer. The safest time to venture offshore in these waters is in the late spring and early summer, but some fair-weather passages from south of Cape Hatteras to the West Indies have been made in late October or early November.

The most dangerous and widely destructive storms are tropical cyclones. Known as hurricanes in the Atlantic, as typhoons in some parts of the Pacific, and simply as cyclones in the Indian Ocean, these storms are revolving lows, similar in many respects to extra-tropical cyclones. Some major differences between the two types of cyclones are that those originating in the tropics are far more intense, they are not frontal in that air-mass temperature differences are not involved, they often move more slowly, and they are quite symmetrical with a calm "eye" at the center of rotation. Tropical cyclones are born near (but not on) the equator, usually at the intertropical convergence zone, where the southeast trade winds converge with the northeast trades. Just as an extra-tropical cyclone can be formed when two winds oppose each other on either side of a front, the two trades may oppose each other when they are acted on by the Coriolis force and start a whirlpool of air which, under the right conditions of temperature, moisture, and pressure, could develop into a severe cyclone. Another factor that frequently influences the formation of tropical storms is the presence of an easterly wave, a trough of low pressure crossing the easterly trade wind flow. As mentioned earlier, tropical cyclones follow

## FIGURE 30: TYPICAL STORM TRACKS AFFECTING U.S. WEATHER

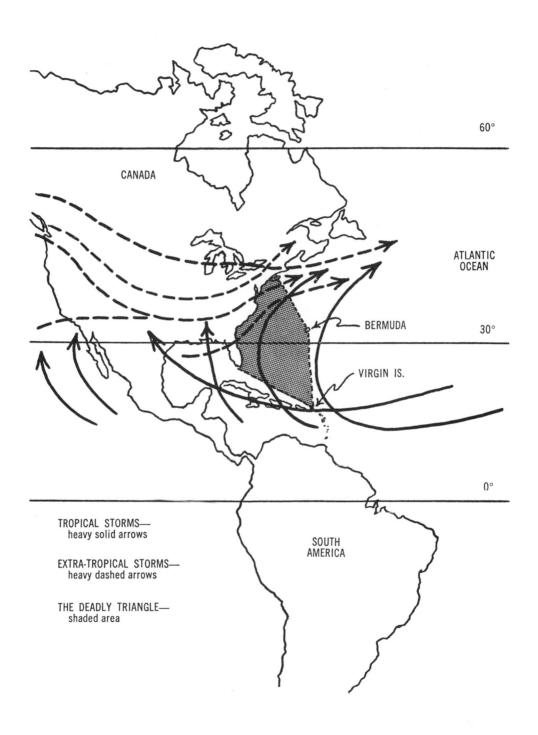

60°

CANADA

ATLANTIC OCEAN

BERMUDA

30°

VIRGIN IS.

0°

SOUTH AMERICA

TROPICAL STORMS—
heavy solid arrows

EXTRA-TROPICAL STORMS—
heavy dashed arrows

THE DEADLY TRIANGLE—
shaded area

somewhat predictable paths that generally run from their point of origin toward the west until they curve northward (in the northern hemisphere) and strike the prevailing westerlies. at which time they tend to recurve towards the east (see Figure 30). These storms are seasonal partly because they are most likely to occur when the intertropical convergence zone moves sufficiently far from the equator, following the seasonal declination of the sun, to be effected by the Coriolis force. Tropical cyclones occur most often in the late summer or early fall of their hemisphere. Indeed, West Indian hurricanes which affect the east and Gulf coasts of the United States occur between early June and late October, with the greatest frequency in September. A hurricane warning rhyme for the West Indies goes: "June, too soon; July, stand by; August, look out you must; September, remember; October, all over." It should be born in mind, however, that hurricanes are not over until the end of October and there have even been a few of these storms in November.

Although hurricane prediction is quite accurate now, especially with the use of weather satellites, and warnings are generally adequate, the careful offshore sailor avoids extended passages offshore in areas subject to hurricanes during the dangerous months. If, however, he should happen to be caught at sea in the path of a tropical cyclone, he must do his best to avoid the storm center and maneuver his craft to sectors of least intensity. His course of action should, in a general way, be based on "the law of storms," devised in the last century by Henry Piddington and endorsed by later authorities on navigation and seamanship such as Nathaniel Bowditch.

Very briefly, the basic principles expressed in the law of storms are as follows: The revolving, circular hurricane is considered to have a "dangerous" and a "navigable" semicircle. In the northern hemisphere, the right side of the circle is signified as being dangerous, because the strength of the whirling winds is reinforced by the forward movement of the storm's center; while in the navigable semicircle, on the left-hand side, the center's forward movement is subtracted from the spiralling wind velocity (see Figure 31). A fairly accurate means of determining the vessel's position with respect to the storm center is with careful and constant observations of the wind. According to Buys Ballot's law, when an observer in the northern hemisphere faces the wind, the center of low pressure is about ten points or 112 degrees to his right. If the wind veers (shifts to the right) he is in the right hand semicircle, but if the wind backs he is in the left semicircle. A constant (non-shifting) wind would indicate that the observer is on the storm track either directly ahead of or behind the center. In this case, if the wind velocity increases and the barometer falls, he is in front of the storm center, but if the wind subsides and the glass rises, he is behind the center. Of course, a hurricane's position might be obtained

## FIGURE 31: TROPICAL STORM STRATEGY

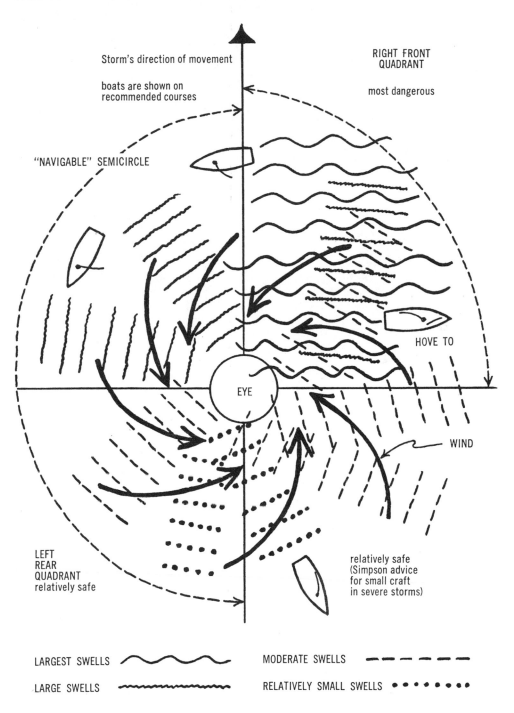

Storm's direction of movement

boats are shown on
recommended courses

RIGHT FRONT
QUADRANT

most dangerous

"NAVIGABLE" SEMICIRCLE

EYE

HOVE TO

WIND

LEFT
REAR
QUADRANT
relatively safe

relatively safe
(Simpson advice
for small craft
in severe storms)

LARGEST SWELLS ⌒⌒⌒⌒

MODERATE SWELLS ― ― ― ―

LARGE SWELLS ∿∿∿∿∿∿∿

RELATIVELY SMALL SWELLS • • • • • •

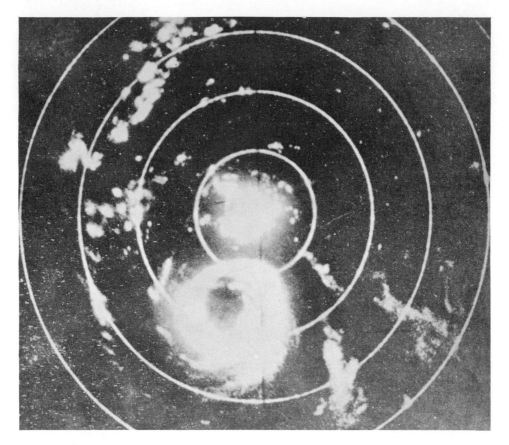

*The eye of a hurricane shown on a radar scope photographed by a Navy "Hurricane Hunter" pilot. (U.S. Navy)*

periodically from radio weather bulletins, but there is often a considerable time lag between an observation of the storm and the report of its position.

After a vessel's position relative to the hurricane has been established, she may be put on the course that will best avoid the dangerous sectors. Standard, accepted rules advise that a sailing vessel in the front quadrant of the dangerous semicircle should sail close-hauled or heave to on the starboard tack so that she will proceed (with speed if possible) away from the storm center. A vessel directly in the center's path should run on the starboard tack with the wind on the starboard quarter, and likewise if she is in front of the navigable semicircle. Powerboats should follow the same general courses, but it may be necessary in very heavy seas for them to keep their bows or sterns facing the waves (more will be said of this in Chapter 8). When it becomes necessary for a sailboat to heave to, the standard rule of thumb is to do so on the tack that allows the shifting wind to draw aft. However, for a modern fore-and-aft-rigged boat in the left front quadrant, it is usually a better tactic to run off under bare poles or storm jib on the starboard tack allowing the wind to draw forward, provided she is well behaved in quartering seas, in order to move as far as possible from the storm center. The principal reason for avoiding the center is that winds reach maximum velocity near the center, and in the "eye," a relatively small area of about 4 to 30 miles in diameter at the center of rotation, the wind is so calm that it does not flatten or give order to the seas. Indeed, vessels have been known to sustain severe damage from rolling in the eyes of hurricanes, where the waves can be huge, confused pyramids caused by the seas converging from all directions.

Although standard advice set forth in the law of storms is generally accepted as being sound even today, it was originally intended primarily for ships and large square-rigged vessels. One original concern, which probably does not have the same significance for the modern fore-and-aft-rigged boat, was the danger of being caught aback by the suddenly shifting winds in a hurricane. Furthermore, advice intended for ships does not necessarily apply in all cases to small craft; thus slight modifications of the standard rules may be necessary for small boats. In fact, one of the most experienced hurricane observers, Robert H. Simpson, believes that in many instances a boat will fare better in the rear quadrant of the dangerous semicircle than in the navigable semicircle. Simpson's advice should not be taken lightly for he is chief of the National Hurricane Warning Center in Miami, a top-ranking meteorologist, and formerly an associate director of the U. S. Weather Bureau. Furthermore, he is an experienced yachtsman, owner of a stock racing-cruising sailboat, and he has flown through hundreds of hurricanes. In an article appearing in *Rudder* magazine (July, 1968), Simpson warned against a small boat being in the left-hand semicircle in a large, severe hurricane. In general, he agrees with standard advice to run away from the center on the left side in small storms, but in large storms, he maintains that seas are more tenable for a small boat in the right rear quadrant. In this location the waves are long, less confused, and are flattened by the high winds. However, Simpson definitely agrees with the standard rule that the right front quadrant is the most dangerous sector of all, because this area has the combination of steep, confused seas with the highest winds, swells of the greatest magnitude, and, in some cases, even tornadoes. Also the wind in this quadrant tends to blow a vessel towards the storm center. Incidentally, it should be kept in mind that we have been discussing tropical cyclones in the northern hemisphere. Storms of this type rotate the opposite way in the southern hemisphere, and their dangerous semicircles are to the left of the storm track.

Warning signs of an approaching hurricane (other than from radio broadcasts) are: first, a long, heavy swell preceding the storm, then bands of cumulo-nimbus clouds and thunderstorms perhaps a day ahead of the hurricane, and then a falling barometer. Next come clouds directly associated with the hurricane, which are normally not unlike the cloud sequence preceding a warm front: cirrus, cirro-stratus, and alto-stratus, perhaps mixed with some alto-cumulus. Movement of the high-altitude clouds and the swells may give a good indication of the hurricane's location and the direction in which it is advancing. As the storm draws near, clouds thicken, the barometer continues to fall, and the wind becomes gusty. Near the times of sunset or sunrise, the sky may develop a sickly greenish-yellow appearance. A heavy black wall of storm clouds, nimbo-stratus, surrounds the center of the storm.

The actual management of a vessel at sea in a hurricane (or other type of storm) will be discussed in later chapters. As for vessels in port during a hurricane, they might be subject to even greater damage in some harbors than if they were far offshore. A major danger in many harbors may come from the extremely high tides that normally accompany hurricanes. It is therefore important to pay out all the scope possible when the vessel is at anchor and to make allowances for a great rise of water when she is made fast to a dock or pier.

An ideal hurricane anchorage should afford protection on all sides, but especially on the sides from which the winds are expected. The wind will seldom swing entirely around the compass, but it may shift through a semicircular arc. Remember that in the Northern Hemisphere a veering wind indicates you are in the right-hand semicircle, while a backing wind indicates you are in the left-hand semicircle. Protecting shores should be sufficiently high to be above the storm tide level, and if there is any choice in the matter, the anchor should be dropped behind a stand of new trees rather than old ones, which are more apt to blow down and drift down on the anchored boat. Of course major considerations are ample swinging room and good holding ground. Soft, oozy mud is a poor bottom during severe blows, unless perhaps a large, deeply imbedded mushroom anchor is used with sufficient scope to allow for the high tide. This book will not attempt a thorough coverage of anchoring techniques and ground tackle. There are many books on seamanship that deal with the subject. However, we might say here that the Danforth, Herreshoff yachtsman type, and especially the C.Q.R. type plow anchors are probably the most highly regarded (of the non-permanent anchor types) by modern seamen. A springy anchor rode to absorb the shock of sudden gusts and steep seas is highly desirable. For this reason nylon is a favorite anchor line material, but it must be carefully protected with chafe preventers, such as split rubber hoses, at the mooring chocks. A chain of moderate length between

*Damage caused by Hurricane "Carol" in 1954. Note how hurricane tides can cause a boat to be impaled on pilings when she parts her lines or is not properly tied off from a pier on her windward side. (Peter Hicks)*

the nylon line and the anchor is highly recommended. It is also helpful if a heavy weight, such as a pig of ballast, can be secured to and slid down the anchor line to a point where the weight is about half way between the anchor and the mooring chock. This will lessen shock, add weight, and help keep a catenary in the line, which will encourage the anchor to dig into the bottom. If there is any question about the strength of the anchor bitt, the rode should be additionally secured around the forward mast of a sailboat.

When the vessel is made fast to a wharf, her docking lines should be set out on both sides in order that she is held away from the wharf. If there are no pilings to which the lines can be secured, then anchors should be set out on the side without pilings. Without lines on both sides, the storm tide might lift the boat above the pier and seas could drop her on top of a piling punching a hole through her bottom. Docking lines should be doubled and well wrapped for chafe prevention. Plenty of fenders should be rigged. Old tires are effective, and normally they are readily available. Whether or not the boat is anchored or at a dock, all loose gear should be taken off her decks, and she should be stripped as much as possible of running rigging, dodgers, weather cloths, sails, or anything that can cause windage. In some cases however, when the boat is at anchor with a crew aboard, storm sails might be left bent, provided they are tightly furled and thoroughly stopped.

As a final thought on hurricanes, a frequent mistake, made especially by people ashore, is to think that the storm has ended when in the storm's

*The seas produced by winds of over 100 knots from Hurricane "Carol." This picture was taken from a Navy "Hurricane Hunter" aircraft just before it entered the eye of the storm. (U.S. Navy)*

eye. Quite often when the wind calms down and blue sky shows above, people rush out of houses, unshutter windows, replace lawn furniture, or perhaps move boats away from their hurricane berths. Soon afterwards, when the eye has passed over, the wind suddenly returns with its former strength but from the opposite direction. This is very often the time when much unnecessary damage and personal injury occurs as a result of safety measures being abandoned too soon. It is the safest policy to wait an hour or so after the weather has cleared before letting down defenses.

## Waves

As all veteran boatmen know, the principal danger of heavy weather is normally not from the wind itself but from the seas produced by the wind. Although concentrated cyclones and sudden squalls can be extremely violent, their winds need not jeopardize a well-found vessel unless she is caught unawares. Although it is possible for a seaworthy sailboat to be knocked down by a sudden wind and sink in smooth water when she

*The way it looks just before being struck by a breaking sea off Cape Horn. (Warwick M. Tompkins)*

is taken by surprise, if her sails are lowered and her hatches are properly battened before the squall, she should be perfectly safe. The real threat to her safety, however, arises when a lengthy blow has had the opportunity to build up heavy seas. Of course, some types of waves are very much more dangerous than others for reasons that will follow.

The size and character of wind-produced waves depend on: the velocity of the wind, the duration of the blow from a constant direction, the wind shifts during the blow, the fetch or distance of open water over which the wind blows, the direction and strength of current, and the depth of water. For small craft wave size is usually of less importance than the character of the waves. Dangerous seas are those that are short, steep, breaking, and chaotic, no matter what their size. Strong winds blowing for a lengthy period over a long fetch of deep water produce high but long seas that usually are not dangerous. In shoal water or with the current flowing against the wind, the seas shorten, become steeper, and break more frequently; and when the wind shifts in such a way that waves move across each other from two or more different directions, the seas can become extremely chaotic.

First of all, let us consider deep-water waves, which are usually defined as wind waves in water whose depth is greater than half the wave length. Off soundings and in areas of little or no current, the three factors that influence wave size, as mentioned above, are wind velocity, duration of that wind from a constant direction, and fetch. At sea, the fetch is not necessarily the distance from a windward shore, but rather the distance from the wind's point of origin, perhaps at the edge of a storm. Without the limiting factors of fetch and duration, waves in very strong gales could be enormously high. Such waves would be called "fully developed." Fortunately for mariners, however, this stage of development is seldom reached in the higher wind velocities, because waves are nearly always limited to some extent by fetch or duration, even in mid-ocean, and the stronger the wind, the greater the distance and time needed for a sea to reach its full potential height. For example, oceanographic tables tell us that fully developed sea heights can only be attained when a 10-knot wind blows for 2.4 hours over a 10-mile fetch; a 20-knot wind blows for 10 hours over a 75-mile fetch; a 30-knot wind blows for 23 hours over a 280-mile fetch; a 40-knot wind blows for 42 hours over a 710-mile fetch; or a 50-knot wind blows for 69 hours over a 1,420-mile fetch. These statistics make it easy to understand why so few monstrous waves are reported from reliable sources. Outside of the high latitudes of the South Pacific or the South China Sea during the monsoons, there are very few places where there is sufficient fetch and duration for a 40-knot wind to produce fully developed seas.

Comprehensive weather reports usually predict the wind strength, direction, and duration, and when the fetch can be estimated (by judging one's distance from a windward shore or storm, for instance), the height to which seas will build up can often be predicted with reasonable accuracy. As a result of extensive oceanographic studies, tables and graphs have been compiled which show the combined effects of fetch and duration on wave size in all strengths of wind. One such wave forecast graph is illustrated in Appendix G. It shows the height and period (the time it takes for one wave length to pass a given point) of deep water waves for wind speeds between 10 and 100 knots over fetch lengths between 1 and 1,000 miles with durations up to 100 hours. Notice that wave height does not increase significantly after 30 hours of duration in the lower wind speeds (under 35 knots approximately), and also, in still lower wind speeds, a fetch of greater than 200 miles will not have much effect on wave height. In using the graph, it should be born in mind that the more limiting of the two factors, fetch and duration, will govern wave height. For example, a 20-knot wind blowing over a 200-mile fetch can produce a wave 8 feet high, but if that wind has only been blowing for 7 hours, the wave will only be about 2.5 feet high. On the other hand, if the 20-knot wind blows for 30 hours the wave could be about 8.5 feet high, but with a limited fetch of only 10 miles the wave would be slightly less than 3 feet high.

Of course, it should be realized that wave forecast graphs are highly generalized. As every seaman knows, the heights of individual seas vary considerably. These wave irregularities are largely due to waves coming from different directions and crossing each other at angles, as, for example, when a new sea runs over an old swell, or irregularities can be caused by the mixing of wave trains (groups or systems of related waves moving at approximately half the speed of the individual waves). When a train having waves of a certain length mixes with another train having waves of a different length or period, some waves are reinforced while others are interfered with so that an irregular pattern is produced similar to that shown in Figure 32. This explains why there is some basis for the seaman's ancient belief that every seventh or eleventh wave will be extra high. Although there is really no invariable magic sequence number for outstandingly high or low waves, their appearance may very well come at regular intervals (perhaps after the seventh, ninth, eleventh, thirteenth, or some other sequence number). Indeed, it is usually possible and, of course, advisable, to pick a "smooth" to perform a difficult heavy weather maneuver such as tacking or wearing ship after the passing of an especially high wave or group of heavy seas.

In similar conditions of wind, fetch, and current, shallow-water waves are generally far more dangerous than those in deep water. Although waves off soundings can build up to enormous heights, and they normally move at higher velocities than those in shoal water, wave speed is not so important as the forward movement of the individual water particles. In other words, what really matters is whether or not the sea is breaking and its manner of breaking. In his book *Safety In Small Craft,* D. A. Rayner explained it rather neatly when he compared a wave's movement to a mouse running along under a rug. No matter how fast the mouse runs, the rug's motion is simply up and down. Of course, the movement of water particles in a non-breaking wave are not strictly up and down, but are circular as shown in Figure 32 with the particles at the crest moving forward (in the same direction as the wave's advancement) and the particles in the trough moving backwards (against the direction of advancement), so that after completing an orbit, each particle returns (almost) to its initial position. Actually, there is some surface drift caused by the wind which makes the particles move slightly away from the direction of the wind. Drastic forward transport of the particles, however,

## FIGURE 32: WAVES

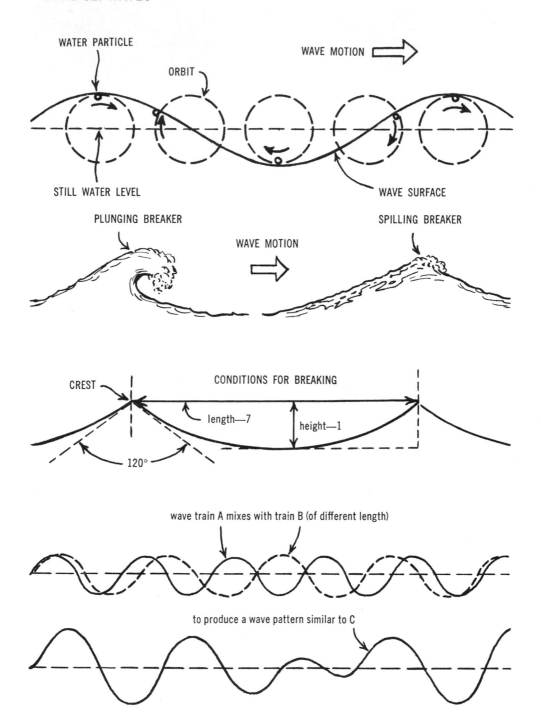

WATER PARTICLE

ORBIT

WAVE MOTION

STILL WATER LEVEL

WAVE SURFACE

PLUNGING BREAKER

SPILLING BREAKER

WAVE MOTION

CREST

CONDITIONS FOR BREAKING

length—7

height—1

120°

wave train A mixes with train B (of different length)

to produce a wave pattern similar to C

*A plunging type breaker in the Gulf Stream. (Jan Hahn)*

occurs only when they tear away from their orbits when the wave breaks, and this helps explain why breaking seas can be dangerous.

As a deep-water wave moves into shallow water, it not only tends to steepen, but the particles' orbits become more elliptical, and although the wave speed decreases, the horizontal particle speed becomes faster. Theoretically, a wave is very likely to break when its crest angle becomes less than 120° or when its height becomes greater than one-seventh of its length, as illustrated in Figure 32. There are two general types of breakers, plungers and spillers. The latter has a more concave back, and its crest breaks gradually and continuously (see Figure 32). A plunger has a more convex back, and its crest falls suddenly and more violently. This type is nearly always the more dangerous. While both kinds of breakers are found near shore and at sea, deep-water breakers are usually the spilling type. Bear in mind, however, that a wave is considered to be in shallow water when it begins to "feel" bottom, and this occurs when the water depth becomes less than half the wave length. Thus with sufficient wave length, it is perfectly possible to have shallow water waves at sea. As Willard Bascom has pointed out in his book *Waves and Beaches,* a wave at the edge of the continental shelf in 600 feet of water with a period of 16 seconds, is considered a shallow water wave, for it would have a length of over 1,300 feet.

$$[T^2 = \frac{L}{5.12}, \text{ where T is the period in seconds and L is the length in feet.}]$$

*Harvey Conover shown at the helm of his newly-built centerboard yawl* Revonoc, *which was lost with all hands in the Straits of Florida in 1958.* Revonoc *was caught between a high pressure system to the north and an intense low to the south. When the winds of each system met, they reinforced each other to produce a sudden northeast gale with gusts up to 70 knots, which opposed the strong flow of the Gulf Stream, producing an untenable condition for the ocean racer and her experienced crew. (Morris Rosenfeld)*

In determining the proper storm strategy, therefore, it is important not only to know your position with respect to shore or shoals on which you could run aground, but also to consider the effect of water depth on the character of the seas in your location. It is nearly always advisable to move towards or stay in the deepest water possible when expecting a lengthy blow, unless of course, a protected harbor can be reached before the blow begins.

As said earlier, dangerous seas can also be caused by a current flowing against the wind. Major offshore currents are well known, and their basic tracks are marked on Pilot Charts, however they can meander considerably. These currents can be dangerous for two reasons: first, because they can "breed" bad weather by bringing warm water into a cool area of the ocean, and secondly, because they often produce short, steep, breaking waves when their flow is opposed by a strong wind over a lengthy period of time. A typical current of this type is the Gulf Stream, and it has been extremely troublesome to small craft off the southeast coast of the United States,

*This dinghy with the small gash in her starboard side was the only trace found of the missing* Revonoc. *(U.S. Coast Guard)*

especially off Cape Hatteras. Many boats, even large ones, have been lost during fall and winter gales in this general area.

A newly-built, 43-foot, Sparkman-and-Stephens-designed, ocean racing yawl, *Revonoc*, was lost with all hands in early January, 1958, off the coast of Florida in a northerly gale blowing against the Gulf Stream. Her owner and skipper, Harvey Conover, was a former commodore of the Cruising Club of America and was one of America's most experienced offshore yachtsmen. *Revonoc* disappeared without a trace except that her slightly damaged dinghy was later found, and it has been suggested that she could have been run down by a steamer. When I asked Rod Stephens Jr. of Sparkman and Stephens about the loss, however, he wrote, "I think the situation in the gale of wind was that three or four knots' current heading directly into the wind is untenable and that was the basic problem."

It is not always easy to tell when you are actually in the main flow of an offshore or coastal current because of its frequent meanderings. Useful signs are: changes in the color of the water, the character of the waves, the water temperature, and sometimes foreign flotsam brought from some other location near the current's point of origin. The Gulf Stream, for example, is generally a deeper blue, has a considerably warmer temperature, and often has steeper waves than the surrounding ocean. It is also usual to see bits of gulf weed carried far north by this current. Obviously, a therometer for measuring water temperatures can be a useful piece of equipment on an offshore boat.

This chapter has attempted to deal with typical storm behavior and general storm strategy, but the next three chapters will be concerned with the actual handling of a boat in heavy weather.

# 6 / SAFE RIGS AND HEAVY WEATHER SAILING

During most heavy weather offshore races there are a rash of gear failures and even dismastings. To some extent these accidents might be a result of poor seamanship, but in many cases they are caused by unsuitable design and construction. Deficiencies in the design and construction of hulls and hull equipment were discussed in previous chapters. It was pointed out that safety shortcomings are commonplace with many stock hulls, but perhaps this is even more true with standard sailboat rigs. Usually the rigging and fittings are simply too light to cope with the stresses of blue water sailing in rugged conditions. This is partly due to the present fetish for reducing weight aloft. It is true that extra weight aloft can reduce a boat's stability far more than many people realize, but nevertheless, safety should be put before every other consideration, especially on an offshore boat. Not only should the mast, rigging, and fittings be of adequate strength for normal heavy weather, but a considerable margin of safety should be allowed for unexpected stresses.

Some commonly seen faults with rigging and fittings on stock boats are as follows:
- Fittings too light and too small.
- Extensive use of cast metal fittings, which may have hidden flaws.
- Pawls and springs of inadequate strength used in some winches.
- Cleats placed at wrong angle to the direction of their lines' pull.
- Some fittings not through-bolted and bolts often placed too close together.
- Certain fittings made of unsuitable materials such as plastics.
- Lack of permanent slide stops at the end of tracks.
- Sail tracks often inadequately secured for heavy weather.
- Blocks of wrong design or construction for their intended purpose.
- Lack of fairleads or separators for halyards running through mast-head sheaves.

- Mast tangs improperly placed or fastened.
- Mast sections too small or walls too thin.
- Standing rigging too light.
- Spreaders too short, allowing a less-than-adequate shroud angle.
- Single lower shroud or other shroud arrangements that allow excessive fore and aft movement of the middle of the mast.
- Inadequate stay support between upper spreaders and masthead.
- Lack of toggles on shrouds or, worse yet, on stays.
- Inadequate staying arrangement on mizzen masts.
- Use of hinged or loosely attached spreaders on offshore boats.
- Too many holes drilled in a mast at one spot.
- Use of improperly swaged end-terminals on shrouds and stays.
- Roller reefing gear and goosenecks too small or of weak construction.
- Booms not tapered for roller reefing.
- Booms too long, creating a hazard of tripping or fouling on the backstay.
- Stays or shrouds made of non-flexible wire cable bent into eyes.
- Use of relatively weak insulators on a stay in order to use it for a radio antenna.
- Lack of proper boom topping lifts and/or boom crutches.
- Mainsheet cleat out of reach of the helmsman.
- Use of shackles in standing rigging.

*Standing Rigging and Related Fittings*

Many of the rigging deficiencies listed above need elaboration. To begin with, fittings are often the weak links in a rig. The noted British author-designer Douglas Phillips-Birt has written that "the capital weakness" of the modern Bermuda rig "is its ultimate dependence upon many small metal parts." Thus it is of the greatest importance that turnbuckles, toggles, tangs, terminal eyes or jaws, and other essential hardware be carefully selected and inspected for any cracks or flaws. Fittings should be forged, extruded, or machined from bar stock best to assure that there are no internal voids or flaws, as are sometimes found in cast metal fittings. Rigging toggles are essential on offshore boats to supply universal joints between stays or shrouds and their attachment to the hull. These joints are especially important on stays, because these wire supports are very much subject to lateral as well as fore-and-aft movements caused by a seaway, the side force of jibs or spinnaker poles against forestays, and the side force of riding sails or topping lift strops against permanent backstays. Without toggles the jaws or threaded portions of fittings can work and fatigue. Furthermore, it is a good idea to lubricate the toggles on head-stays and backstays, because they are often set up so tight (to prevent a large catenary in the jib luff) that the joints are reluctant to move. Despite the extra weight aloft, it is the safest policy to have toggles at the top as well as the bottom of the headstay and the backstay if it is subjected to forces from various directions.

Turnbuckles must be extra strong because they are held together by screw threads. Very often failures in turnbuckles and screw shackles will occur at the threads. Care should be taken to see that an ample length of shank is screwed into the barrel at the top and bottom of a pipe turnbuckle. Lock nuts, or preferably cotter pins, should be used to assure that the turn-buckles will not come unscrewed. Threads should be kept lubricated, and great care should be taken not to bend the barrel of an open turnbuckle by sticking a lever through its barrel to turn it forcibly. Although one frequently sees screw shackles used for linkages in standing rigging, this practice can be dangerous. It is safer to use threadless, toggle-type, clevis pins with strong, heavy cotter keys. Be sure that cotters are not fatigued from frequent bending and that they are the same material as their pins (normally stainless steel or bronze), because galvanic corrosion can weaken the keys. As a matter of fact, this corrosion can even occur aloft, where the fitting is out of range of normal salt water spray. On alumi-num masts, when fittings of dissimilar metal, such as stainless steel or espe-cially bronze are attached, they should be isolated with plastic tape or some other barrier material. It is generally considered acceptable, however, to use stainless steel screws on an alloy mast, partly because the area of the more noble metal (stainless steel) is relatively very small. Top quality stainless steel fittings have greater tensile strength than those of bronze, but the latter material is satisfactory when there is sufficient size to the fitting, and steel turnbuckles are sometimes subject to binding and almost welding their threads when under great stress. It is sometimes recom-mended that turnbuckles, especially those on headstays, have a safety factor of at least five times the normal working load. One simple test for appraising the strength of a stainless steel fitting (not wire) is with the use of a magnet that is held in contact with the fitting. When there is a definite attraction between the metal and the magnet, the fitting should be suspect. It could be dangerously weakened from having been bent or overly stressed.

Standing rigging is generally composed of stainless steel cable of the 1 x 19 construction (one strand made of nineteen wires). This construction is highly satisfactory in most respects, because it is strong and has minimal stretch. However, there is one drawback in that the cable is non-flexible and very difficult to splice. In fact, the vast majority of shrouds and stays made of 1 x 19 wire have swaged end eyes or jaws. These terminal fittings, which are squeezed onto the wire under high pressure have a holding strength of up to 100 percent of the wire strength when the swaging is properly done, but there have been more than a few cases of swages letting go, and I have seen old and even brand new rigging with minute longitudinal cracks in the terminal fittings. Swaged fittings should be carefully examined periodically with a magnifying glass. One recommended method is to use a dye penetrant and developer. The dye may be visible (Ardrox 996), fluorescent under ultraviolet light, or visible and fluorescent (Ardrox 9VF1). The dye is applied to a thoroughly clean surface, allowed to penetrate any cracks, wiped off, and then shows up on developer applied to the dry surface. Fluorescent penetrant is more sensitive and shows up smaller defects. Traditionally the same technique, using light oil on a cleaned surface and chalk as the developer, was used on metals to detect cracking, etc. It has also been argued that fish oil or primers (Rustoleum 769) will help to prevent stress corrosion of stainless fittings, but this is a debatable point. Certainly they must be applied before the fitting has had any chance to pick up salt from spray or sea air. Use of any such preparation must not be assumed to give complete protection, and fatigue-reducing design coupled with regular inspection are necessary.

Since failures in swaged fittings do occur (although not very often when the fitting is properly swaged and periodically inspected), some offshore cruising sailors prefer to use flexible cable that can be bent into eyes and spliced for standing rigging. Flexible rigging is not as strong and has more stretch than 1 x 19 wire, and a splice only gives up to 80 percent of the cable's strength; but nevertheless, small amounts of stretch can be tolerated on a cruiser, and a well-spliced eye over a large, solid thimble may instill more confidence by the fact that it will seldom let go suddenly, without warning. It is interesting to note that Captain John Illingworth, a noted authority on rigging, specified wire of the 7 x 7 construction (seven strands of seven wires each) with spliced ends for the yawl *Lively Lady,* which Sir Alec Rose sailed around the world single-handed in 1967-68. Several experienced offshore sailors with whom I have talked prefer to use 1 x 19 wire, but with removable terminals with swage inserts such as the "Norseman" brand, because these can be renewed easily, and their installation is simple and almost foolproof. A few ocean racing skippers have their rigging hardware x-rayed for hidden defects. This is a troublesome procedure but prudent when extensive offshore work is anticipated. If the keel bolts are to be x-rayed (see Chapter 3), perhaps vital fittings could be done at the same time. Ordinarily, however, when fittings are not cast, are of top quality and ample size, and are carefully inspected, x-raying should not be necessary.

Breaking strengths of rigging wire and fittings are listed in marine supply catalogs. A typical size for a small boat would be ¼-inch-diameter stainless steel cable, which is given a breaking strength of 8,200 pounds in 1 x 19 construction, and 6,100 pounds in 7 x 7 construction. The recommended forged bronze turnbuckle size to accompany the ¼-inch wire is ½-inch, which has a breaking strength listed from 10,500 to 12,000 pounds depending on the make. As said before, it is important to allow an ample safety margin with turnbuckles because of their vulnerability to fatigue. A very simple rule of thumb in choosing the proper wire size for a boat is to select an upper shroud with a breaking strength equal to the displacement of the boat if she is extremely stiff, or, if she is not particularly stiff, the next smaller size wire (normally 1/32 of an inch smaller) may be used. This rule usually gives a shroud size slightly larger than that found on stock boats, but it allows a good margin of safety for offshore sailing. The shrouds on stiff boats, particularly on multihulls, should be heavier than those on tender boats that yield more to the wind's side force. A headstay and backstay should generally be the same size as the upper shrouds, but lower shrouds can be a little lighter, especially if there is a pair on each side of the boat.

The use of solid rod rigging is somewhat controversial at the present time. A rod allows minimal stretch, but if it fails from stress corrosion, the mast may very well go by the board, whereas the breaking of one wire in a 1 x 19 cable will still leave 18 wires for support. Furthermore, there seems to be a greater likelihood of fatigue failure in the terminal fittings with solid rod as compared with 1 x 19 cable. There have been a rash of rod headstay failures in ocean races recently, but it is my understanding that at least one manufacturer of rod stays, the Nautical Development Company, has had a very good safety record. Most authorities agree that the initial (at anchor) tension put on a rod headstay before getting underway should be very much lower than the tension given a cable stay. Recommended tensions for a precipitation-hardened, stainless steel rod are from 15 to 20 percent of its breaking strength. Rod rigging certainly has its place in "around-the-buoys" racing, but for greater safety in ocean sailing, I would prefer 1 x 19 stays. The latter rigging has at least some stretch and therefore the ability to absorb unanticipated loads before failure. Furthermore, this stretchability imposes less strain on the mast and hull in rugged conditions.

Aluminum masts on many stock boats are very light and thin walled. It is of the greatest importance, therefore, that these masts be properly rigged and tuned. In my opinion, they should be kept straight at sea, and the rigging should be positioned and set up sufficiently tight to prevent excessive mast movement. Compression bends from overly taut stays

# FIGURE 33: STANDING RIGGING

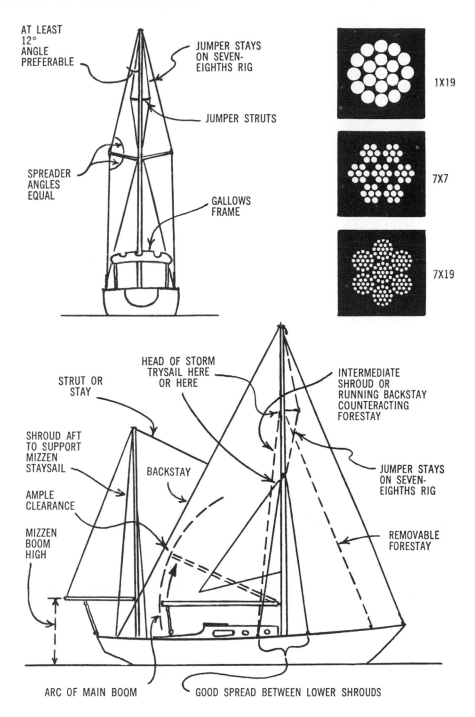

AT LEAST
12°
ANGLE
PREFERABLE

JUMPER STAYS
ON SEVEN-
EIGHTHS RIG

JUMPER STRUTS

SPREADER
ANGLES
EQUAL

GALLOWS
FRAME

1X19

7X7

7X19

HEAD OF STORM
TRYSAIL HERE
OR HERE

STRUT OR
STAY

INTERMEDIATE
SHROUD OR
RUNNING BACKSTAY
COUNTERACTING
FORESTAY

SHROUD AFT
TO SUPPORT
MIZZEN
STAYSAIL

BACKSTAY

JUMPER STAYS
ON SEVEN-
EIGHTHS RIG

AMPLE
CLEARANCE

MIZZEN
BOOM
HIGH

REMOVABLE
FORESTAY

ARC OF MAIN BOOM

GOOD SPREAD BETWEEN LOWER SHROUDS

should not be allowed; at the same time, the rigging should be tight enough to hold the mast in column in a seaway, otherwise, it can collapse without breaking a stay, shroud, or fitting. I have seen this happen. Normally there should be a pair of lower shrouds on each side with sufficient spread between the forward and after lowers to hold the middle of the mast steady in a seaway. On masthead-rigged boats with a lot of distance between the upper spreaders and the masthead a removable forestay with counteracting after intermediate shrouds or running back- stays (shown by dashed lines in Figure 33) may be necessary to prevent excessive fore-and-aft mast movement. The forestay may also serve the desirable function of counteracting the pull of a reefed main or the head of a tall storm trysail. Seven-eighths-rigged boats may carry jumper stays and struts to control the bending and movement of the upper mast, but struts will interfere with a masthead jib. Of course, there are many different rigging systems, and any of these may be satisfactory as long as they hold the mast straight and reasonably steady. Also, the simplest plan that can do the job adequately is usually the one most desirable.

Yawls and ketches sometimes lack adequate mizzen support forward because of the difficulty in rigging a mizzen forestay that will not be fouled by the main boom. One solution to this problem is a jumper stay running from the mainmast's head to the mizzenmast head or a strut or wire from the mizzen's masthead to a point approximately halfway up the main backstay, as shown in Figure 33, but the trouble with any connection of rigging between masts is that if the mainmast goes by the board, it will probably carry away the mizzenmast. It is important that shrouds and stays be properly tensioned. Headstays and backstays are often set up tighter than they should be for the greatest safety offshore. As a general rule, upper shrouds should be carried tighter than intermediates, and inter- mediates should be tighter than lowers, because the longer shrouds have more stretch and usually pass over spreaders. Several boats lost the tops of their masts recently, because their intermediates were tighter than they should have been as compared with the tautness of the uppers.

A modern trend is the extra flat trimming of Genoa jibs. Sheeting angles (angles the chord of the sail makes with the centerline of the boat) have moved inboard from about twelve degrees to nine degrees on some modern boats. This means that shrouds have been moved inboard and spreaders have been shortened to make possible the small sheeting angles. In my opinion, this practice can be dangerous on offshore boats, because it reduces the angle between the upper shrouds and the mast. When this angle becomes smaller than twelve degrees, shroud loading increases con- siderably. Many of the newer boats, have shroud angles of eleven degrees, and a few of the most recent boats have angles far less, as little as seven-

and-a-half degrees. This is creating an unnecessary risk, to my way of thinking.

It is surprising how often one sees a boat with horizontal spreaders. Actually, the spreaders should nearly always be cocked up slightly so that the angles between the shroud and spreader above and below are exactly equal (see Figure 33). Otherwise, compression on the spreader will be out of column and the tip may tend to slip. Of course wooden spreader tips should have metal ferrules to prevent their splitting, and they should be securely lashed to the shrouds and then wrapped with felt or fitted with rollers to prevent chafe on the Genoa jib.

Tangs and mast tracks should be very securely fastened, but care should be taken to see that there are not too many fastenings at the same vertical location on the mast. Not long ago I examined a broken aluminum mast which had nine holes drilled entirely around it not more than a few inches apart in the vertical direction. The break ran from hole to hole. Mast tracks sometimes pull away from the mast, and so they should be bolted in the areas of greatest stress. An especially important area is that adjacent to the head of a fully hoisted storm trysail. Mast tracks, tangs, pins, sheaves, and all fittings aloft need very careful inspection before the vessel is taken offshore. Indications of weaknesses which could possibly lead to failures are: tangs with drilled holes having elongated oval shapes; masthead tangs which have sunk even slightly into the mast; poorly seated screws indicating possible slippage of the tang; bolts showing evidence of being bent or worn; eye splices with wire snags or enlarged eyes; worn lips on halyard sheaves; spreader fittings or tangs which show even a slight shifting of position; masthead cranes which may be bent or slightly crushed; spreaders with considerable play or looseness at their inboard ends; and so forth. All cotter pins should be carefully examined for crystallization or corrosion, vertical bolts should have their heads up, and nuts should be locked on by peening or with cotters. Of course, all mast fittings should be examined for hairline cracks, weak weldments, distortion, wear, or serious corrosion.

*Running Rigging and Related Fittings*

It is generally agreed that the best materials for running rigging are Dacron (called Terylene in England) line and 7 x 19 (seven strands, each made from nineteen wires) flexible, stainless steel, wire rope. Dacron is generally used for sheets, and the wire is used for halyards because of its low stretch and windage characteristics. When a reel halyard winch is used, the halyard is wound up on a drum which has a friction brake to stop rotation, thus the halyard can be composed entirely of wire. When non-reel ratchet winches are used, however, the wire halyard has a rope tail that can be cleated easily and coiled. The rope tail is joined to the wire either with two eye splices or with a wire-to-rope tail splice. Although tail splices are commonly used, I think they can be risky when reefing, because when sail is shortened, the weight of sail and boom are supported by the relatively weak linkage of the wire-to-rope splice. In fact, I was once on board a boat that lost her internal main halyard when the tail splice let go. From the standpoint of reefing, it is better to use reel winches, or two eye splices joining the wire and rope tail, or in some cases it may be possible to rig a head pendant to extend the length of the halyard so that its wire part will go around the winch a few times when the sail is reefed; thus avoiding excessive strain on the tail splice.

An important consideration with wire halyards is to be sure that proper blocks and sheaves are provided for them. Standard blocks on stock boats are not always adequate in construction and design. A common failing is the use of non-swiveling blocks when the line or wire running through the sheave may change direction and pull somewhat laterally so that the line presses against the shell of the block. In this case the shell can break, or the line will chafe, or a wire may become jammed between the sheave and the shell. A sometimes satisfactory substitute for a swivel is the addition of an extra shackle to the fitting by which the block is hung. Be sure the block is large enough for its line, especially when using natural fiber rope that can swell when wet. Blocks for wire should have deeply grooved sheaves and minimal space between their sheaves and shells to lessen the possibility of a wire jam. Side-by-side sheaves mounted in the masthead should have metal separators between them, or else fairleads to prevent one halyard from jumping its sheave and jamming another. There is hardly a worse feeling than attempting to lower a sail in a squall only to discover its halyard is jammed aloft. If the halyard has very forcibly been pulled between the sheave and shell, quite often the block must be disassembled to remove the wire. It is important that sheaves or winches intended for wire be of sufficient diameter. A rule of thumb is that for 7 x 19 wire, the sheave or drum diameter should be at least 20 times the diameter of the wire rope. Otherwise, the wire will be weakened, and it may develop sharp snags or "fishhooks" when it is sharply bent.

On stock boats, some fittings may be made of unsuitable materials. For instance, I have seen Tuphnol blocks without metal straps connecting the sheave pins to the eyes by which the blocks are hung. Small cruising boats are sometimes fitted with Genoa jib leads made of nylon, and sail slides are sometimes secured with nylon shackles. These fittings frequently carry away in heavy weather. Weak or improperly secured fittings are not just annoying; they can lead to serious injuries. In my sailing area, a young man was killed recently when a block let go and hit him in the head. It is especially important that turning blocks be extra strong and well secured, because when a line enters a block and then reverses its direction of pull by 180 degrees, the strain on the block is doubled. In other words, if the pull on the line leading to the block is 500 pounds, the line also pulls with a strain of 500 pounds after it turns and leaves the block, which puts a total load of 1,000 pounds on the fitting.

Winches can be dangerous to handle. In fact, there have been more than a few serious accidents where crew members have been "beaned" by runaway winch handles. It is true that some of these injuries could have been avoided with careful seamanship, but in most cases the accidents were a result of winch failure, often from broken pawls, pawl springs, or faulty brakes. It is the safest policy to avoid buying cheap, unfamiliar equipment, but even the most costly winches fail occasionally. With a pair of new, expensive sheet winches made by a well-known firm, I had two pawls and three springs break within the period of one year. The sailor can best protect himself by handling his winches very cautiously. This subject was discussed in Chapter 4. Brake handles on reel winches should be fitted with locks so that they cannot be accidentally tripped. The safest kind of brake is probably the toggle-and-screw-pin type that allows the gradual easing of friction.

Roller reefing mechanisms on stock boats are often undersized. They should be very strongly made and be fitted with a large flange to prevent the sail from sliding forward at the tack and getting tangled in the mechanism. Although booms are seldom tapered for roller reefing, I think they should have a larger diameter aft than forward, because otherwise the after end will droop when a deep reef is rolled in. The gooseneck should also be very strong, and its track should be bolted to the mast, especially if the boat carries a vang which secures at the base of the mast. Such a vang will impart a powerful lateral thrust against the gooseneck and track when the boom is broad off.

It is not at all unusual to see a main boom so long that it can strike the permanent backstay during a goose-wing or "Chinese" jibe. Such a jibe can occur if the mainsheet is not bowsed down sufficiently when wearing ship or during an inadvertent "all-standing" jibe. When this happens, the outboard end of the boom rides up and moves closer to the backstay. If the boom should strike the stay it could break the stay or boom, strain the transom, pull out the chainplate, or at least cause a severe knockdown in heavy weather. Be sure the vertical arc made by raising the end of the main boom is well clear of the backstay. This point is shown in Figure 33.

A pet peeve of mine is the lack of proper main boom topping lifts on stock boats. Standard practice is a short wire strop secured to the permanent backstay with a compression sleeve which holds up the main boom while the boat is at anchor. Quite often, at the end of the strop, there is a weak snap hook to facilitate clipping the strop to the boom. Failure of the snap hook, which lacks the strength of a pin shackle, could allow the boom to fall on a crew member's head. A major difficulty with the strop lift is encountered when lowering or raising the sail in a fresh breeze. The boom must either be held up by hand, a difficult and possibly dangerous task in heavy weather, or else it is necessary to leave the strop attached to the boom while the sail is being hoisted or lowered, in which case the boat is subjected to a possible knockdown, unless she is held exactly head to wind. If the sail is going up or down while the boat is underway, it may be very nearly impossible to hold her head into the eye of the wind without auxiliary power. Furthermore, there is always the possibility of a sudden wind shift, not uncommon in gusty northwesters in certain areas, which might cause the sail to fill. A proper topping lift, adjustable at the mast, can be used to top up the boom when running off in heavy seas; facilitate raising, lowering, and reefing the sail; and also it can be used for an emergency halyard. In addition, I think boats should be provided with boom crutches to support the boom when sail has been lowered. Actually, it is preferable that an offshore cruiser have a sturdy gallows frame with boom positions on both sides as well as amidships.

Cleats are often incorrectly mounted. They should be placed so that their longitudinal axis are angled slightly away from the direction of pull of their cleated lines. If a cleated line under tension runs exactly the same way as its cleat axis, it is liable to jam and be difficult to free in a hurry. A common mistake in mounting headsail sheet cleats is to place them in exactly the same position on one side of the boat as on the other. This symetrical placement is seldom correct, because sheet winches usually turn clockwise on both sides of the boat, and this means that a sheet will lead off the outboard side of the winch to starboard and the inboard side of the winch to port.

In many cases on stock boats, the mainsheet cleat is out of reach of the helmsman. Such an arrangement is not advisable, because there are times when the helmsman might have to release the sheet in a hurry. This is especially true when the boat is being sailed shorthanded.

### The Offshore Rig

Some 50 years ago, many seamen felt that the Marconi rig, with its tall, intricately stayed mast, was unsafe to take offshore. In fact there are still a few non-racing sailors who think the gaff rig is the most suitable one for blue water cruising, but by and large, the Marconi or Bermudian rig, as it is sometimes called, has become almost universally accepted as the superior system for spreading sail, even at sea. Of course, both rigs have their good and bad points, but most agree that there are many more advantages with the Marconi system. Arguments in favor of the gaff rig are: that the mast is low when sail is down, rigging is simpler and there is often no need for spreaders, a great area of sail can be spread with a relatively low center of effort (geometric center of the sail, where the wind's force can be considered concentrated), and gaff sails may have less area blanketed in the troughs of waves at sea. Advantages of the Marconi rig, however, are: that it avoids a heavy, movable spar aloft which detracts from stability and creates chafe; it more successfully avoids excessive sail twist and is more efficient to windward with its long leading edge and high aspect ratio; more sail can be carried aloft (without the use of topsails) for effective light weather sailing; there is little need for long booms which interfere with backstays, are subject to tripping, and move the center of effort outboard when reaching; and for a given sail area the rig can be more inboard or compact longitudinally, allowing greater safety for the crew from the standpoint of sail handling.

An outboard rig or one that is extended longitudinally requires a bowsprit and perhaps a boomkin, and, when sail is lowered in heavy weather, it is usually necessary that crew be stationed on these spars, which are nearly always less secure than skid-proof decks protected with adequate rails, pulpits, and life lines. Although there are some advantages in having a bowsprit from the standpoint of versatility in rig balance and also in having a convenient place to cat an anchor, there seem to be many more disadvantages. Not only does a bowsprit normally add to the risk of losing a man overboard, it supplies less structural support for a headstay than when the stay is properly attached to the vessel's stemhead. Furthermore, there is often the problem of chafing the anchor rode on the bobstay. If it is necessary to have a bowsprit for the sake of balancing the rig, the spar should be short, broad, and flat with toe rails, life lines and a pulpit if possible. The bobstay must be tremendously strong, perhaps a solid rod type, and the anchor chocks or rollers should be mounted at the outboard end of the sprit to avoid anchor rode chafe.

To elaborate on the advantages of a short boom, it is obvious that for a given mast height such a boom produces a high-aspect-ratio sail (one that is tall and narrow). This kind of sail shape not only has a high lift-drag ratio and great efficiency to windward, it normally permits easier handling and reefing. Although the aerodynamic advantages of a high-aspect sail are less apparent when sailing off the wind, the tall configuration has merit even on a broad reach. In the first place, lift (rather than drag) can be utilized, when bearing away from the wind, much longer

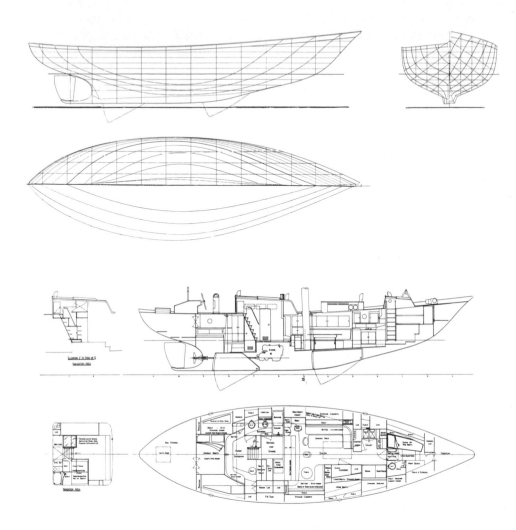

*The plans of the Angantyr, designed by MacLear and Harris. Her dimensions are: LOA—60 feet, 7 inches; LWL—45 feet; beam—17 feet, 2 inches; draft (boards up)—5 feet, 4 inches; draft (boards down)—7 feet, 10 inches; displacement—35 tons; sail area—1,647 square feet. Developed for extensive cruising, she has a number of interesting features, including tandem centerboards, flush deck, small mainsail and large fore triangle, and wide choice of downwind sails setting on spinnaker poles that house when not in use.*

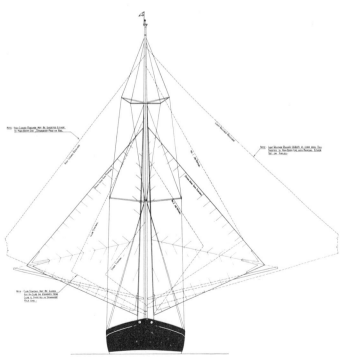

*Angantyr* has been successfully sailed single-handed. She has demonstrated the advantages of the single-stick, mast-amidships rig, even for a large boat. She might be called a Bermuda cutter, but her owner-skipper, James Crawford, uses the appelation, "single-masted schooner." (Beken)

than most sailors realize. It may very well pay, in terms of speed and efficiency, to trim the sail so that it makes a small angle to the wind (a low angle of attack, roughly 30 degrees) in order that the sail will produce optimum lift, even when the apparent wind is abaft the beam (see Figure 34). Thus the sail shaped for high aerodynamic lift efficiency is not merely suitable for close-hauled work, but it is also of value when the sheet is well started. A definite advantage in having a high aspect sail when reaching is that the center of effort (CE) of the sail is further inboard as compared to a low aspect sail with a long boom. The further outboard the CE is located, the greater the lever arm between the CE and the boat's vertical turning axis, and hence the greater the boat's weather helm or her tendency to round up into the wind. This point is illustrated in Figure 34. Another, more obvious, advantage of a short boom is that it is less subject to tripping or dipping its end in the sea when the boat is rolling while sailing down-wind.

To assure that the boom will not trip, it is often advisable, in my opinion, for the seagoing cruiser to carry a slight or moderate mast rake aft. If the sail is cut so that the boom is horizontal when the sheet is trimmed

## FIGURE 34: CENTER OF EFFORT & BALANCE

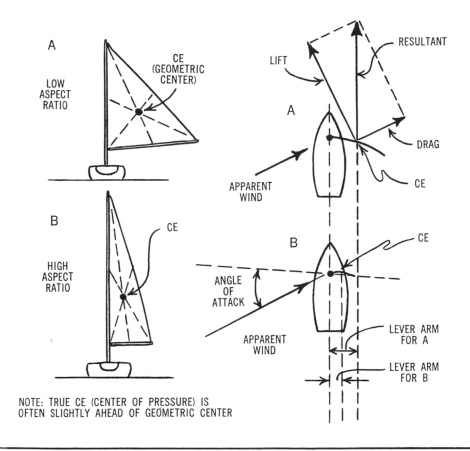

NOTE: TRUE CE (CENTER OF PRESSURE) IS
OFTEN SLIGHTLY AHEAD OF GEOMETRIC CENTER

## FIGURE 35: ANTI-TRIPPING

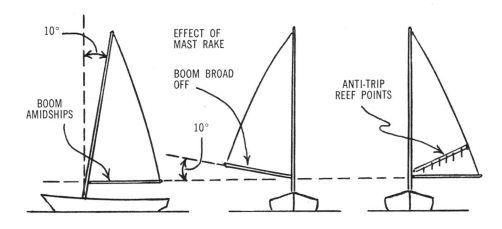

flat (with boom on the boat's centerline), the end of the boom will rise when the sheet is slacked off. This is illustrated by the exaggerated example in Figure 35. Notice that if the tack angle is to remain constant, the angle of mast rake (angle between the mast and a vertical, 10 degrees in the example) will equal the angle of boom rise (the angle between a horizontal and the boom) when it is broad off. Of course, there are other considerations relating to mast rake, a vital one being how it affects the boat's balance. Ordinarily a rake aft will increase a boat's weather helm, but since a short main boom on a single-masted boat will decrease weather helm, theorctically there should not be a great deal of difference in the effect on helm balance between a vertical mast with long boom and a raked mast with short boom.

Divided rigs are necessary, of course, on large vessels in order that individual sails can be small enough for easy management. At the present time, the most popular divided rigs are yawls and ketches. For offshore cruising the ketch rig offers the advantage of having the smallest mainsail for a given amount of sail area. The schooner rig, of course, provides still another means of dividing sail area, but this rig is far less popular today than it was in former times. One reason for this loss in popularity is the schooner's short foremast, which doesn't permit the setting of extremely large headsails and parachute spinnakers for running and beating in light airs. Then too, when hard on the wind, the schooner's powerful mainsail is backwinded to some extent by her forward sails, and her narrow gaff foresail twists into a relatively inefficient shape for windward work. With very large vessels, of course, the three masted schooner rig provides a balanced plan with sails small enough for easy management. For small boats, however, when the largest sail is not so large that it can't be easily handled, I think there are many advantages in a single masted rig. Although it is true that a two or three-masted rig keeps the total center of effort low in heavy weather at sea, the CE should not be so low that the sails become blanketed in the troughs of seas. Captains of square-riggers realized this, and they often hove to under topsails rather than lower courses. A single-masted boat can carry a tall storm trysail or a Swedish mainsail (a tall, narrow, small mainsail for windward efficiency in heavy weather), which will reduce heeling but will keep enough sail area aloft to help damp rolling and to avoid excessive blanketing from the seas when offshore. An advantage of the modern sloop, and especially the cutter, is that the rig can be concentrated amidships. The cutter rig allows efficient use of a small mainsail, and the mast is almost amidships near the point of maximum beam where there is a wide base for efficient staying and a relatively stable platform for crew safety when handling sails. The sloop or cutter enables a more continual use of a venturi slot between sails for aerodynamic efficiency even in heavy weather, and concentrates mast weight amidships to help alleviate harmful pitching tendencies.

Another point in favor of concentrating shortened sail amidships, rather than at each end of the boat, is that a chance heavy sea breaking over the side and striking the foot of a sail will not unduly affect the boat's directional stability when the sail is amidships. Solid water hitting a sail at the bow or stern will tend to turn the boat, especially if she has a short keel. An example of this happened when the 40-foot yawl *Puffin* broached to and suffered severe damage while running before a strong wind in the Mediterranean Sea in 1966. A following sea broke against her mizzen and, in the opinion of her owner, Edward R. Greef, greatly contributed to the turning moment that caused the broach. Under most conditions, a sail amidships is better protected and less vulnerable to wind and water forces that could weathercock the boat in the event that a sail is struck by a sea, a sail blows out, or a sheet parts. When running off, sail should usually be concentrated somewhat forward of amidships, of course, in order that the center of effort is kept forward to alleviate any broaching tendencies. I would be wary of carrying considerable sail extremely far forward, however, partly because the downward component of sail pressure at that location would tend to bury the bow, and this could move the center of lateral resistance forward which might encourage rooting and broaching to.

Although with yawls and ketches there is the advantage of being able to drop the mainsail to reduce sail during a sudden squall, progress to windward under jib and mizzen alone is usually poor, and it is not always the safest policy, in my opinion, to sail for lengthy periods in steep head seas with no sail set in the area normally occupied by the hoisted mainsail. One reason for this is that almost any sail (storm trysail, Swedish mainsail, or reefed mainsail) secured to the mast will help hold the mast steady and alleviate excessive fore-and-aft whipping. There have been more than a few cases of masthead rigs under heavy compression going by the board soon after the mainsail was lowered (but not replaced by a smaller sail) when in rough seas.

Figure 36 illustrates a seagoing cutter rig, which, in my opinion, has many advantages for offshore cruising. Notice that the mast is stepped well aft, it carries a small mainsail, and it has a moderate rake that lifts the boom when it is broad off and further concentrates the weight amidships to lessen pitching in a seaway. The cutter's mast location also affords maximum safety for the crew when handling her working sails, and it allows a wide shroud angle to minimize compression on the mast. Her fore triangle gives a large area for versatile headsail combinations. The forestaysail is sufficiently far aft to allow reasonably good helm balance under that sail alone if it becomes necessary to drop the mainsail during a real blow. Running backstays, not ordinarily needed may be set up to reduce mast whip in heavy head seas. The staysail with a boom and traveller is self-tending, and its stay is far enough aft to permit fairly easy tacking of large masthead jibs. Twin booms are shown housed against the mast. Their upper ends are lowered to hold out twin headsails for safe and comfortable running in fresh winds. This arrangement permits easy self steering with the wind astern. The tiny riding sail shown in the illustration may be used to help hold the head up when lying a-hull. When reaching or sailing close hauled, the wind vane and pendulum takes over the automatic steering. Notice that in addition to the main rudder and pendulum, which controls the main rudder, there is a keel trim tab with its heel well raised (to prevent damage from groundings). The tab serves as an emergency spare rudder and may be adjusted to control helm balance when reaching. Also, there are times when it might be turned in the opposite direction from which the rudder is turned to act as a brake in heavy weather.

The full-length battens shown on the cutter's Marconi mainsail are not allowed by major handicap racing rules, but they have several advantages for cruisers. In addition to holding out a substantial roach for a more efficient sail shape, the long battens allow complete and variable draft or camber control. The deeper a batten is inserted in its pocket, either manually or by adjusting tension on a leech line, the greater the sail's camber at the batten's location. In a strong breeze, the battens are kept straight with minimal insertion in their pockets to minimize sail camber. Also the long battens minimize luffing from headsail backward and permit the use of a narrow slot between the mainsail and an overlapping jib for greater efficiency, as Dr. Manfred Curry observed many years ago.

Another advantage in long battens is that they will hold a sail steady in a breeze and let it "sleep" to a great extent, even when headed into the wind, thus lessening damage from flapping. In addition, when the battens are properly placed and adjusted they can simplify reefing. Earings or downhauls are rigged at each end of the battens so that the sail can be pulled down, and lazy jacks, shown in the illustration, hold the sail and battens on top of the boom. A minimal number of reef points are also needed to secure the battens to the boom. In a strong breeze, the battens are kept straight with minimal insertion in their pockets to minimize sail camber. Battens should probably be made of fairly stiff plastic, fiberglass, or moderately heavy wood strips covered with glass cloth to guard against risk of breakage. This full-length-battened, jib-headed mainsail has some of the virtues of a Chinese lug sail but retains most of the advantages of the conventional Marconi rig sail.

FIGURE 36: A MODERN OFFSHORE CRUISING CUTTER

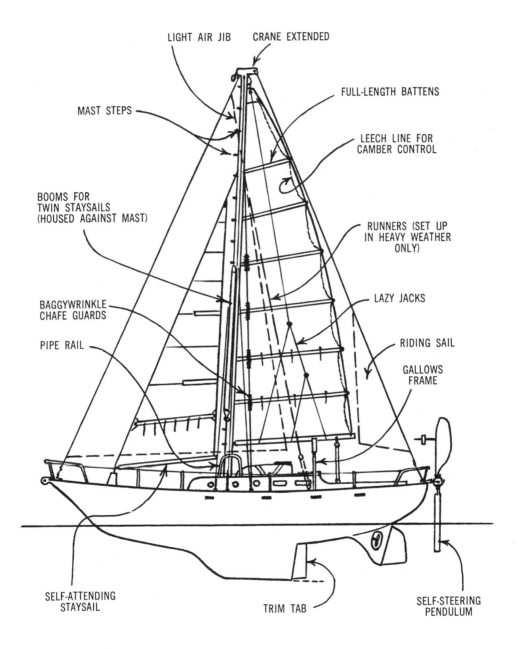

LIGHT AIR JIB

CRANE EXTENDED

FULL-LENGTH BATTENS

MAST STEPS

LEECH LINE FOR
CAMBER CONTROL

BOOMS FOR
TWIN STAYSAILS
(HOUSED AGAINST MAST)

RUNNERS (SET UP
IN HEAVY WEATHER
ONLY)

BAGGYWRINKLE
CHAFE GUARDS

LAZY JACKS

PIPE RAIL

RIDING SAIL

GALLOWS
FRAME

SELF-ATTENDING
STAYSAIL

TRIM TAB

SELF-STEERING
PENDULUM

The Chinese lug rig, shown in Figure 37, has some special advantages in ease of handling for singlehanded cruisers, but it has some decided drawbacks when there is an adequate crew and speed or windward performance is a major consideration. The rig is very ancient, but it was modernized in the late 1950s by the offshore innovator, Colonel H. G. Hasler. Advantages of such a sail are: twist can be controlled by the multiple sheets; the sail can be hoisted, handed, or reefed easily by one man from a central control position near the helm; as with other sails (such as the lateen) that extend forward of the mast, the center of effort is kept inboard to reduce weather helm when reaching or running (see Figure 37), and there is minimal compression on the mast and few metal parts that can break, as compared with the modern Marconi rig. Of course, the Chinese lug sail also enjoys some advantages of any full-length-battened sail in that the strain on the sail is more evenly distributed and violent flogging is avoided in a strong breeze. Reefing the modern lug sail is done with the four lines

Jester, *a modified 25-foot Folkboat with a modern Chinese lug rig. Her skipper, offshore innovator H. G. Hasler, is shown in the hatchway where he can hoist, trim, reef, or hand the sail without moving from his station. With this rig* Jester *completed three Singlehanded Transatlantic Races. (Eileen Ramsay)*

FIGURE 37: MODIFIED CHINESE LUG RIG

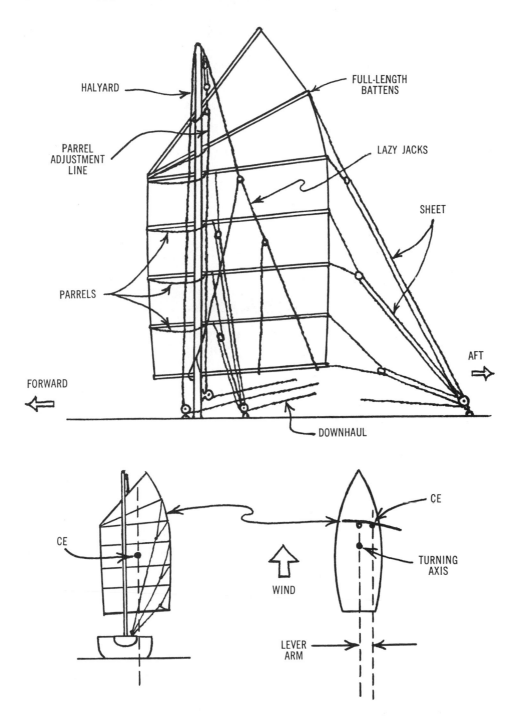

HALYARD

FULL-LENGTH BATTENS

PARREL ADJUSTMENT LINE

LAZY JACKS

SHEET

PARRELS

AFT

FORWARD

DOWNHAUL

CE

CE

TURNING AXIS

WIND

LEVER ARM

*R. M. Ellison's* Ilala, *a two-masted Chinese lug-rigged single-handed ocean racer. Note the details of her running rigging. One possible drawback of such a rig for offshore work is the complete lack of standing rigging for mast support. (Eileen Ramsay)*

shown in Figure 37. First the halyard is slacked, which drops the lower battens down to the boom. Then the sheet and downhaul are tightened to pull snug and secure the lowered battens at each end, and finally the parrel line is adjusted so that the yard is in the proper fore-and-aft position.

A major consideration with any rig is the mitigation of chafe. At sea, when a vessel is constantly rolling and pitching, chafe is an insidious foe eroding the sails and rigging. With a mainsail or mizzen, especially one with full-length battens, care must be taken to protect the sails where they lie against the shrouds when the boom is broad off. Vulnerable areas of a sail may be protected with baggy wrinkle or other chafing gear on the shrouds (see Figure 36). Spreader tips should be fitted with rollers or soft padding. Sails can be protected with reinforcing patches at vulnerable spots, and it is often wise to have vulnerable seams glued as well as sewn. Topping lifts must be kept clear of leeches, and spinnaker halyards must

*One of the U.S. Naval Academy's 44-foot Luders yawls shortened down with small Genoa jib and reefed main. Note the jib's foot is well raised so that it will not scoop up seas. (U.S. Navy)*

be rigged so that they do not chafe on stays. It is important that all lines subject to chafe are fitted with proper fairleads, and whenever chafing cannot be avoided, that the lines be protected with chafe guards.

## Heavy Weather Sailing

The question of when to shorten sail as the wind increases is usually not a very difficult one to answer on a cruising boat that is not concerned with maximum speed every moment, but on a racer, the question often demands some agonizing soul searching on the part of the skipper. He must carefully consider such matters as the strength of his boat, her sails, rigging, fittings, and equipment; the weather conditions; character of the seas; behavior of the boat; the number and quality of the crew; and the competency of the helmsmen. The decision to reduce sail is easier to make

*One of the hazards of carrying a spinnaker in too much wind. This knockdown to windward might have been averted by trimming the sheet and sailing higher. This is a 5.5 meter. (Roger Smith)*

when the boat is beating or reaching in a steady wind; because if the boat is heeled beyond her optimum sailing angle, she will slow down, and usually the mainsail can be reefed with little or no loss of boat speed during the operation, especially if the boat has roller reefing. The optimum angle of heel can be determined without too much difficulty if the boat is fitted with an inclinometer to give the exact heeling angle and a speedometer. Even without these instruments, the experienced seaman can usually feel when his boat is not doing her best. What often creates a problem, however, is a wind that constantly varies in strength. In this case, some skippers carry sail suitable for the average wind strength or even the lulls when puffs are not too frequent. While this policy may produce a greater average boat speed, it might be hazardous under certain circumstances. Any skipper who matches his sail to the lower wind velocities should be as sure as possible that the hardest puffs will only slow the boat and not expose her to danger. Safety must be the first consideration, whether racing or cruising.

The real problem of deciding when to reduce sail comes when racing downwind in heavy wind and seas with the spinnaker set. On almost any race course in heavy weather, it is a common sight to see spinnaker-carrying boats careening out of control, knocking down, and broaching to,

*In the heat of competition, when the wind pipes up, many skippers are tempted to carry parachute spinnakers, when a single-luff spinnaker, half-winder, boomed-out jib, or twin headsails would give much better control and perhaps as much or more speed. (Morris Rosenfeld)*

especially those craft with high aspect ratio fins and free-standing spade rudders that are raked aft considerably (see Chapter 2). Such a sight might indicate an alarming lack of seamanship, but many competitive racing sailors, who are in most respects highly competent seamen, are frequently enticed into carrying a parachute spinnaker despite the risk of damage, because the sail provides such tremendous power. In this respect, the 'chute is a dangerous temptress. The problem is well recognized, and ocean race committees have even tried limiting the weight of spinnaker cloth in order that the sails will blow out before the boat is endangered. However, this attempted solution has not been entirely successful, partly because of the differences in stress on a small spinnaker as compared to a large one of the same weight. Heavy weight "storm spinnakers" with little camber and narrow shoulders have been allowed, and these are a safer design for heavy weather. They permit spinnaker sailing in winds stronger than those in which the normal, full, high-shouldered 'chute can be carried in safety, but even a storm 'chute has its limits, and after a certain velocity of wind, boat control will become very difficult.

Spinnaker knockdowns are of two types, those that heel the boat to windward and those that heel her to leeward. The former kind is the most spectacular and frightening perhaps, but it is usually easier to control. If the boat tends to roll over to windward while running off before it, the helmsman luffs up to bring the wind more on the beam, the spinnaker sheet is flattened, and in some cases the pole is guyed forward. The leeward knockdown is often more difficult to avoid especially when the wind is on the beam. At the first sign of a possible knockdown to leeward, the helmsman should bear off and the sheet should be eased. A major problem with the parachute spinnaker on a broad to beam reach is that the after leech curves around to such an extent that the after half of the sail exerts its drive laterally causing a strong heeling moment. Some knowledgeable sailors feel that the old-fashioned, single-luff spinnaker, which is somewhat like a parachute spinnaker cut in half, is a more sensible rig in strong winds when frequent jibing is not necessary. Certainly it is more snug, and its shape helps avoid the aforementioned leeward heeling force. Another approach to the problem is with the use of a half-winder spinnaker, devised by British sailmaker, Jeremy Howard-Williams and described in his book *Sails*. Although this sail is still exeprimental, it has some good points, in theory at least. Such a sail is similar in shape to a conventional double-luff 'chute, but its after half is somewhat porous so that it lets a certain amount of air flow through the sail (see Figure 38) thereby eliminating a great deal of harmful side force. Ventilation of the after half might be accomplished with porous cloth, mesh, or ventilating holes, but, as Williams points out, too much air-flow through the sail will probably lead to premature collapsing.

More often than not, the most seamanlike rig for running off in a fresh breeze is the twin-headsail rig, or simply the mainsail and a jib "wung out" on the spinnaker pole; of course, when it really comes on to blow, these sails may very well produce more speed than any kind of spinnaker. A boomed-out jib can usually be set quite easily by: rigging the spinnaker pole to windward as though it were being set for the spinnaker, clipping the outboard end of the pole onto the windward jib sheet, and then outhauling (with the windward jib sheet) the jib's clew to the end of the pole. It is important that a pole lift be rigged in order to keep the outboard end of the pole high so that it will not dip in the sea when the boat rolls.

In deciding when to change from spinnaker to boomed-out jib or

FIGURE 38: HEADSAIL SIDE FORCE WHEN RUNNING
OR BROAD REACHING

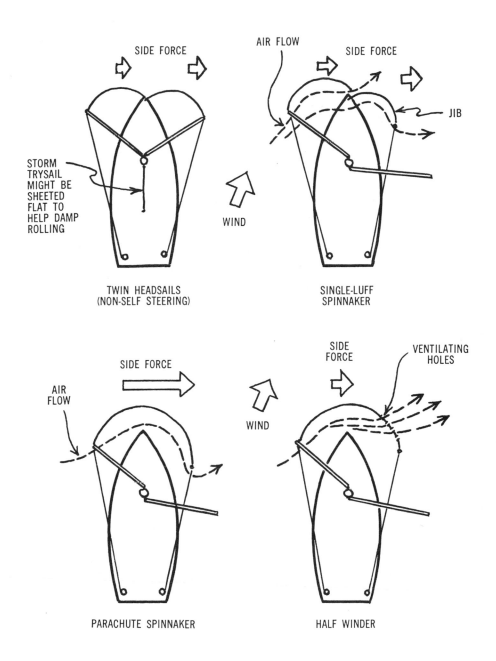

TWIN HEADSAILS
(NON-SELF STEERING)

SINGLE-LUFF
SPINNAKER

PARACHUTE SPINNAKER

HALF WINDER

twin headsails, a foremost consideration is the quality of helmsmanship. A skilled helmsman will anticipate waves and puffs, and he will not oversteer when the boat yaws or rolls. Quite often leeward knockdowns can be averted if the helmsman bears off immediately after being struck by a puff. Should he hesitate for a moment, the rudder might stall and lose its bite on the water. This is especially true with spade rudders. They normally provide very good response if the boat is run off at once and not allowed to heel a great deal. After a racer takes her first spinnaker knockdown, the skipper should try to determine the cause. If it was due to poor helmsmanship, then greater attentiveness in steering or perhaps a new, more experienced helmsman would be required. Should the boat take a second knockdown, then a change to heavy weather spinnaker or a boomed-out jib would certainly be advisable, especially if weather and sea conditions seem to be getting worse. At sea, repeated knockdowns should not be allowed, in my opinion. Even when the hull and crew are sound, and all vulnerable deck openings are closed, repeated spinnaker knockdowns impose tremendous stress on the rig. Not only is there danger of ripping sails and breaking booms, but the shock of a collapsed 'chute suddenly refilling with wind can put a dangerous load on the backstay and its fittings.

An important point to remember when a knockdown seems possible is that there should be a man standing by to instantly slack the main boom vang when the boat heels down. There is no quicker way to break a boom than to dip its end in a sea while its middle is bowsed down with a vang. As a matter of fact, when the mast is not raked aft considerably, it is a wise plan for offshore boats to have their mainsails fitted with anti-tripping reef points (see Figure 35) in order to raise the outboard end of the boom. In a very fresh following breeze, it is advisable to lower the main and run under twin headsails alone; or, if rolling is severe, a storm trysail sheeted flat amidships might be carried (in addition to the twins) to help damp the motion.

As said previously, it is easier to determine the proper time to reduce sail when the wind is on or forward of the beam. This judgment should largely be based on the vessel's angle of heel, but of course there are other important considerations as well, such as how the hull, rig, and crew are withstanding the strains of the heavy weather. If the boat is slamming violently into the seas, green water is running over the decks, the cockpit is being filled, the mast is whipping excessively, the leeward rigging is overly slack, gear is breaking down under the strain, or the crew is exhausted and sea sick, then obviously the time has come to shorten sail, perhaps drastically.

Normally, the first step in shortening sail is to set a smaller headsail, reef the mainsail, and, on a modern yawl, to lower the mizzen. A modern

*Broken booms are often caused by overly taut boom vangs, especially when the boom trips on a sea. (Morris Rosenfeld)*

racing sloop with roller reefing might roll down her main and keep up her large Genoa jib when on a short windward leg, but at sea on a long beat it is usually better to change to a smaller Genoa or a double-head rig with staysail and jib topsail. A heavy weather jib should have a short tack pendant to raise its foot well clear of the deck or otherwise it might scoop up seas. If the foot has a roach, it might be fitted with a grommet at its lowest point so that it can be lifted with a halyard or piece of shock cord fastened to a jib hank to keep it clear of the bow wave when reaching.

The basic principle of reducing sail when reaching and beating is to keep a balanced sail plan, in order that the boat will neither develop a lee nor a weather helm. Theoretically, the total center of effort should be in about the same location for the reduced plan as for the non-reduced plan. In actuality, however, it is usually advisable to move the center of effort forward somewhat, because most boats develop some weather helm when heeled. Thus a more forward position of the CE will help counteract the

*Four identical U.S. Naval Academy yawls using different heavy weather sail combinations. From left to right these are: No. 2 Genoa, reefed main and mizzen; No. 2 Genoa and mizzen; No. 1 Genoa and storm trysail; and No. 3 Genoa and full main. The extreme left and right boats seem to have the more powerful combinations and more effective slots between sails for driving to windward in the wind and sea conditions illustrated. (U.S. Naval Institute)*

additional weather helm caused by a high angle of heel. Of course, this means that a greater amount of sail will be carried forward than aft. A great advantage in reefing a sail is that its CE is automatically moved forward as its area is reduced.

Roller reefing has several advantages over conventional (reef-point) reefing in that the former system allows variable sail reduction quickly and with minimal crew effort. There is always the possibility, however, that the roller mechanism at the gooseneck, which rotates the boom to roll up the sail, will break down during a lengthy passage; thus it is advisable for offshore boats to have an alternate reefing system, such as rows of reef points or eyelets for lacing lines in their working sails. If the boom fitted with roller reefing is not tapered to prevent its after end from drooping, as was discussed earlier, then tapered shims (wedge-shaped battens of wood) might be inserted at the leech as the sail is wound around the boom. If this is done, care must be taken not to let the shims fly out of

*Adlard Coles' Cohoe, a Tumlare type, narrow, double-ender using a double slot heavy weather rig. (Bill Kuenzel)*

the sail when it is being unrolled. A better idea might be to secure the shims to the boom permanently when droop is a serious problem. If the mast is fitted with a gooseneck slide on a track, it may be advisable not to slack the halyard off until the boom has been rolled up to the top of the track. Despite the fact that this will slightly raise the center of effort, it will allow ample clearance for the after end of the boom. An important point to remember with conventional reefing is that reef points should be passed around the foot of the sail, not around the boom, in order that the sail's bolt rope will provide some elasticity or "give" to distribute the strain evenly on all reef points. On offshore boats, the tack and especially the clew earings (the pendants that hold down the luff and leech of the reefed sail) should be permanently rigged, in my opinion, in order that reefing can be done as quickly and easily as possible.

Sail area can often be reduced very conveniently with roller furling. By this method a sail is rolled up on the rod or stay to which it is attached by hauling on a furling line wound around a drum near the tack, which rotates the stay. Roller furling is not always appropriate, however, for a lengthy thrash offshore, when specialized headsails will do a better job. Then there is always the possibility that roller sails will jam, or unroll, or a rod luff might break. As said earlier, there have been more than a few cases of rod failure offshore. In any case, the roller furling jib stay or luff wire should not be used as the only means of forward mast support, for the wire might have to be lowered in the event that it becomes necessary to repair the jib. Nevertheless, twin headsails which roller furl on wire luffs have been used successfully for easy downwind cruising and even trade wind passages since 1930 when the rig was first introduced by Captain Otway Waller.

When wind and seas necessitate a further reduction of sail, deeper reefs are put in and smaller headsails are bent. A sloop without roller furling might carry a small, flat, working jib or large storm jib forward of the mast, while a cutter might carry her working staysail without a jib. A modern yawl with a small mizzen should probably have her mizzen furled and carry a reefed main and small jib, or a staysail if she is double-head rigged. A ketch might carry the same combination but with a reefed mizzen; however, a double-head rigged ketch may balance well under main and staysail and thus avoid the need to reef except in a hard blow. A schooner could carry a small jib, foresail or mainstaysail, and a deeply reefed mainsail. Many sail combinations are possible, and some experimentation is often necessary to find the best plan for each individual boat. Nevertheless, in choosing the right combination it is important to bear in mind the aforementioned sail reduction principles, which are: to lower and move forward the total center of effort; keep some sail bent to the after side of the mainmast to minimize whipping in head seas; try to keep the rig somewhat centralized (not spread out to the extent that no sail is amidships while large sails are at the boat's extremities); and raise the foot of any heavy weather sail, particularly one at the bow or stern.

Sail reductions should not be delayed when they are needed, for not only does a boat lose speed and risk damage when she is overburdened, but procrastination increases the difficulty of shortening down.

Further reduction of sail would require special storm sails: the storm trysail or Swedish mainsail (mentioned earlier) and a small storm jib, or spitfire as it is sometimes called. The Swedish mainsail is often the best sail when it is necessary to drive a long distance to windward or claw away from a lee shore. The storm trysail may be sheeted to the main boom, and it will give some drive, but the sail is primarily for the purpose of heaving to. This storm tactic and the trysail will be discussed fully in Chapter 7. Storm jibs should be cut flat, and they should have tack pendants of ample length to keep them well above the deck. In general, storm sails need not be much heavier than working sails because their areas are so small. It is generally agreed that soft dacron is the most suitable material, and when chafe is anticipated, it is advisable to have the seams glued as well as sewn together. In my opinion, it is usually better to tie the sheet to a storm sail with a bowline to eliminate the risk of a crew member being struck in the head with a metal shackle.

When sailing in heavy weather, frequent checks should be made on the condition of the hull, rig, and fittings. The bilge should be looked at periodically to determine if the hull is leaking from spewed caulking, stress at the garboards, failure of a through-hull fitting, or any other cause. It is advisable to sight up the mast occasionally to see that it is not whipping violently or bending seriously. An especially important part of the mast to check for bending is that point near the head of the storm trysail or reefed main. The head may exert a considerable pull aft on the mast. It is the safest practice to raise the trysail or reef the main to a point where their heads are nearly opposite a shroud or forestay that pulls forward to counteract the pull aft. In addition, frequent checks should be made to see: that spreaders are not sagging or working loose; that turnbuckles are not coming unscrewed; that mast and sheet lead tracks are not bending; that halyards are not chafing and are not becoming wrapped or fouled aloft due to the motion; that sail slides or hanks are not popping off; that the jib is not scooping up waves; that no sail seam is beginning to split; and so forth. If the motion permits, it is often a good plan to look at the heads of sails through the binoculars. Head boards occasionally pull off and then there is the devil to pay in retrieving the halyard. For this reason, it is sometimes wise to rig downhauls on the halyards before bad weather commences. By all means do not let the sails flog in a real breeze of wind, as this is a sure way to damage them. A fairly new Dacron sail of proper weight and construction with unchafed seams will rarely blow out in almost any strength of wind if the sail is kept full and is not allowed to flap. However, be sure that ample heavy weather sails are aboard the boat in case it becomes necessary to replace blown-out or damaged sails.

Sailing in a prolonged blow at sea is seldom pleasant, but it is made more bearable when the skipper and crew have confidence in the soundness of their sails and rigging. In general, a sound rig is one engineered to have a great margin of safety, made of proven materials, with the primary emphasis on strength and reliability, while low windage and light weight are merely secondary considerations. The skipper (or designer or builder) who chooses a flimsy rig over a strong one in hopes of gaining a slight advantage over his competition in fair weather racing, may sorely regret his choice when sailing in heavy weather offshore.

# 7 / SAILBOAT MANAGEMENT
## IN STORMS OFFSHORE

The chances are that sooner or later every boat frequently venturing far offshore will be subjected to a real blow with heavy seas. In such a circumstance there is obviously no means of seeking shelter, and the vessel has no recourse but to stay and take her punishment. Of course, her skipper is faced with the important decision of choosing the method of boat handling that will result in the least possible damage. This decision is not easy to make when experience is limited, because the variety of alternatives and advice given by seamanship manuals and by experienced sailors often seems confusing and conflicting. Actually, there can be no hard and fast rules for offshore storm management, because courses of action will depend on the particular combination of conditions and circumstances, as for example: the design, rig, and construction of the boat; location of the boat with respect to a lee shore, shoal water, offshore current, and the storm area; size, number and fitness of the crew; nature and severity of the weather disturbance; and size and character of the seas.

There might be considered five courses of action for sailboats in extremely heavy weather at sea: (1) Pressing on under reduced sail, (2) heaving to under reduced sail, (3) lying a-hull under bare poles, (4) riding to a sea anchor (either from the bow or stern), and (5) scudding (running off with little or no sail and with or without drags astern). Each of these storm tactics will be discussed separately with consideration of the aforementioned conditions and circumstances that would affect the choice of tactics.

*Pressing on Under Reduced Sail*

Methods of progressively shortening sail in increasing wind and seas were discussed in the last chapter. On a non-racing cruiser far offshore sail should be reduced early, because she is not involved in competition, and there is no shelter which must be reached before the blow commences. Of course, a racing yacht will carry on under the fastest sail combination, without shortening down or heaving to, for the longest possible time. The ocean racing skipper has the very difficult task of trying to determine the exact point at which high speed sailing begins to involve an undue element of risk. Factors that influence his judgment were discussed in the last chapter.

An ocean racer is usually able to press on, without heaving to, under full or reduced sail for a much longer period of time than a cruising yacht of similar size. This is due primarily to the fact that the racer normally carries the larger crew. One of the major problems in contending with heavy weather at sea is that of crew sickness and fatigue. Seasickness can knock a man off his feet; while fatigue can cause carelessness, inability to steer and reef or change sails, and it can adversely affect one's judgment and even cause halucinations. It is very important for the crew to get all the rest they can, to take sea sickness pills well in advance of the expected bad weather (some remedies may act quicker in liquid form), and to have adequate nourishment in the form of quick energy food and hot drinks (preferably prepared before the blow and kept in thermos bottles). It is also a wise plan to stow warm clothing in plastic bags to keep them dry during the blow. The navigator should determine the boat's position before the arrival of the heavy weather.

Other preparations for bad weather would include: inspection of the bilge, gear, and fittings; closing all deck openings; placing all needed gear so it will be readily available; securely lashing down all loose equipment that will be needed on deck; taking below all gear not needed on deck; carefully stowing all loose gear below; donning foul weather clothing, life or buoyant jackets, and safety harnesses. It is important that all seacocks be shut except those on cockpit drains and deck scuppers. If there is no seacock on the engine exhaust, it is often a good idea to close the outlet with a tapered wood plug. Ventilators should be removed and replaced with screw plates. This even holds true for Dorade trap types if extremely heavy weather is expected. Slides should be inserted in the after end of the companionway and the sliding hatch should be kept shut except when entering or leaving the cabin during the storm. Of course, all hatches and ports must be securely dogged. It is important to see that the bilge pumps are working and that the bilge is reasonably dry and clear of wood chips, paper labels from canned goods, or anything else that could clog the pumps. The radar reflector should be hoisted and have a downhaul rigged from its bottom to hold it steady, and at night a powerful, waterproof flashlight, a fog horn, and flares should be readily available from the cockpit. It is often a good idea to rig lines for hand grips across or around the cockpit when the motion becomes violent. See that storm sails are bent or are handy and that extra sheets, tackles, anchor (when near shore) or sea anchor, drags (that might be needed to slow speed) and properly coiled anchor rodes or warps are available. Great care must be taken in stowing gear so that it cannot break loose and become projectiles. Pay special attention to heavy equipment such as extra batteries or anchors to see that they will not shift and fall against seacock handles, wires, pipes, or tanks. See that all life saving equipment is accessible and in working order.

In deciding whether or not to press on under reduced sail (rather than attempting to stop headway), the primary consideration should be given to the vessel's location. If she is near a lee shore with the weather deteriorating, then she must drive to weather in order to get all the sea room possible. For the competing ocean racer an extreme alteration of course away from the rhumb line may not always be necessary unless extremely bad weather is expected, because, in addition to having the advantage of a large crew, the normal ocean racer is more weatherly and better able to claw off a lee shore than the average sailing cruiser. Facing the possibility of a full gale, however, it is always wise, even for a racer, to get a decent offing. One possible comfort for some yachts engaged in competition is that some ocean racing sponsors provide escort vessels that may be able to come to the rescue of a racer in trouble; but there could be a drawback in having escorts if their presence should happen to give any yacht skipper a false sense of security. It is well to remember that even if signal contact (flares or radio) can be made, rescue at sea in a storm is extremely difficult, and it might well be impossible for an escort vessel to reach a yacht grounded on a lee shore.

As a matter of fact, in bad weather it could be dangerous to be near any shore, even one to windward that reduces fetch, not only because of the possibility of a wind shift that would put the shore to leeward, but because if the shore is high and mountainous it can produce strong gusts called williwaws that drop down to the water with tremendous force soon after passing over the mountains. Also, as said in Chapter 5, shoal water waves can turn relatively harmless deep water waves into dangerous, short, breaking seas. In addition, it was pointed out that strong coastal currents can produce dangerous seas in bad weather, especially when the wind opposes the current's flow. Needless to say, every attempt should be made to avoid strong currents and shoal water in heavy weather offshore.

Another very important consideration that will affect the decision of whether or not to press on under reduced'sail is the vessel's location with respect to the track of the storm. As said previously, most severe storms are circular, and they usually travel in somewhat predictable paths. Obviously, weather reports should be obtained from the radio, and continual observations should be made of the sky, barometer, and wind direction in order to keep track of the boat's location with respect to the storm center. This was discussed in Chapter 5. If the vessel is not headed for dangerously shoal water or a lee shore and she can keep sailing without undue risk of damage, then of course, she should attempt to move away from the storm, out of its path, and into the safest sector in accordance with advice given in Chapter 5.

If the decision is made to press on, it is important to keep careful track of the vessel's position through dead reckoning and/or radio navigation (RDF, consolan, or loran). It is very doubtful that celestial navigation could be used in bad weather. To assure reasonable accuracy of the dead reckoning position, the helmsmen should continually note the compass heading, while the navigator consults the speed indicator or taff rail log (or else estimates the boat's speed) and keeps track of the time spent on each heading. Of course, allowance has to be made for any current, and leeway must be estimated. In heavy weather it is almost impossible for the helmsman to hold a steady course on any point of sailing, but he must do his best to "average out" his course alterations. In other words, if his desired course is SE, but some heavy seas force him down to SSE for about five seconds, he should try to work up to ESE for about five seconds or else try to hold up to SE by E for about ten seconds in order to make good a southeasterly course. Remember that leeway may be considerable in heavy winds and rough seas.

*Heaving to Under Sail*

When sailing becomes risky, that is if the boat is being damaged by taking aboard green water (solid water and not merely spray), if the hull is leaking or showing signs of stress, if the sails or rigging are being strained or damaged, if the boat is extremely difficult to steer or any play begins to develop in her helm, if there is a strong tendency to broach to or take extreme knockdowns, or if the crew is sick and exhausted, then sail should be further reduced and headway should be slowed or almost stopped.

*The sequence of pictures on the following four pages dramatically illustrates why the words "lee shore" fill the hearts of many coastal sailors with dread. The boat shown was reduced to kindling wood within an hour after grounding on the coast of Normandy. (Edward Tadros)*

In such a case, unless the desired course lies downwind and the boat can be made to run off comfortably under bare poles or greatly reduced sail, she should probably heave to. In a very broad sense, heaving to implies stopping headway by any means (other than anchoring or mooring), but in the strictest sense, a vessel is said to be hove to when she lies nearly dead in the water with the wind and seas between beam on and broad on the bow or somewhat further ahead, while she carries a single storm sail or counteracting sails. When one sail is trimmed to work against another it is counteracting, and of course this tends to stop headway or forereaching. Heaving to in this manner is very often the next step to take after it becomes too rough to press on, particularly when the desired course is to windward.

The classic means of heaving to is to carry a small spitfire jib or storm staysail sheeted to windward counteracting the drive of a deeply reefed mainsail or storm trysail. This method is illustrated in Figure 39. Normally, the helm is lashed down so that when the trysail or reefed main, which is sheeted in flat, drives the boat slowly ahead, the rudder turns her towards the wind. When the trysail or main begins to luff, the backed jib will not only slow headway, but it will cause the bow to fall off, until the main or trysail completely fills and again begins to drive the boat ahead; thus the cycle is repeated. In the meantime, the boat is making considerable leeway due to the fact that her headway is nearly stopped, she is heeled somewhat, and her keel is stalled (not supplying lift) and this causes a noticeable wake to windward which in moderately heavy weather, may have some effect on smoothing the seas and possibly encouraging them to break before they reach the boat. The less she forereaches and the more leeway she makes, the more effective the drift-wake to windward will be. Actually, the effect of the drift in smoothing seas may be somewhat overrated in very heavy weather. I think the main advantages in heaving to this way are to reduce headway (in order to allow riding over rather than smashing into the seas), to put the boat in an advantageous attitude to the waves, and to allow her to retreat from or yield to the force of the seas. Leeway or drift might be as much as two or three knots, but of course this will vary with individual boats. Naturally, a shoal-draft centerboarder with board up will make more leeway than a deep keel boat with great lateral plane. A very shoal draft boat generally should be hove to with the board part way down but no deeper than necessary, because extreme depth might cause the boat to knock down as a result of tripping on her board, or the board could be bent or otherwise damaged in very heavy weather when it is lowered too far.

Exact methods of heaving to under sail will vary greatly with individual boats and their rigs. Usually the center of effort of the reduced

## FIGURE 39: HEAVING TO (UNDER SAIL)

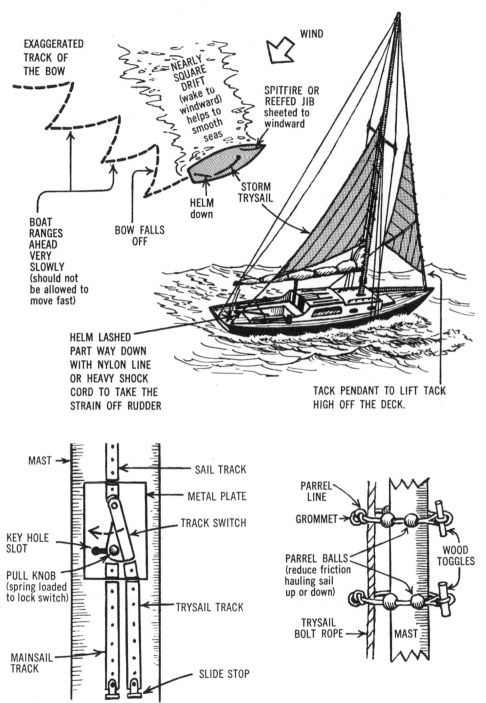

EXAGGERATED TRACK OF THE BOW

WIND

NEARLY SQUARE DRIFT (wake to windward) helps to smooth seas

SPITFIRE OR REEFED JIB sheeted to windward

BOAT RANGES AHEAD VERY SLOWLY (should not be allowed to move fast)

BOW FALLS OFF

STORM TRYSAIL

HELM down

HELM LASHED PART WAY DOWN WITH NYLON LINE OR HEAVY SHOCK CORD TO TAKE THE STRAIN OFF RUDDER

TACK PENDANT TO LIFT TACK HIGH OFF THE DECK.

MAST

SAIL TRACK

METAL PLATE

TRACK SWITCH

KEY HOLE SLOT

PULL KNOB (spring loaded to lock switch)

TRYSAIL TRACK

MAINSAIL TRACK

SLIDE STOP

PARREL LINE

GROMMET

PARREL BALLS (reduce friction hauling sail up or down)

WOOD TOGGLES

TRYSAIL BOLT ROPE

MAST

sail plan (used when hove to) should be kept near or abaft the total center of effort (the center of effort of the full working sail plan). Seldom should the CE of the reduced sail be located much more than slightly forward of the designed TCE, or the boat may tend to pay off and pick up speed, even with the helm lashed down. The increased headway could be dangerous for two reasons: first, the hull may be deprived of time needed to lift to the seas, and secondly, headway will improve the keel's lateral resistance which will reduce leeway and make the hull more vulnerable to beam seas. In other words, the boat will tend to plow into the seas and not yield to them.

This situation is exemplified by the experience of Fred M. Slavic's *Nightingale,* a 44-foot, Sparkman-and-Stephens-designed, keel yawl in a Force 9 gale (see Beaufort scale, in Appendix E) in the Bay of Biscay. The *Nightingale* was comfortably hove to under her mizzen with a storm jib backed and the helm down, when suddenly she was rolled down and damaged by a huge sea. On past occasions the yawl had weathered several gales successfully under bare poles or with the storm trysail and spitfire, but on this occasion, Slavic theorized, the mizzen sheet let go, and the removal of wind pressure on the after sail (which moved the CE far forward) caused the boat to bear off and pick up headway. She then plunged her bow into a sea which led to her being rolled down to an extreme angle of heel. Although the sea which did the damage was possibly an unusually large "rogue" or "freak" sea, the *Nightingale* might have fared better with her bow closer to the wind and especially with less headway. This experience also shows us that if it is necessary to heave to under two counteracting sails spread far apart on opposite sides of the designed CE, great care must be taken to see that the after sail and its gear is of ample strength. If the forward sail blows out, there is probably little danger unless the boat turns so far that she lies head-to-wind, in which position the rudder could be damaged by the boat making sternway while the helm is lashed down, or the mizzen could be damaged by violent flogging. As said in the last chapter, if a sail is carried far aft or forward in extreme weather, it must be raised high enough to avoid a sea breaking against its foot.

Some boats will lie to reasonably well with only a riding sail aft. A ketch might carry a reefed mizzen or storm trysail set on her mizzenmast. A yawl with a small mizzen with a high foot might carry it unreefed, but it is usually better to have a smaller, strongly made storm mizzen cut very flat. Wright Britton, a famous offshore sailor and winner of the Cruising Club of America's Blue Water Medal, claims that his yawl *Delight,* a *Finisterre*-type centerboarder, will lie to comfortably with her bow quite close to the wind under mizzen alone and with the helm loosely lashed amidships with shock cord. The *Delight* once weathered a succession of gales in this manner for nineteen days in the waters east of Iceland. It should be pointed out, however, that a yawl under mizzen alone should not lie so close to the wind that her mizzen flogs violently. Furthermore, in this attitude, there is some danger of the boat being pushed backwards by the wind and seas fast enough to put a great strain on the rudder. Actually, many modern yawls with cut-away forefoots and small mizzens will not hold very close to the wind under mizzen alone. Some will head little if any higher than beam-on to the wind and seas. Heaving to in this manner requires a high mizzen boom and strong rigging, stronger than that found on many racing yawls. Humphrey Barton has stated that when the mizzen is carried in extremely heavy weather, most yawls and ketches he has seen need a special mizzen forestay rigged to hold the mast forward and counteract the mizzen's backward pull. A satisfactory substitute may be a jumper stay to the mainmast head or a strut from the mizzenmast head to the main permanent backstay, as shown in Figure 33, but it should be kept in mind that with these rigs, if the mainmast ever goes by the board it would probably take the mizzen with it.

On boats with no mizzenmast, a riding sail might be rigged on the permanent backstay provided that stay is strong enough. Such a sail is illustrated in Figure 40. This particular riding sail is cut flat, has a full-length plastic or fiberglass batten that is removable, and has wires in both the luff and leech, all of which are for the purpose of strengthening the sail and keeping it quiet. In this particular design, there has been an effort to make a very versatile sail, one that will serve primarily as a riding sail, but also one that can double as a storm trysail when its foot is secured to the mast, and a spitfire jib when it is turned around backwards and hanked to the jib stay (see Figure 40). Some sailors object to battens in storm sails, but they help prevent flogging and the rapid leech flutter that can damage a sail in strong winds. Furthermore, flexible plastic or fiberglass battens can be almost unbreakable, and short battens can be permanently sewn into a sail if there is concern over their working loose.

It is often said that a great advantage of the storm trysail over a reefed mainsail is that it need not be secured to the main boom. The trysail may be trimmed similarly to a jib with a pair of sheets, one leading to the deck on each side of the boat. If it becomes necessary to jibe in exceptionally heavy weather there probably would be less strain and shock with such a boomless trysail than with the trysail sheeted to the boom, but there are certain times when it may be advantageous to secure the trysail's clew to the boom and use the main sheet to trim the trysail. Such a time might be when the trysail is used in conjunction with other sails to impart headway while beating to windward, as for example, when it is necessary to claw off a lee shore. With the trysail secured to the boom it is generally easier to tack, because this rig avoids the necessity of casting off one sheet and hauling in on the other. When a small trysail is made fast to the boom, there can be quite a strain on the sail from the boom's weight and the leverage of a boom-end main sheet; thus it is important to set up on the topping lift to relieve this strain. If the trysail is trimmed to the side decks, be sure that the lead blocks are secured to through-bolted eye straps. Some Genoa tracks are not through-bolted and cannot accept the strain of a storm trysail sheet.

A trysail intended for really heavy weather should be considerably smaller than the deeply reefed mainsail. As a matter of fact, this is required if the boat is raced. Both the Cruising Club of America and the International Offshore rules state that storm trysails "must be materially smaller than a normal close-reefed mainsail . . ." On a boat with a single set of spreaders on her mainmast, the trysail's head might come fairly close to the point where the spreaders are secured to the mast (see Figure 33). It is a good idea to keep the head of the trysail fairly near the point where the forward lower shrouds attach to the mast in order that the head's after pull is opposed by the shroud's forward pull to prevent the mast from bending. If the trysail is materially higher, then its head should probably be at a point where its pull is opposed by a forestay. The trysail should have a tack pendant so that its tack is well above the furled mainsail, and the trysail clew should be slightly higher than the main boom (in normal topped-up position) in order that the clew can be secured to the boom, or so that it will clear the boom in its crutch when tacking if the sail is sheeted to the deck.

There are several ways to secure a trysail to the mast. In former times, it was customary to use parrel lines (lashings passed around the mast, securing the luff to the mast) fitted with beads or wooden rollers to reduce friction when the sail was hoisted (see Figure 39), or sometimes the beads were omitted and the parrel lines were passed diagonally around the mast passing from one grommet to the next one above. With the latter method, the slant of the line reduces friction, but not as much as with parrel beads. Nowadays, however, trysail luffs are usually secured to the mast with slides on a mast track similarly to the mainsail's method of attachment. Quite often there are two side-by-side tracks on the mast, one for the mainsail and the other for the trysail, for the purpose of saving time and effort in changing from one sail to the other. Sometimes, the extra track for the trysail is a very short section, just long enough to accommodate all the slides when the sail is lowered, and there is a switch above the trysail track which routes the trysail slides over to the main track after the mainsail has been lowered (see Figure 39). It is highly

FIGURE 40: A TRIPLE-PURPOSE STORM SAIL

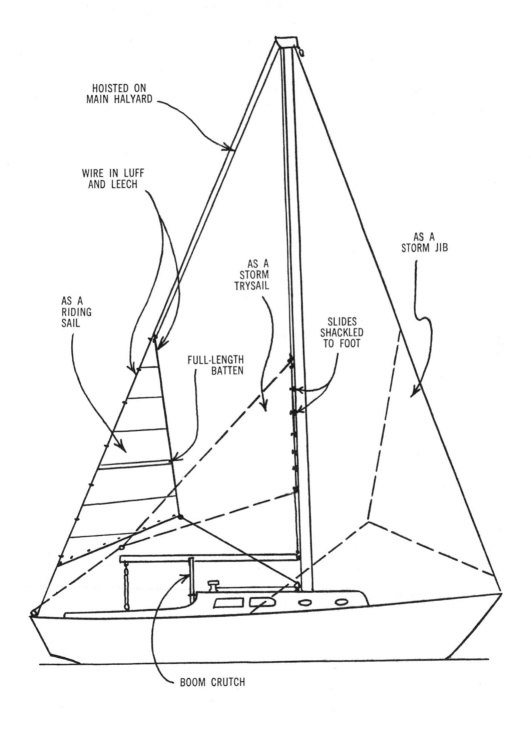

HOISTED ON
MAIN HALYARD

WIRE IN LUFF
AND LEECH

AS A
STORM
TRYSAIL

AS A
STORM JIB

AS A
RIDING
SAIL

SLIDES
SHACKLED
TO FOOT

FULL-LENGTH
BATTEN

BOOM CRUTCH

advisable to have the track through-bolted to the mast at the normal position of the trysail's head and tack, however, every effort should be made to avoid drilling holes very close to a location where there are several other holes, as, for example, where spreaders or tangs are secured, because too many holes and fastenings in the same area can weaken the mast. Some boats have specially made, heavier-than-normal track sections and slides at the trysail tack and head positions. Slides may be wired to the luff or special stainless steel shackles can be used, but be wary of nylon shackles as these can break in a strong wind.

Traditionally, the storm trysail has been vertically cut (cut with the cloth panels running parallel to the leech) for the purpose of achieving great strength while minimizing bias stretch at the leech, but some modern trysails are miter-cut with the cloths running at right angles to the foot and leech. With the latter construction, bias stretch is minimized at the foot as well as the leech, but there may be greater stress at some of the seams, and so it is often a good plan to have them glued as well as sewn. Contrary to what many people think, the trysail does not have to be extremely heavy, because it is such a small sail. Many sailmakers recommend a cloth weight similar to the mainsail's. By the same reasoning, the spitfire need not be extra heavy when it is made of Dacron. The old-time storm sails of soft cotton were a delight to handle, but alas, they lacked the strength of modern synthetic sails. Some years ago after setting a cotton trysail, I found myself praising the sail for its softness and resistance to violent flogging, when all at once, the sail seemed to explode into ribbons. Since that experience, I have cheerfully put up with the comparatively slippery stiffness of Dacron for its extra strength and resistance to rot. Actually, if one is not overly concerned about stretch, and this is not a very important point except in a racing sail, then Dacron can be had which is moderately soft and fairly easy to handle.

The most satisfactory method of heaving to can only be discovered after considerable experimentation. Not only does the most effective reduced sail plan depend on the rig, but also it very much depends on the underwater shape of the hull and the amount of windage of the deckhouse and topsides. Boats with cut-away keels forward will normally tend to fall off the wind, and this might mean that the helm should be lashed down further and that the CE of the storm sails should be moved further aft. Moderately heavy boats with long keels might be hove to easily and be made to look after themselves, but lively fin keelers are often very hard to control, as they often tend to fall off the wind and forereach. The racing boat with a short fin keel might lie to with a small riding sail aft, however, or if more sail is carried, she might need constant tending by a helmsman who would allow just enough headway to give some rudder control. In such a case, the boat is generally luffed slowly into the seas, but her bow should be brought off slightly at the crest to lessen the water's impact. The helmsman must be careful to keep the speed low by *slightly* luffing the sails, but if this threatens to injure them, sail should be further reduced.

Of course, the vessel's rig will have a great bearing on the method of heaving to. Some of the possible sail plans and combinations are as follows: a cutter or modern sloop with a large foretriangle might lie to under a backed spitfire or storm staysail in combination with a storm trysail; but a sloop with her mast well forward might be hove to under the storm trysail alone, provided it is very small so as not to drive the boat ahead too fast. It is also possible that these single-masted boats could use the aforementioned riding sail hanked to the backstay either alone or in combination with a backed storm staysail. A schooner might carry a storm forestaysail with a main storm trysail, or carry a reefed foresail alone. A yawl or ketch might lie to under the storm trysail alone, under storm mizzen alone, or (in the case of a modern yawl with a large base to her foretriangle) under storm staysail and trysail. There are all sorts of combinations possible, especially when the rig is divided. Spaulding Dunbar, the naval architect, once told me that he hove to successfully in a lengthy gale with a small jib hanked to the leeward shrouds.

The main considerations in heaving to under sail should be: to reduce headway, to hold the bow fairly high, and to prevent the sails from flogging violently so that they will not blow out. Experimentation to find the proper heavy weather sail plan should be accomplished *before* one is caught in a gale. It is a wise plan for the skipper to get some idea of how his boat will behave in a severe blow by taking the boat out in a moderate blow with a good crew and proper storm sails and trying out various sail combinations. This will not only provide clues concerning the boat's heavy weather behavior, but also it will afford sail handling practice for the "real McCoy." It should be remembered that when caught in a gale at sea, especially when short handed, sail changing experiments can be extremely difficult. One should at least have some idea beforehand of how his boat will behave in a gale.

### Lying a-hull

When the wind increases to such an extent that sails cannot be carried or the boat's headway cannot be slowed, then sail should be removed, and quite often the proper tactic is hulling, or lying a-hull. This means that the boat is simply left to drift and look out for herself under bare poles. Usually, the decision to remove all sail will result primarily from the desirability of stopping headway rather than concern over sail damage, because modern Dacron sails that are new and properly made will not easily blow out if they are not allowed to flog. Also an important consideration in determining the proper time to remove all sail will be the height of the seas. Even if the seas are long and not especially dangerous, the boat carrying sail might be alternately blanketed in the trough but exposed to the wind's force on the crest, and this could cause erratic turning with dangerous knockdowns that might result in damage to the rig or cabin trunk.

Although the tactic of hulling has been practiced from early times, some seamen, especially many small craft sailors from former days, are opposed to letting a boat "wallow in the trough" or lie broadside to the seas, as most boats will do when left to drift freely. Today, however, it seems that hulling is becoming a more and more acceptable and seamanlike practice. This may be due in part to differences in design, displacement, construction and rig of most modern offshore yachts as compared to those of former times, and partly it may be due to the growing record of successful hulling experiences in recent years.

One of the first American sailors to advocate and publicize such a tactic as hulling was Thomas Fleming Day, the editor of *Rudder* magazine who made an early Atlantic crossing in the 25-foot yawl, *Seabird*. In 1911, he wrote, "My long experience in small boats has taught me this: that if a boat is a good boat, when real trouble comes she is best let alone. She knows better what to do than you, and if you leave her alone, she will do the right thing; whereas nine times out of ten you will do the wrong." This same general philosophy is expressed in a different way by William Albert Robinson, the circumnavigator. In his book, *To the Great Southern Sea*, Robinson speaks of a vessel's "drift tendency," and how it is important in extremely heavy weather to let a boat drift the way she will, whether her attitude is beam on or stern up to the wind and seas. He suggests that the best seamanship is that which encourages rather than fights against this natural tendency. Drifting freely, a boat will back away and yield to the seas, somewhat as a boxer rolls with the punches.

A boat's natural drift attitude (I prefer the word *attitude* rather than *tendency* to describe a boat's position relative to the wind while she drifts freely) will depend on her underwater shape and the windage of her hull, deckhouse, and rig. It is interesting, however, that the attitude is not always entirely predictable. Some boats that look as though they might fall off the wind and begin to run with the helm unattended, will actually lie fairly close to beam-on. The naval architect and aerodynamicist, Walter J. Bloemhard, gives us a clue when he tells us that elongated bodies traveling in the direction of their longitudinal axis tend to be unstable, and the natural attitude of a flat plate in a flow is to lie across the flow. Bloemhard goes on to say that when the normal sailboat is brought broadside to the wind with her sails let completely out (with no forward and little side pressure on them), she is directionally stable and will not turn her bow to port or starboard. Commander D. A. Rayner who wrote the book, *Safety in Small Craft,* is more dogmatic. He says that an untended boat with normal hull shape, keel, masts, etc. will lie beam-on and "nothing on earth will stop her doing so." I think this is probably overstating it a little, because while many boats will lie beam-on, some with short keels located aft and considerable windage forward will undoubtedly lie with their quarters more or less up to the wind, and a very few with deep forefoots and windage aft will lie with the wind forward of the beam. As a matter of fact, some boats do a considerable amount of switching around with constantly changing attitudes while hulling, but by and large the wind and seas are mostly on the beam.

Those seamen who oppose lying a-hull in bad weather argue that when beam-on, a boat is more vulnerable to the seas because most of the hull is exposed to them, and furthermore there is danger of being rolled over by a large breaking sea. Some experienced blue water sailors such as Eric Hiscock, Erroll Bruce, and Humphrey Barton have said that they approve of hulling up to a certain point, perhaps to Force 9 winds (depending, of course, on the type of boat and the particular weather and sea conditions).

Despite the fact that there are arguments against lying a-hull, there are a great many sound reasons for using the tactic up to whole gale winds, and there are also arguments for hulling in survival conditions (the most extremely bad weather). Some of the advantages of drifting beam-on under bare poles are as follows: the boat is presenting her maximum buoyancy to the seas; headway can be kept to the minimum, especially as compared with scudding; backing down on the rudder is minimal when compared with holding the bow up; sails are not subject to damage since they are removed; there is little danger of broaching to or pitch-poling (somersaulting end-over-end), as there is when running off before it; the boat will yield to the seas by making leeway to a much greater extent than if she were held by a sea anchor; and drift is not extreme (a definite advantage when near shore), as compared with drift when running off. Buoyancy is obviously important in order that the vessel can lift to the seas rather than have them break aboard. Forereaching can be dangerous, because the boat may drive into a sea even if she lies beam-on, and also headway tends to reduce leeway so that the boat will not readily yield to the seas.

Surprisingly, some boats (usually racing types) will make considerable headway beam-on even under bare poles, and also if a boat tends to bear off with helm unattended, then naturally she will pick up forward speed; therefore it is customary to lash the helm down when hulling. With the rudder turned to windward, any headway will tend to make the boat turn towards the wind which will slow forward progress. A few boats have been known to make some sternway when hulling, and if such is the case, special precautions should be taken with lashing the tiller or even the rudder itself. This will be elaborated on when we discuss riding to a sea anchor off the bow, a tactic which makes the rudder especially vulnerable.

When comparing lying a-hull with broaching to, it might be argued that a vessel is in approximately the same attitude with respect to wind and seas in both cases. However, there are important differences, a boat lying a-hull is in a directionally stable position drifting sideways, but a broach is associated with forward speed downwind which results in a sudden turning to bring the boat broadside to the seas. In the latter case, the momentum of the turn is added to the heeling moment produced by the side force of the wind and seas. Furthermore, the vessel that broaches to is often carrying at least some sail, which might add considerably to the heeling moment. Then too, the broaching vessel carries some headway after she has turned beam to the seas, and this tends to decrease leeway, gives her less opportunity to rise to the seas, and reduces her ability to yield.

Although some sailors have expressed concern over a hulling vessel directly exposing her side to the seas, at the crest of a wave the normal boat will heel sufficiently to present the rounded turn of her bilge to the wave force. This part of a vessel is usually very strong, and when it takes the brunt of a sea, it lessens the remaining force that would strike against a weaker part such as the cabin house. Also, as said earlier, the boat will be side slipping and yielding to wave smashes.

Lying beam-on, a vessel may roll quite violently, and this is one reason for heaving to under sail until this method gets out of hand. When the wind is so strong that it is impossible to carry sail, however, there is often sufficient wind pressure on the masts and rigging to inhibit excessive rolling. Rod Stephens, Jr. wrote me, "It seems that lying a-hull is generally a satisfactory expedient when it is really too severe to carry any sail, but this presupposes a wind that will keep the boat pretty steady by virtue of the wind pressure on the spars, and with less than extreme conditions it would be very undesirable rolling to weather." Of course, a major problem is that in high, steep seas the vessel is very apt to be becalmed in the troughs and with her keel immersed in the backward-moving water particles she would tend to roll to weather. However, the motion might very well be tolerable if the wave (or wavelet) period and the boat's period of roll did not coincide in such a way that accumulative or rhythmic rolling began to develop. Unless normal (non-accumulative) rolling is very extreme, the motion will be more uncomfortable than dangerous. An individual boat's behavior when lying beam-on in a particular condition of wind and sea can only really be determined through actual trial.

Hulling is very definitely more desirable under certain circumstances than under others. To be very general, the tactic seems most appropriate, when the following conditions can be met: (1) the boat has a high range of stability, (2) she is light but strongly built with a round hull, low cabin trunk and moderately high freeboard, (3) the keel is of such shape and depth that it permits ample leeway when the boat has no headway, (4) the boat is directionally stable when lying beam-on and her headway is controllable when lying a-hull, (5) the seas are of the deep-water kind, long and with spilling-type breakers, (6) the wind is not so strong as to cause prolonged extreme heelings under bare poles, and (7) the wave period and period of roll do not reinforce each other in such a way that they produce dangerous accumulative rolling. As to the first point, a boat has the least transverse stability (she is most tender) when beam to the wind and seas; therefore it is of the utmost importance that she have a high range of stability if she is to lie a-hull. A fairly low initial stability is not dangerous, and it may even be helpful in alleviating extremely quick rolling and for exposing the turn of the bilge, but ultimate stability is vital.

A sailor who is unfortunate enough to be caught in the most extreme survival conditions at sea should be, as well as possible, prepared for the worst. The worst that could happen when running off is undoubtedly pitch-poling, but the worst when hulling is capsizing or turning turtle. The boat must be of such a type, with the necessary ballast and sufficiently low center of gravity, that she can recover from a bottoms-up position, otherwise I don't think hulling in a severe storm is worth the risk. In such weather conditions in a boat lacking ultimate stability, there is probably less chance of turning bottom up if the boat can be kept end-on to the seas. When hulling, the crew should expect an occasional extreme, perhaps momentary, knockdown, even when the boat has ample stability. Many injuries have been inflicted on those closed up in the cabin during knockdowns, because heavy gear was not properly stowed or the crew not adequately secured in their bunks. In extreme conditions ordinary bunk boards may not be sufficient. Bunks should perhaps be equipped with automobile-type seat belts.

When Jerry Cartwright was sailing the 29-foot Cascade sloop, *Scuffler*, in the 1969 Singlehander's Transpacific Race, he received a horrible head injury, a fractured skull and partial loss of memory, from being thrown out of his bunk. It is almost a miracle that he made it alone safely to Hawaii. The *Scuffler* is a light-displacement fin-keeler, and although somewhat tender, she lay a-hull successfully in winds up to 50 knots. On one occasion, she took a severe knockdown while hulling, but she recovered without damage to her hull or rig.

In considering hull characteristics most suitable for the tactic of lying a-hull, I think a low, strong cabin trunk with small windows is of tremendous importance. High deckhouses are especially vulnerable to seas breaking aboard, and surprisingly, the leeward side of the trunk is what is usually damaged during a violent knockdown. On seagoing boats cabin trunks should be molded to the deck or strongly secured with bolts or metal straps, and it certainly helps if the trunk has a rounded shape. Many windows on modern yachts are dangerously large. They should be small, strongly secured with metal frames, be equipped with storm shutters, and should be made of Plexiglass, safety, or perhaps even bullet-proof glass for the very worst conditions.

Freeboard should not be excessively high because of windage and vulnerability to seas, but the topsides should be high enough for ample reserve buoyancy, reserve stability, and also to delay submerging the rail. I believe that if the rail is deeply buried when hulling, a sea, exerting considerable thrust against the boat's windward side and bottom, could produce a dangerous capsizing force. Naturally, the boat must be strongly built to lie a-hull in extreme conditions, and I think that rounded topsides with moderate tumble-home should be helpful. One has only to observe how offshore lighthouses are rounded to stand up to years of awesome wave pounding. Another advantage of reasonably high freeboard (combined with a fairly straight or reversed sheer) is that it allows the use of a small cabin trunk in a small to medium size boat, without sacrifice to headroom below.

Many moderately light displacement boats are particularly suited to hulling because a light hull has great buoyancy and will rise easily and also give to the seas. This does not mean, however, that all heavy boats are not well suited to the tactic. Sir Alex Rose, who made an outstanding one-stop solo circumnavigation in 1967 and 1968, is a great advocate of hulling, and his vessel, the 36-foot *Lively Lady,* was of considerable displacement. One advantage of a heavy hull is that it has more body underwater which allows a lower cabin trunk for a given freeboard in order to have full headroom below decks.

In the opinion of many authorities, draft has an important bearing on the success of hulling. However, I think the really important matter is not merely draft alone, but the combination of draft with the area and shape of the lateral plane. What we want is low lateral resistance (when there is no headway) combined with sufficient draft to allow low placement of ballast, but not so deep as to result in an extremely low center of lateral resistance. As pointed out in Chapter 1, when there is great distance between the CLR and the center of wind pressure on the sails, the heeling moment is high, therefore if a major consideration in hulling is the angle of heel, the rig must not only be reasonably low, but also the CLR should be reasonably high. Draft alone does not determine the CLR's location. Figure 41 shows how keel shape can alter the vertical height of the CLR. Of course, stability depends primarily on a vessel's beam and her ballast, with the beam and hull shape contributing more to stiffness at low angles of heel and ballast supplying the greater righting force at high angles of heel. The lower the ballast is located, the greater the range of stability; therefore the ballasted keel must be reasonably deep to assure recovery from an extreme knockdown, but not so deep (or so large in area at its bottom) as to make the CLR excessively low or to prevent reasonable leeway when hulling.

A reasonable amount of leeway is important, as said before, in order that the vessel yield or give to the force of seas striking the hull on her beam. As everyone knows, draft has an important effect on lateral resistance, and shoal-draft boats generally tend to make considerable leeway. For this reason some authorities, such as sailor-builder-designer Robert Derecktor, feel that keel-centerboarders have a safety advantage over deep-keel boats when struck on the beam by breaking seas in extreme conditions. Since water particles only move forward significantly at the very crest of a wave, a shallow hull is most likely to be carried bodily sideways with the particles and without excessive solid water sweeping over the deck or any great capsizing force resulting. But a deep-draft boat will have her keel buried in relatively steady water, while the crest exerts a strong lateral force against the upper hull thereby creating a powerful tendency to capsize. In other words, the boat with a very deep draft is vulnerable to tripping on her keel. For this reason, centerboarders should usually lie a-hull with their boards retracted (unless, perhaps, a very small amount of board is used to correct balance). In 1964, the 39-foot, centerboard yawl *Doubloon* was rolled over (through 360 degrees) twice in a gale off the coast of Georgia. The *Doubloon* was lying a-hull when the accident occurred, with her board down as a result of attempting to make her lie closer to the wind. Her owner-skipper, Joe Byars later reflected that the lowered board tripped the yawl and contributed to her roll-overs.

It is interesting to note that when Richard Carter tested the stability of his controversial retractable-keel design, the *Red Rooster,* in actual sailing trials, the boat could not be knocked down to any great extent with her keel up. She merely heeled over and slid off to leeward. Despite this apparent attribute, however, it could be dangerous to lie a-hull in the *Red Rooster* with her keel retracted in the most extremely bad weather in heavy seas, because there is so little draft that undoubtedly ultimate stability would suffer. Centerboarders and retractable keel boats may have an advantage in low lateral resistance, but leeway should never be achieved at the expense of high ultimate stability. As said earlier, in my opinion, normal, small, sea-going centerboarders should have a draft of at least one-seventh of the load water line length in order that the rudder can be kept low (when it is not retractable) for good steering control and in order that the ballast can be kept low for reserve stability. Of course this is merely a rule of thumb, and exact draft to LWL ratio would depend on hull shape, displacement, weight of ballast, and hull size (large boats require relatively less draft). Rod Stephens, Jr. writes, "In spite of a certain amount of propaganda from centerboard enthusiasts, I certainly feel a reasonable keel with the stability range provided, would be my choice for bad weather off-shore."

Although fin-keelers have traditionally been shunned for ocean cruising, principally because of their lack of directional stability, we are seeing more and more of them offshore today. In the 1969 Singlehanders Transpacific Race, for instance, four out of five contestants were light or moderately light displacement fin-keelers. In lying a-hull, the boat with a short (but not excessively deep) keel may have a special advantage, because a high-aspect-ratio, cambered keel particularly depends on hydrodynamic lift to prevent leeway. When there is no headway (as when hulling) a fin keeler will move sideways in a somewhat similar way in which an airplane will drop when its forward speed is reduced and its wings are stalled (see Figure 42). For a given draft, a fin keeler will be less likely to trip on her keel than a boat with a long keel, because, as the English author-designer, Douglas Phillips-Birt, tells us, when the keel is stalled, its lateral resistance depends on area rather than aspect ratio. Thus with a fin keeler, we might be getting the greatest draft (to permit low placement of ballast) for the least stalled-lateral-resistance (to help avoid tripping). Any difficulty from lying a-hull in a fin keeler will most likely come from lack of directional stability. This type of boat might tend to fall off the wind and forereach, however, this fault might be corrected by lashing the helm down, or, when conditions are not too extreme, by setting a very small riding sail aft.

Although reasonable leeway is desirable when hulling, excessive leeway might not be desirable, especially when near a lee shore. In such a case, if hulling is still the preferred course of action, it might pay to stream warps or some sort of drag over the windward side, provided leeway is not slowed too much. Warps might also help smooth the seas. John

FIGURE 41: SHAPE OF KEEL AND THE CENTER OF
LATERAL RESISTANCE

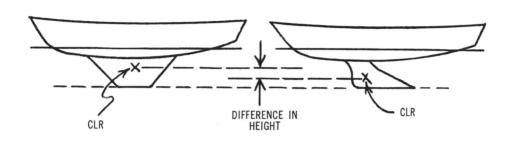

FIGURE 42: LATERAL PLANE AND LEEWAY WITHOUT
HEADWAY

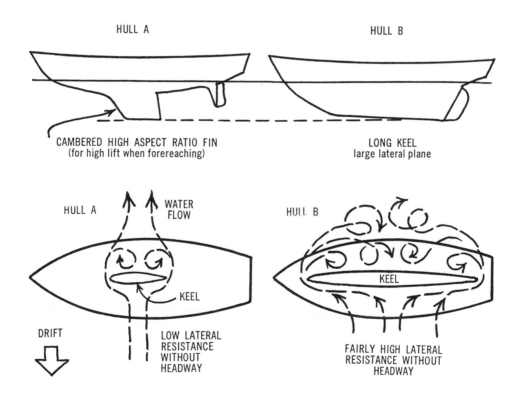

Guzzwell, who made a circumnavigation in the 20-foot, light-displacement, fin-keeler, *Trekka,* wrote me that he usually lay a-hull, beam-on, with the helm down in bad weather. On one occasion, in a lengthy gale off Queensland, Australia, he became worried about his offing, and so he streamed two long warps attached to an eight-foot piece of lumber to windward. *Trekka's* drift was noticeably lessened, but it is interesting to note that she did not lie to as comfortably as before, when she had no drags to windward.

If the tactic of hulling seems too dangerous for any of the aforementioned reasons, such as: the seas being short with plunging breakers, or the boat having less than adequate reserve stability, or the cabin house or windows being vulnerable, then the boat should be kept, as much as possible, end-on to the seas. Her bow or stern will present the smallest target, and the hull will be in the position of greatest transverse stability when end-on. To be held in this position she must either run off before it, or ride to a sea anchor.

### Riding to a Sea Anchor

Sometimes a distinction is made between a drogue and a sea anchor, but essentially each is a floating anchor designed to slow a vessel's drift and to help hold her in a desired attitude. We could differentiate between the two to some extent by saying that the sea anchor is intended to reduce drift to a bare minimum, while the drogue is merely a drag to lessen drift. The most familiar sea anchor is the conic, cloth bag, the mouth of which is held open by an iron or steel hoop. This type, as well as several other kinds of sea anchors and drogues, is illustrated in Figure 43.

The traditionally accepted way for a small boat to weather a storm at sea was to ride to a sea anchor streamed from her bow, but today this tactic is very rarely used. A great many modern, experienced sailors who have logged thousands of miles offshore have never used a sea anchor or even seen one in use. Is this tactic a lost art, or is there a good reason for abandoning the sea anchor? Perhaps there is some truth in the affirmative answer to both these questions. It is certainly true that the typical modern boat is not well adapted to riding to a sea anchor (especially off the bow), but on the other hand, there is at least one circumstance when a sea anchor might be considered imperative. If a small vessel were caught near a lee shore in deep water, and conditions were too severe to claw off under sail and power, I think this undoubtedly would justify the use of a sea anchor. In order to be prepared for such an emergency, it certainly seems advisable to carry a sea anchor and to practice handling it if an extended coastal or offshore passage is to be made in a small boat.

## FIGURE 43: SEA ANCHORS AND DROGUES

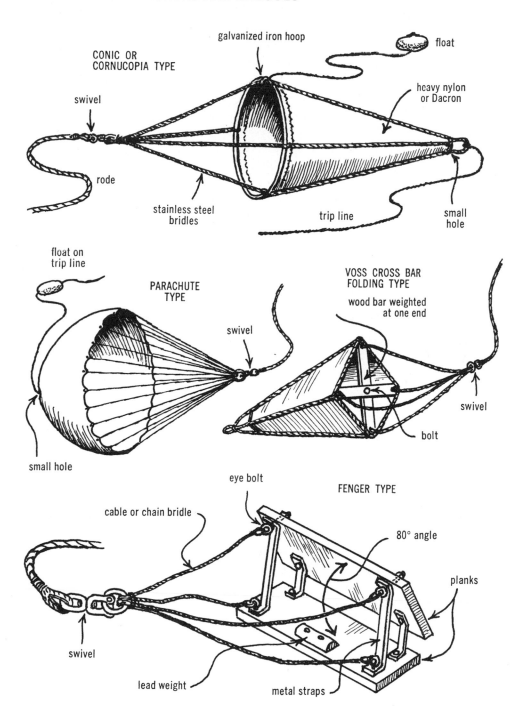

CONIC OR CORNUCOPIA TYPE

galvanized iron hoop

float

swivel

heavy nylon or Dacron

rode

stainless steel bridles

trip line

small hole

float on trip line

PARACHUTE TYPE

swivel

small hole

VOSS CROSS BAR FOLDING TYPE

wood bar weighted at one end

swivel

bolt

eye bolt

FENGER TYPE

cable or chain bridle

80° angle

planks

swivel

lead weight

metal straps

The great champion of the sea anchor was Captain John C. Voss who sailed the 37-foot Nootka dugout canoe, *Tilicum*, almost around the world in the early 1900's. His classic book *Venturesome Voyages of Captain Voss*, contains a great deal of advice, some of which is still valuable, on the handling of small boats at sea. It is said that his small boat seamanship theories greatly influenced polar explorer Ernest Shackleton who made an incredible passage of 800 miles in an open boat through Antarctic seas after his ship, the *Endurance*, had been crushed in the pack ice. In his book, Voss gives instructions on the use of the sea anchor and praises its effectiveness in helping to hold a vessel's bow up to the wind. It should be born in mind, however, that most of the boats sailed by Voss were better able to lie bow to the wind than are most contemporary boats. The *Tilicum* especially, with her long, shallow keel, low windage forward and means of setting a satisfactory riding sail aft, seemed well suited to riding to a sea anchor off the bow. Lifeboats, dinghies and other small, shoal-draft boats have successfully used this tactic (often without riding sails) to weather bad storms. It is interesting to note that when Robert Manry's 13½-foot dinghy, *Tinkerbelle*, encountered her first real blow during her Atlantic crossing in 1965, she did not keep her head up when the sea anchor was put over the bow; but when Manry unshipped her deep outboard rudder, she immediately swung head-to-wind and rode out the blow successfully.

Despite the success of many older, long-keeled boats and shoal-draft small craft with the sea anchor streamed from the bow, most modern boats with short, deep keels and great windage forward cannot be held head to the wind by this means. In many cases a modern boat might be held fairly close to the wind with a riding sail aft in addition to the sea anchor forward; but there are often severe jerking strains from the anchor line that might pull the bow into the wind momentarily and cause the riding sail to flog violently. In this case, when a riding sail is used, it should be a specially-made, flat-cut, extra strong storm sail. On a yawl this could be a storm mizzen, but on a sloop, I think the riding sail should be similar to the type illustrated in Figure 40. Although it has been suggested that a small working jib can be hanked to the permanent backstay as a substitute riding sail, I don't think the usual jib is suitably designed or cut to stand up to the punishment of a lengthy gale if it is set backwards for use as a riding sail.

Even if the modern boat can be made to lie reasonably well to a sea anchor forward and a riding sail aft, there are certain disadvantages in this method, a major one being that the boat will at times be thrown backwards, and this could very possibly damage the rudder. An example of this danger is the case of the 20-foot, fin-keel yawl, *Nova Espero,* when she broke her rudder blade while riding to a sea anchor during an Atlantic gale in 1951.

*Shown at the helm of his famous Nootka Indian dugout canoe, the* Tilicum, *at Samoa in 1901, is Captain John C. Voss, who sailed this craft across the Pacific, Indian, and Atlantic oceans. Voss was a pioneer of small-boat, blue-water sailing and a champion of the sea anchor. (Provincial Archive, Victoria, B.C.)*

As a matter of fact, even Voss broke his rudder post on two occasions when using this tactic. To alleviate the strain on the rudder caused by sternway, the rudder itself (instead of the helm) should be lashed amidships whenever this is possible, as in the case of an outboard rudder. Captain Voss suggested securing two blade ropes (he called them heel ropes), one on each side, to a hole or eye in the above-water trailing edge of the rudder, after which each rope is pulled taut and secured to the deck at each quarter. Adlard Coles has suggested that such a hole in the rudder could be filled with soft putty that could be poked out easily in an emergency. Of course, most rudders could not be secured easily because they are deeply submerged, but it might be possible to lash a spade rudder in the manner described. Since the top, after corner of many a modern spade rudder is located very close to or slightly above the waterline, blade ropes might be rigged just prior to bad weather, or they might be left attached to the rudder's corner when cruising offshore. In the latter case they could be carried slack over the stern as shown by the dashed line in Figure 44 in fair weather, but in a storm the ropes could be led to each quarter where they would be hauled taut and belayed. Another possible justification for blade ropes is that they could also serve as jury steering lines in certain kinds of rudder damage. With some spade rudders, if the propeller allows clearance, it might be possible to turn the rudder around backwards to lessen strains due to sternway (see Figure 44).

Of course, one way to solve the problem of rudder damage is to stream the sea anchor over the stern. This will obviously tend to bring the stern up to the wind into an attitude that is more natural for a modern boat with her deepest draft aft and considerable windage forward. However, it should be kept in mind that the sterns of some boats, especially those with long overhanging counters, are less able to rise to the seas than their bows and may pound badly. A sea anchor should not be used astern, unless the boat has a small, self-bailing cockpit. Cockpit scuppers must be large, the companionway must be high above the cockpit floor, and the companion hatch must be fitted with proper slides (not doors) of unquestionable strength. It is usually much easier to stream a sea anchor over the stern because the cockpit is more handy to work from than the foredeck, but it should be secured to a very strong fitting, such as a heavy bitt located aft on the boat's centerline, or the mizzenmast of a yawl. The strains imposed by a sea anchor are so great that they can wrench off an ordinary cleat, and the anchor will often break up or part its bridle lines before a lengthy blow will moderate. For this reason, the anchor and its gear must be tremendously strong. Of course, the rode must be extremely well parcelled or protected with durable (perhaps rubber) chafe guards at the chock. Authorities often recommend a short length of chain at the chock, or where the rode crosses the bobstay if the vessel has a bowsprit and the sea anchor is streamed from the bow.

A possible danger in using the sea anchor is that the boat might be tethered or held too firmly against the seas so that she cannot yield. This might increase the force of the waves against the hull and cause them to break aboard. When Humphrey Barton streamed a sea anchor over the starboard quarter of the *Vertue XXXV* during a storm near Bermuda in 1950, a sea broke aboard with such force that two cabin windows were smashed (see Chapter 2). Barton said that the anchor, a 21-inch diameter conical type, had stopped his small boat "almost dead." It seems very possible that the force of the damaging sea was increased by tethering the boat to a nearly immovable sea anchor, and perhaps the sea would have caused less damage if the warp had been secured on the boat's centerline instead of her quarter, in order that the stern could have been held more squarely to the seas. Apparently, Barton himself, who is a very knowledgeable and experienced blue water sailor and yacht surveyor, now believes that the trouble encountered by the *Vertue XXXV* was at least partly due to her being overly tethered. Although a standard rule of thumb for the diameter of a conical sea anchor is one-tenth of the boat's waterline

# FIGURE 44: REDUCING RUDDER VULNERABILITY
## WHEN DRIFTING BACKWARDS AT SEA

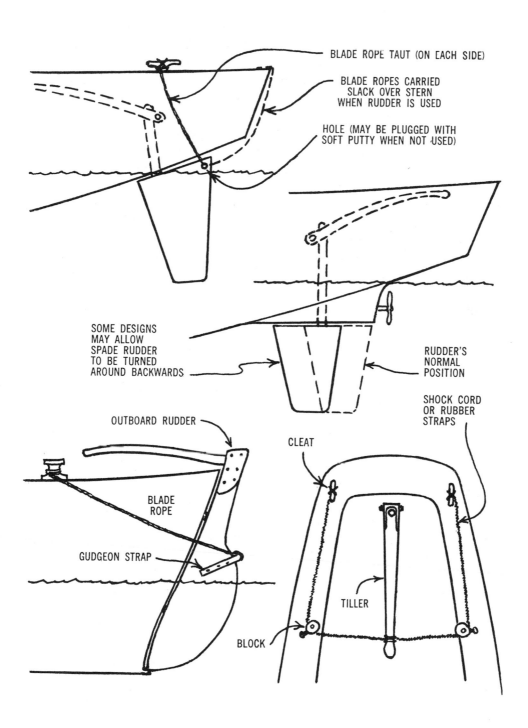

BLADE ROPE TAUT (ON EACH SIDE)

BLADE ROPES CARRIED
SLACK OVER STERN
WHEN RUDDER IS USED

HOLE (MAY BE PLUGGED WITH
SOFT PUTTY WHEN NOT USED)

SOME DESIGNS
MAY ALLOW
SPADE RUDDER
TO BE TURNED
AROUND BACKWARDS

RUDDER'S
NORMAL
POSITION

SHOCK CORD
OR RUBBER
STRAPS

OUTBOARD RUDDER

CLEAT

BLADE
ROPE

GUDGEON STRAP

TILLER

BLOCK

length, a smaller size, perhaps one-twelfth or less, would lessen the tethering risk.

Another offshore sailor who has had experience with sea anchors, Dr. Paul Sheldon, also believes that the anchor should allow a fair amount of drift in extremely bad weather. Dr. Sheldon recommends the parachute type (see Figure 43) when it is necessary to stop excessive drift in winds up to perhaps 25 m.p.h., but in stronger winds he believes in towing astern the Fenger drogue (also shown in Figure 43), made from two heavy wooden planks, a type that allows more drift or give. Thomas Fleming Day suggested that an easily stowable drogue could be made by securing a plank across the flukes of an ordinary fisherman-type anchor. Most sea anchors comprised of planks will not overly tether a boat, but a very large conical type and especially the parachute type may very well hold too fast. As a matter of fact, some parachute anchors have printed warnings against their use in extreme conditions because of their lack of "give" in heavy seas.

When I discussed this subject with Eric Hiscock a few years ago, he expressed some concern over a boat being held too firmly to the seas, and he seemed to disapprove of sea anchors in general, especially when streamed from the bow. However, Hiscock said that he believed in keeping a sea anchor aboard for an emergency, and in streaming it, nearly always from the stern, if it became essential to slow a vessel's drift. His *Wanderer III,* a 30-foot, transom-sterned sloop, once lay for four days in heavy weather to a sea anchor off the stern for the purpose of lessening drift away from a destination that lay to windward and to stay well clear of a small island and reef to leeward.

In order to minimize the jerking strains of a sea anchor, an ample length of springy nylon rode should be used. Naval architect-author Juan Baader and others have suggested a scope equal in length to the length of the wave or a multiple thereof, in order to synchronize, as much as possible, the motion of the boat and anchor. When both the anchor and boat are in wave crests simultaneously, both are carried forward by the water particles, but when boat and anchor are in troughs at the same time, both are opposed by the orbiting water particles. This synchronization should help alleviate severe jerking strains. It might be necessary, however, to use a scope equal to two wave lengths when the seas are not very long to help assure that the anchor will stay immersed and that the rode will be sufficiently springy. As said, a stern bitt should be on the boat's centerline, but when there are only cleats on each quarter, a bridle might be improvised by securing the rode to one cleat and then securing a second line with a rolling hitch to the rode a few feet outboard of the stern and then hauling in on the second line until the knot is directly astern on the centerline (see Figure 46).

The typical conical sea anchor is usually pictured with a float attached by a short float line and a trip line, as shown in Figure 43. Yet some sailors who have had experience with drogues, prefer not to use these extra lines, because they not only add to the difficulty of streaming the drogue, but also these lines can become fouled or badly twisted if the drogue begins to rotate on its rode. More will be said of this when we discuss running inlets through surf in the next chapter. Although a float might be needed in shallow water, it certainly seems desirable to avoid the unnecessary complication of extra gear when in deep water. It is not extremely difficult after using a sea anchor to bring it back aboard without a trip line. The rode is hauled in, or the boat is sailed up to her drogue when conditions have moderated, and when the drogue is alongside, its apex (small end) can be reached with a boat hook so that the bag can be capsized to spill its water. A strong swivel is recommended between the rode and the drogue's bridle lines to prevent twisting the bridles in the event the drogue should start spinning.

Despite a great deal of confusion and controversy about sea anchors, it seems reasonably safe to draw the following general conclusions, in my opinion:

• Sea anchors or drogues still have their place for small, very shoal-draft boats, especially open boats, either motor, sail, or rowing boats. It is the safest policy for boats of these types to carry some kind of drogue (even if it is only a *strong* bucket, on a very small boat) when in unprotected waters. An open or undecked boat should usually not be allowed to lie broadside to the seas in heavy weather.

• A modern, moderate sized offshore boat should carry a suitable sea anchor for emergency use, but in most cases it should be used only when it is essential to lessen drift and when there is no other means of doing so in reasonable safety.

• Care should be taken to see that the sea anchor and its gear are tremendously strong; that, if it is the conical type, the bridle ropes run all the way down the bag to its apex (see Figure 43); that there is a strong swivel, ample nylon rode, and proper bitts and chocks (on the boat's centerline, aft); and that the anchor is a type or size that allows the boat some yield in extremely heavy weather. The rode should be well parcelled or fitted at the chock with a rubber chafe guard.

• Since most modern boats with short keels and great windage forward will not lie much closer to the wind then beam-on (and some will even lie with the wind abaft the beam) with a sea anchor over the bow, it is usually best to stream the anchor astern. However, this requires a small, self-draining cockpit with large scuppers, and a high companionway hatch fitted with proper slides. Also the stern should be a buoyant type without a long overhanging counter. A strong stern bitt should be on or near the boat's centerline, but perhaps a bridle can be rigged from two quarter cleats.

• If the sea anchor is streamed from the bow, the average modern boat will require a strong, flat, riding sail aft. When using this method, it is preferable that the rudder blade be lashed as described previously. If this is not possible, it may help to lash the helm with elastic shock cord or rubber straps to help alleviate jerking strains on the rudder caused by sternway (see Figure 44).

• If a sea anchor is carried, it should be inspected periodically, and occasionally it should be used in practice sessions in moderately bad weather.

## Scudding

The remaining tactic we have not yet discussed is scudding or running off before the wind and seas with little or no sail set. Despite several potential dangers in this tactic, it is widely endorsed under certain circumstances by contemporary seamen. The potential dangers are the possibilities of being pooped (having a following sea break over the stern), broaching-to (inadvertently rounding up, beam to the wind and seas), and being pitch-poled (capsized longitudinally, end-over-end). The principle circumstances that might very well justify scudding, however, are: (1) the necessity of vacating a dangerous area, (2) the desirability of proceeding towards one's destination when the wind is favorable and the boat is completely manageable, and (3) conditions requiring that the boat be kept end-on to the seas, and yet, because of her drift attitude, vulnerable rudder, lack of proper riding sail, or some other reason, she cannot or should not be kept bow to the seas.

To elaborate somewhat on these circumstances, it would certainly seem desirable or necessary to vacate an area if there were a strong current opposing a gale, if you were in the path or dangerous quadrant of the storm (see Chapter 5), or if you were on shoals that were producing dangerous seas. When the wind is blowing towards your destination, naturally it is desirable to gain all the distance possible in the right direction, provided there is no danger of the boat being close to a lee shore before the bad weather dissipates.

Scudding, whether fast or slow, also requires: that the boat is manageable; that she answers to her helm and shows no alarming tendencies to root (bury her bow) and broach-to or pitch-pole; that heavy pooping seas are not breaking over her stern; and that the stern is not squatting (being sucked down) excessively. Similarly to riding with a sea anchor off the stern, scudding also requires a small, self-bailing cockpit and a high companionway with proper slides. In severe weather with the threat of pooping seas, companion slides should always be kept in and the sliding hatch kept closed except, of course, when entering or leaving the cabin. Conditions that might require keeping the vessel's end to the seas have already been discussed, but to summarize briefly, they are: lack of reserve stability or capability to self-right; excessive draft and lateral plane which might encourage tripping laterally on the keel; vulnerable topsides, cabin house, and especially windows; excessive rolling when lying a-hull; extreme, initial tenderness of the boat and/or such a severe wind that beam-on and stripped of sail, she lies with her rail submerged in solid water; and seas that are dangerously short and steep, with frequent breakers of the plunging type. Difficulties with keeping the bow of a modern boat up to the seas were discussed in the previous section on sea anchors. In general, there seem to be fewer problems involved in keeping the stern towards the seas, especially if the bow tends to fall off the wind below beam-on when the vessel is allowed to assume her natural drift attitude (under bare poles with the helm free).

Although most contemporary offshore seamen agree that scudding is an entirely acceptable storm tactic under the right circumstances, there is considerable disagreement and controversy about the exact proper technique. Some advocate running off at fairly high speed, others feel that speed must be kept low, many recommend trailing lines or drags, others do not, some believe in taking the seas on the quarter, while others insist on taking them squarely on the stern, and so forth. Which technique is used will depend to a large extent, on the type of boat, the size and character of the seas, and the general severity of the weather.

The classic means of scudding is that first popularized by Joshua Slocum when he ran off before a gale in the *Spray* near Cape Horn in 1896. The *Spray* carried no sail other than a reefed forestaysail sheeted flat, and she ran dead before it with her helm lashed amidships while towing two long hawsers over her stern. The small scrap of sail forward and the drags aft helped hold her off before the wind. This method of scudding was appropriate for the *Spray*, because of her exceptionally good directional stability (mainly due to her flat run and long keel), and because she had ample buoyancy in her ends. Then too, the *Spray* did not have the ultimate stability of most modern boats, and this would suggest that hulling should be avoided in the most extremely bad weather, especially in the waters off Cape Horn. Of course, the big disadvantage of Slocum's method was that it carried him a little too rapidly towards a lee shore, and as a result, he narrowly escaped being wrecked on a group of submerged rocks known as the Milky Way off Cockburn Channel.

Although the subject of speed while scudding is somewhat controversial, I believe that most experienced offshore sailors are in favor of a boat going moderately slowly, or at least not extremely fast, when her speed can be controlled. This is one of the main reasons for towing lines and drags astern. Even a single long, heavy line streaming astern can cause a fair amount of friction, while tying many knots in the line and towing the line in a bight can cause a greater drag. Of course, drags attached to the ends of the lines such as buckets, sails, anchors, spars towed sidewise, or a swamped dinghy can create far more drag. Incidentally, heavy floating objects such as a dinghy or spars should be towed very far astern, because they can be thrown a considerable distance forward by a breaking crest. A swamped dinghy would probably break up or pull away from or part her painter in a lengthy gale, and so it would be preferable to tow it in a cargo net. I have been told by quite a few blue water sailors that automobile tires make excellent drags. Then, of course, there are drogues such as the Fenger type (shown in Figure 43) that are designed to slow a boat's speed but not to stop headway in the manner of a true sea anchor, but drogues can be difficult to handle if they are fitted with floats and trip lines.

Another reason for towing lines or drags astern is that they may have a smoothing effect on the seas and help prevent the crests from breaking in most weather less severe than survival conditions. Irving Johnson and others have suggested towing sails to help smooth the seas. Frik Potgieter, who sailed the 35-foot, Piver-designed trimaran *Zulane* from South Africa to the West Indies, told me that he rode out a bad storm near the Cape of Good Hope by towing his mizzen boom with the mizzen attached while running off under bare poles. In addition to slowing the boat, the sail had a calming effect on the seas.

There are a number of potential dangers in scudding at high speed in steep seas, especially for heavy displacement vessels. The deep, heavy hull makes a large stern wave when travelling at hull speed (1.34 times the square root of her waterline length) and this might have a disturbing effect on a following sea that could cause it to break over the stern. Furthermore, such a speed may cause the stern to squat or be sucked down which would encourage being pooped. Scudding requires a buoyant stern but there should not be so much buoyancy aft that there is risk of depressing the bow. High speed in heavy following seas might cause the bow to dig in or root, which could lead to broaching-to or even pitch-poling in the most extreme case. Of course, the shape of the bow has a considerable influence on this matter. The buoyant bow with shallow forefoot would probably be the most desirable to avoid rooting. The late professor of naval architecture at M.I.T., K.S.M. Davidson, pointed out some years ago that a deep forefoot can temporarily move a vessel's center of lateral resistance far forward when the stern is lifted in running before heavy seas, and this could disturb directional stability and lead to broaching. Although Dr. Davidson suggested that full blunt bows have less tendency to dig in, high-speed scudding can be risky even for boats with this type of bow. Naval architect-author Howard Chapelle tells us: "The fallacy of the full entrance as a prevention of 'sailing under' by hard driving sailing craft was exploded by the middle of the last century. As a matter of fact, full-ended heavy displacement sailing yachts tend to 'bore' if pushed."

If a vessel does inadvertently turn and broach-to, the inertia of her forward speed will be added to the capsizing force of the wind and seas when she turns to the beam-on position. If the bow roots but the vessel does not turn, there is the possibility of pitch-poling, when the stern's momentum carries it over the buried and thus much slowed bow. In other words, the boat trips on her bow and somersaults. The tendency to pitch-pole or broach-to is aggravated not only by high speed, but also by the size and shape of the seas. A short, steep sea with a wave length of about twice the vessel's length will not only lift her stern considerably higher than her bow, but it will expose her stern to the forward-moving, orbiting water particles at the very same time her bow lies in the backward moving particles in the trough (see Figure 45). Although a small headsail set forward might help hold the bow off before the wind, this sail would increase speed and it might tend to depress the bows of some modern boats and add to the danger of rooting.

Another argument in favor of scudding at a low speed is that the faster a vessel travels, the longer she stays on the crest of a sea. Even if the crest is not breaking, it can be dangerous because the orbiting water particles are moving ahead, and also, when a boat is on the crest, she is supported or buoyed up amidships but relatively little at her ends. In this position, she has minimal transverse stability. Tank tests have shown that a vessel's righting moment is generally greatest when she is in the trough while running before a following sea, but that the righting moment is minimal when the crest is amidships. Furthermore, while on the crest, the rudder's control is minimal because of the forward speed of the water particles and the likelihood of the rudder emerging. It seems desirable, therefore, to slow down and let the crest pass quickly.

Although there are very convincing arguments against high-speed scudding (when this can be prevented), most experienced offshore seamen believe in maintaining enough speed for good steering control. A moderately low speed allows the vessel to yield to the seas and gives her reasonable helm response without the danger of drawing a large stern wave, carrying excessive forward momentum, or driving her bow under. Furthermore, when there is enough headway to allow rudder control, breaking crests can sometimes be avoided and the stern can be kept towards the seas. Just how fast a boat should be run off, provided her speed can be controlled, for adequate steerage way depends to a large extent on the boat's size and design, or such factors as her length of keel, hull shape, and rudder size and position, and especially on the wind and sea conditions. To be very general, the ideal speed for a small offshore boat (perhaps 25 feet on the waterline) might be three or four knots in moderately short seas, but somewhat faster in long, regular seas. In my opinion, it could be dangerous for a heavy displacement hull to exceed a speed-to-square-root-of-length ratio of 1.0 (5 knots for a 25-foot LWL) in steep seas, since beyond that speed a sizeable quarter wave would develop. Furthermore, there are the problems of momentum and boring or rooting the bow, as mentioned earlier.

One disadvantage in towing warps or drags is that these hamper steering control. When one vessel tows another of comparable size, an adverse effect on steering is noticed at once by the helmsman of the towing vessel when her tow line is secured abaft her rudder head. This is why tug boats have their towing bitts located well forward of the rudder. Warps or drags secured to a boat's stern have a similar effect on steering. When the French circumnavigator Bernard Moitessier ran his ketch, *Joshua*, off before a gale in the South Pacific in 1965, he streamed lines and drags over the stern to slow his boat's speed. But in the Roaring Forties between Tahiti and Cape Horn, the seas can be so enormous, steep, and so conducive to surfing that even a heavy, steel, 40-footer such as the *Joshua* could not be slowed. Moitessier claimed that in those conditions not only did the drags (five long hawsers with iron ballast attached and a heavy cargo net) fail to slow the boat, but they hampered steering as though he were towing a "motor boat." When the *Joshua* appeared to be in imminent danger of being overwhelmed, Moitessier cut loose the drags and immediately his boat gained steering control. The successful technique developed by Moitessier under these particular conditions was: to strip the boat of sail and steer her, without drags astern, dead before the wind until she was overtaken by a steep following sea. At this time, he would luff slightly in order to let her heel somewhat and allow the sea to pass under her quarter. *Joshua's* stern was held about fifteen to twenty degrees from being square to an approaching crest line. Although one might expect a quartering sea to exert a strong broaching force, Moitessier explained that this force was readily controlled by the rudder, that there was somewhat less tendency for the boat to plane, and that the slightly heeled hull presented the curve of its leeward bow to the trough "like a ski," and this helped prevent rooting. Moitessier referred to advocates of high-speed scudding as belonging to the "Vito Dumas school," because the Argentine circum-

FIGURE 45: FORCES WHEN SCUDDING IN SHORT
STEEP SEAS

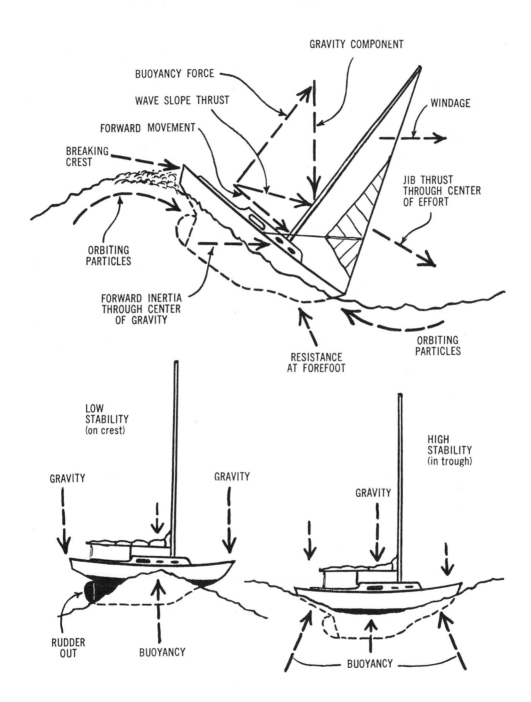

navigator Vito Dumas often ran off at high speed (usually carrying sail) in his Colin Archer-type double-ender *Lehg II*. However, this thinking should probably be called the Moitessier school, because Dumas gave very few details of his technique, while Moitessier is very explicit. I first read of the Frenchman's ideas in The Cruising Club of America's *Cruising Club News* (February, 1967), then later in Adlard Coles' fine book *Heavy Weather Sailing*. More recently Moitessier has told his story in his own book, *Cape Horn: the Logical Route*.

While the technique of Moitessier worked well for him, we must remember that he was discussing the great seas of the South Pacific where the fetch is enormous and where gales are often of unusual duration. He doubted that *Joshua* would lie a-hull without being rolled over, and he had no use for sea anchors in those conditions; thus he elected to scud. He adopted the technique described because there was no way of slowing his boat. Although the drags he trailed often hampered steering, they had "no more effect than a tuna line" in slowing the ketch. Moitessier therefore decided that if he had to run fast, he would do so in the manner that allowed maximum steering control. A point I would like to suggest, however, is that Moitessier's technique is not necessarily suitable for all conditions. In lesser seas that are not so conducive to surfing, it would certainly seem prudent to attempt slowing the vessel down at least to a speed equal to the square root of her waterline length, which would allow steering control but minimize most of the risks associated with high speeds. If the vessel could not be slowed, then the Moitessier technique might be considered, but in my opinion, the slowing should be attempted first. The scientist-sailor, C. A. Marchaj, suggests that high-speed scudding is often suitable in long, fast moving seas, but when the waves are short, he recommends a slow speed and towing drags that would help hold the stern up when the boat is on a crest, at which time the rudder has very little control.

As for the problem of steering being hampered by towing drags, there have been suggestions made that could help alleviate some of the difficulties. It was mentioned earlier that the towing bitts on tug boats are located well forward of the rudder and propeller in order that the tow load does minimal harm to steering control. Possibly a similar effect could be achieved by a ketch towing a drogue (or drags attached to a single line) when the line is made fast around the mizzenmast, high enough to avoid the need of a chock aft (see Figure 46). Of course, this would require a very strong mizzen, and it would be desirable to have the mainmast's permanent backstay attached to the mizzenmast near the drogue line's point of attachment as shown in the illustration. This method would probably require removal of the mizzen sheet and perhaps the stern pulpit, and great care would have to be taken to see that the drogue line was

FIGURE 46: TOWING DRAGS

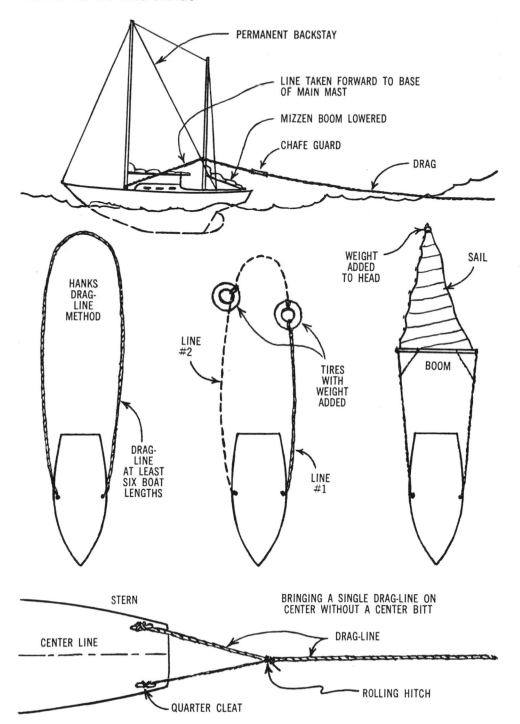

PERMANENT BACKSTAY

LINE TAKEN FORWARD TO BASE OF MAIN MAST

MIZZEN BOOM LOWERED

CHAFE GUARD

DRAG

HANKS DRAG-LINE METHOD

DRAG-LINE AT LEAST SIX BOAT LENGTHS

LINE #2

LINE #1

TIRES WITH WEIGHT ADDED

WEIGHT ADDED TO HEAD

SAIL

BOOM

STERN

CENTER LINE

QUARTER CLEAT

BRINGING A SINGLE DRAG-LINE ON CENTER WITHOUT A CENTER BITT

DRAG-LINE

ROLLING HITCH

protected against chafe at the point where it would bear on the after rail.

A technique of streaming drags astern in a manner to have steering relatively unhampered was suggested by E. F. Hanks in an interesting article published in the *Cruising Club News* (December, 1968). The article was written as a result of its author's concern over Moitessier's inability to find a means of slowing his scudding ketch in the South Pacific. Hanks, who once ran the seamanship department of an indoctrination school for ship's officers, suggested towing astern a heavy warp (or docking lines made fast end to end )in a great bight with each end of the bight made fast to each side of the vessel near her maximum beam (nearly amidships) instead of being secured at the customary locations on each quarter. In this way, the warp is made fast well forward of the rudder post. In my opinion, securing the warp on each side would not allow as much steering control as would a tug boat's arrangement with a single tow line secured in a similar fore and aft location but on the boat's centerline. A line towed in a bight would tend to smooth the following seas, however. Hanks claimed that in actual trials in heavy seas, the bight of the towed line "not only knocked down the crests of curling breakers but provided a steadying, controlling effect and a wide slick astern." Furthermore, he claimed that this technique allowed the stern to swing and it did not unduly hamper steering. Hanks' method of towing a bight while running at moderate speeds was tried in shallow water breakers and also offshore in heavy weather with good results. Although the experiments were tried with various kinds of power craft, Hanks also recommends the method for sailboats. For best results, he suggests that the drag line have a length of at least six boat lengths. Incidentally, Robin Knox-Johnston, the first man to circumnavigate alone, non-stop, had success using this drag towing method while scudding under a tiny storm jib set forward and sheeted flat on his 32-foot double-ender *Suhaili*. He used the method in winds as strong as Force 10. It seems to me that the Hanks method would be well worth trying, but I have some reservations about its efficacy in the kind of conditions to which Moitessier was exposed, because the drag line could be thrown forward in the crests of those tremendous seas.

Drags might be added to a towed bight to help slow the vessel's speed in the manner suggested in Figure 46. As shown, an automobile tire is attached to the end of line number one. Then the end of a second line is secured to the tire, and a short distance (perhaps twice the beam of the boat) from the end of line number two, a second tire is secured to the line. The drags are dropped over the stern and each line is payed out and secured amidships. The bight would be quite narrow, but perhaps it would be of some help. It might be necessary to add weight to the tires to keep them well submerged.

As with the sea anchor, the use of storm oil seems to be a dying art. In former times, few well found boats would put to sea without a supply of oil that could be dripped overboard for the sake of helping to calm the seas in the event of bad weather. Perhaps there is some justification for modern seamen abandoning the use of oil, however, because today's boats usually cannot be held head to the wind, and in most other attitudes they may tend to run away from a slick unless a large amount of oil is used continuously. Of course, oil is quite messy to use also. It can get spilled below, seas wash it on board and make the decks slippery, and the highly effective fish oils have, for most people, a nauseating smell that may encourage sea sickness. However, there are certain occasions when, for brief periods of time, oil might be of some real value. Oil might be helpful when entering an inlet in rough seas or when it is necessary to board a wreck, especially if the crew on the wreck can spread oil as well as the crew of the rescue vessel. Nevertheless, for a small, modern boat weathering a lengthy, severe gale, it seems doubtful that enough oil could be carried for any sustained significant effect on the seas. If oil is used in limited amounts, a recommended method is to spread it from canvas bags pricked full of holes, filled with rags or oakum soaked in oil, and then hung over the topsides or towed astern. If a sea anchor is used, an oil bag can be fastened to it. Modern mariners who have tried using oil in heavy weather most often use motor oil or other petroleum products, but oceanographer Willard Bascom tells us that these have relatively little effect as compared with fish or viscous animal oils.

## Survival Tactics

Fortunately, the vast majority of blue water sailors can spend a lifetime at sea without experiencing survival weather or the ultimate storm. Nevertheless, the most optimistic offshore seaman can't be absolutely sure he will never be caught in such conditions, and so it is important for him to give this improbable but perfectly possible contingency some serious thought.

Of course there is no sure way to guarantee survival in an ultimate storm at sea, and so, obviously, every possible attempt should be made to avoid exposure. The deep sea sailor should make a careful study of all coast pilot books, pilot charts, and oceanic wind and current charts covering the general area of his proposed passage. He should know the general weather pattern of the area, the typical paths of tropical or extra-tropical storms, the safest time of year to make the passage, the location of shoals or currents that could cause dangerous seas, and the whereabouts of regions notorious for dangerous weather. In addition, of course, he should have a safe boat, soundly designed, constructed, and equipped. If the passage maker absolutely insists on sailing in potentially dangerous waters, as for example, off Cape Hatteras in the fall or winter, in mid-Atlantic during the hurricane season, or in the South Pacific near Cape Horn, then he should be prepared for the worst. As the ocean sailor, Edward Allcard, has said, "assume that one day the boat will turn upside down."

When Marcel Bardiaux rounded Cape Horn alone in the 30-foot sloop, *Les 4 Vents,* in 1952 sailing the "wrong way" (from east to west) against gale-force winds, he expected the worst. His sloop was, as well as possible, built and fitted out to survive a capsizing, and it was just as well, because near Cape Horn she twice rolled bottomside up. Her recovery and survival were largely due to her extra strong water-tight construction, her rounded cabin house and decks designed to withstand green water, small portholes instead of the large picture windows found on many modern boats, and ability to self-right, due, not only to her outside lead ballast, but also to numerous buoyancy tanks bolted to her frames at a high level. The lesson for blue water sailors seems clear: first, avoid exposure to survival conditions (they can usually be avoided with careful planning); and secondly, if you are compelled to take the ultimate risks like the mountaineer who must meet the challenge of Mount Everest, expect and be ready for anything, and this includes turning bottomside up.

In most cases, there are probably only two ways for a modern boat to weather a lengthy ultimate storm at sea: by scudding or lying a-hull. In the most extreme conditions, it is doubtful that any sail can be carried, because even if the sail could survive, it might impose too great a strain on the boat or her rig. It seems advisable to avoid using a sea anchor on the typical modern boat, unless it is essential to slow the drift towards a lee shore, because the anchor will overly tether the boat, and there will be such strains that the anchor might pull itself to pieces or even damage the boat. Dr. David Lewis nearly pulled the transom off his *Cardinal Vertue* with a sea anchor during a North Atlantic gale in 1960.

If we eliminate the tactics of heaving to and riding to a sea anchor, the remaining choices are running off under bare poles or hulling. The advantages and disadvantages of both these methods were discussed earlier in this chapter. Which tactic is used should depend primarily on the design and construction of the boat and also on the need to evacuate the area. In such conditions, it is most probable that there is only one direction in which to evacuate, and that is downwind. Thus, if the boat is fairly close to a lee shore, hulling would be the better tactic to minimize drift, and vice versa, if there is ample sea room and it is necessary to vacate, then running off would accomplish this in the quickest time.

As for the boat's design, consideration should be given to the boat's natural drift attitude, in accordance with William A. Robinson's thinking. It is probably better to let the boat do what she will naturally, rather than try to make her resist and fight against overwhelming forces. As said before, design and construction features that are desirable or mandatory for scudding are as follows: buoyant ends; good directional stability when making headway downwind; a small, self-bailing cockpit (preferably located amidships); a moderately long keel without an excessively deep forefoot; a deep rudder (preferably with a skeg when the keel and rudder are separated); moderate beam; a strong bridge deck or high companionway; strong well-placed towing bitts located aft; and the absence of a long, flat counter. For lying a-hull, the most important design virtues are: ample reserve stability and self-righting ability; a low, strong, preferably rounded cabin trunk; small ports or windows of ample strength; a keel that allows adequate leeway when stalled (probably a fin type or moderately shoal-draft keel); a natural beam-on drift attitude; an adequately buoyant hull (preferably of moderate to light displacement) with adequate freeboard; and a round (rather than a flat surface, V-bottom) hull adequately strong at the turn of the bilge.

It is probably true that there are some weather and especially sea conditions so severe that no small boat can remain undamaged or stay upright no matter how she is handled. After the 46-foot ketch *Tzu Hang* pitch-poled in the Roaring Forties about a thousand miles from Cape Horn, many sailors offered various suggestions on how the accident might have been prevented. These suggestions ranged from towing more drags or a sea anchor astern, to scudding with speed, to lying a-hull. Of course, there are problems in all of these methods. The sea anchor would be apt to hamper steering, impose dangerous jerking strains, overly tether at the wrong moment, or else be thrown forward in a crest and allow surfing. High-speed scudding has many dangers, discussed earlier, but it is possible that Moitessier's method might have worked in those great seas. Lying a-hull would probably have resulted in the *Tzu Hang* capsizing or turning turtle, as the seas were too steep and the ketch seemed unsuitable for the tactic with her deep draft and great lateral plane. Indeed, she did roll over while hulling on another occasion. No one can say with any certainty that any tactic could have kept her upright in the particular wave that tumbled her. John Guzzwell of *Trekka* fame was aboard the *Tzu Hang* when she pitch-poled, and he contributed much to her survival by repairing the serious damage and constructing a jury rig which enabled her to make port in Chile. John has written that he suspects there might be uncharted shoals in the general area of the South Pacific where the pitch-poling took place. He described the state of the sea at that time as being similar to "what would be encountered with a long swell passing over a shoal area,

very steep seas, some of which toppled over and broke like surf." It seems
that the ketch simply could not cope with those unusually bad seas.

If a non-negotiable freak sea is met or conditions are so bad that
turning over is extremely probable, it is undoubtedly better to capsize,
turning over laterally, than to pitch-pole, end-over-end; and so this is an
argument for hulling in the worst possible conditions. The *Tzu Hang* was
damaged far less when she rolled over while lying a-hull than when she
somersaulted while scudding. Even Moitessier, the advocate of running off
at high speed, maintains that the force of seas taken beam-on when hulling
is softer and less damaging than when they are taken end-on with speed.
He writes, "Even an enormous breaker taken full broadside reminds me of
the image of the blow of a giant bludgeon—made of foam rubber. The
blow can be extremely powerful, but it will remain relatively soft, with
very little breaking effect." There are more than a few records of seagoing
boats capsizing offshore, and in most cases, the rig has been badly damaged; but when the hull, cabin, decks, and cockpit were properly designed
and constructed, they were seldom seriously damaged, and in many cases
the rig was not destroyed.

If the seas seem negotiable end-on (that is, without due danger of
pitch-poling), then it would seem advisable to try scudding with just
enough speed (when it can be controlled) to provide good steerageway,
provided the boat is suitably designed and constructed for this tactic.
It might be well worthwhile trying the Hanks method of towing drags to
control speed and help smooth the following seas with minimal harm to
steering, and/or (if the boat is ketch rigged) drags might be attached to
the mizzen as suggested in Figure 46. But when the seas do not seem
negotiable end-on, or when the helm cannot be manned due to illness,
injury, extreme fatigue, or weather that prevents prolonged exposure, then
hulling may be the only answer. Carleton Mitchell has described the wind
in the worst survival weather as "a raving, mad demon, totally unfamiliar,
capable of picking up a man and throwing him down like an empty paper
bag; of tearing off his clothes; of deafening, blinding, and smothering him."
If conditions can get that bad, it certainly seems doubtful that any man
could stay on deck for very long, much less steer effectively. It would
probably be best for him to go below, batten down all hatches, stow and
secure all movable objects, and fasten himself in his bunk. The boat
would then be left to look out for herself, and hopefully, as Thomas
Fleming Day said, "She will do the right thing." This is the means by
which Jean Gau in the 30-foot Tahiti ketch *Atom* weathered hurricane
Carrie, the same blow that sank the large training bark *Pamir*, drowning
all but six of her eighty-six crew members.

Before going below and leaving the boat to look after herself, however, careful preparations should be made on deck. The boat must be made completely watertight (this includes removing all vents, even Dorades); all gear that cannot be taken below should be thoroughly secured, especially poles and booms that might have to serve as jury masts in the event of a dismasting; oil bags should be put over the windward bow, and it is often advisable to stream many lines to windward or astern; to lessen windage, working sails should be unbent and perhaps even storm sails, unless it might be necessary later to attempt beating away from a lee shore; and also to reduce windage, it may be advisable to remove halyards, except those that might be needed to set emergency storm sails when conditions moderate. If the boat's natural drift attitude should be nearly beam-on or slightly stern-up, the helm should probably be lashed down (with shock cord) to prevent forereaching. Of course, this advice is based on the premise that there is high risk of pitch-poling when lying end-on and that capsizing is the lesser of two evils. If the seas are not so steep as to induce surfing and serious rooting of the bow which could result in broaching-to or pitch-poling, then it might be advisable, when the boat has a stern-up tendency, to run off with the helm lashed amidships, while towing all the drags possible astern. When the helm cannot be manned, then obviously there is no need to be concerned about steering control, and the drags over the stern may help hold the stern to the seas, slow the boat's speed, and smooth the seas. It is probably the safest policy, however, to avoid towing a sea anchor astern, because of the strains and the risk of over-tethering.

Some knowledgeable sailors have suggested cutting down the masts when faced with the ultimate storm in order to reduce windage and weight aloft, but I would certainly hesitate to recommend such a drastic measure. There is no guarantee that a mastless boat will not capsize. Joe Byar's *Doubloon* was rolled over twice in the same day, once with her masts and once without them. In one respect a mast may even be helpful in that its windage will damp rolling when the boat lies beam-on. Furthermore, during a lull in the storm, a mast (or even a stump of the mast) might be needed to carry a stormsail for the purpose of evacuation or clawing off a lee shore, and obviously, sail will be needed to reach port after the blow has moderated. As said before, there are cases of boats keeping their rigs intact despite a capsizing. Thus there is probably far more to be lost than gained in a deliberate dismasting.

A fact of some encouragement to those caught in extremely bad conditions offshore, is that there are more than a few cases of boats surviving when left abandoned. This gives support to the theory of hulling and letting a boat assume her natural drift attitude; because time and again, when vessels have been given up for lost, abandoned by their crew and left to their own devices, they have survived. A few examples are: *Black Duck, Dutch Treat, Curlew,* and *Compass Rose,* and, more recently, *Integrity.*

The old Crowninshield-designed schooner, *Black Duck,* broached-to while scudding before a gale in the Gulf Stream off Cape Hatteras in March, 1948. The accident left her half swamped, with little more than a foot of freeboard, and her main pump had become clogged and broken. She was repeatedly swept by seas while lying beam-on and appeared to be leaking badly. Her crew were taken off by a tanker, but the *Black Duck* did not sink until the next day just before she was to be taken in tow by a freighter. Incidentally, there are few quicker ways of sinking a damaged vessel than towing her faster than her hull speed. Alain Gerbault's cutter *Firecrest* foundered while under tow.

The *Dutch Treat,* a 45-foot steel ketch designed by A. Mason was abandoned during a blow off the coast of Charleston, South Carolina, in 1960. Although the wind in this case was not extreme, its direction opposed the flow of the Gulf Stream, and this caused a dangerous sea. The *Dutch Treat* wallowed in the trough and was swept by short, steep, breaking waves. Her crew sent out a distress signal and were soon rescued by a tanker. The abandoned ketch then proceeded to drift for eight days until she grounded on the sand banks off Cape Hatteras. Amazingly, she sustained no serious damage and had very little water in her bilge.

The 67-foot schooner, *Curlew,* broached-to and was pooped while scudding under bare poles before a Force 12 storm near Bermuda in November, 1962. Her crew were taken off by a U. S. Navy ship, and three days later she was found drifting, half swamped but still afloat, having cared for herself during the latter part of a real survival storm. In the case of the *Compass Rose,* a hard-chine, keel yacht, abandonment occurred after grounding on a sand bar in the Bahama Islands during a gale in October, 1967. Her skipper, the only crew, was rescued by a helicopter. Somehow, the vessel refloated herself and drifted for six days, most of the time in gale-whipped seas, after abandonment. In November, 1970, the 52-foot schooner *Integrity* was abandoned about 400 miles southeast of Cape Fear, South Carolina after she had broached-to. Three weeks later she was still afloat and was towed to safety by a salvage tug. All of these derelicts with the exception of the *Black Duck* were saved. In most of the above mentioned cases, the skippers of the damaged craft should not be blamed for their decisions to abandon, because when a rescue ship is available, and there is a real possibility of foundering, obviously it is better not to gamble in a matter involving human life. Nevertheless, these incidents clearly show how well a vessel can look out for herself, even in the worst conditions.

Abandoning at sea in the middle of a survival storm is not as simple as it may sound. In fact, there can be tremendous difficulties involved.

*Salvaged after eight days of drifting as a derelict, following her abandonment, is the steel ketch,* Dutch Treat. *Surprisingly, the boat was hardly damaged and had little water in her bilge. (Salt Water Sportsman)*

It is generally agreed that the rescue ship should go to windward of the boat being abandoned to create a lee, however, the problem in this tactic is that the ship will make the more leeway and will soon drift down on the boat and damage her. Despite this risk, however, I think this approach is nearly always preferable to one on the lee side of the boat unless, perhaps, the ship has a Lyle gun (line throwing gun) that can shoot a line a considerable distance. In this case the ship might stand clear to leeward, shoot a line to the boat and transfer the crew in a rubber raft. When the rescue ship is close aboard to leeward, she not only fails to make a lee, but the reflection of the waves off her windward side can make a dangerously steep and confused sea. The suggestion has been made that the ship go some distance to windward of the boat and float down to her, at the end of a long line, a rubber raft or rescue mat (a floating mat usually made of buoyant PVC). It seems to me, however, that this operation would be next to impossible when the vessels lie parallel, beam-to-beam, because a raft or mat would drift very little, if any, faster than the ship, and it is

likely that the two vessels would collide and perhaps even crush the abandoning crew before they could be taken aboard the ship. A far better
variation on this maneuver would be for the ship to approach the distressed
boat from the windward side and then turn into the wind and hold her
position while the raft or mat is drifted down to the boat. However, in such
a position the ship makes a small lee, and of course great care must be taken
to avoid her propeller. A faster and perhaps more certain means of rescue
is for the ship to come alongside to windward of the boat and close aboard
even though the boat will probably be damaged. When side-by-side, the
two vessels can perhaps be lashed together, and the crew of the boat can
climb or be hauled up the side of the ship. This is a very dangerous operation because the man going up can be crushed between the vessels, thrown
against the side of the ship, or be struck by the boat's rigging when the ship
rolls. David Q. Scott, who was taken off the *Black Duck* when she was
abandoned, told me that he considered it far safer to be hauled up the
ship's side rather than climb up on a rope ladder or cargo net. He said
that when the rescue ship came alongside the apparently sinking schooner,
lines were thrown down with double bowlines tied in their ends. The
*Black Duck's* crew were able to slip into the loops of the bowlines, and
then they were pulled aloft quickly before they could be smashed by
either boat. It is far preferable that the ascent, whether climbing or being
pulled, begin when the boat is on the crest of a wave in order that she will
drop away from the man going aloft. Another point to consider is that an
ascending crew member should be as far as possible away from the masts
so that he will not be struck by the rigging or speared by a spreader. In
some cases, perhaps, when the boat being abandoned is a trimaran with
her awkward amas, for example, the rescue might be effected more easily
from the rescue ship's lifeboat.

## Multihulls in Heavy Weather

Chapter 2 contained a discussion of the suitability and disadvantages
of multihulled craft for blue water sailing. Although multihull enthusiasts
abound and many successful offshore passages have been made in these
craft, there have been a great number of unsuccessful passages, and there
are several inherent drawbacks in the multihull design concept for extensive
offshore work. One of the most serious drawbacks is the lack of ultimate
stability and of the ability to self-right. As said earlier, most multihulls have
tremendous initial stability, but when heeled beyond a certain point, they
will turn over and their normal tendency is to remain bottomside up. Of
course, the usual unballasted multihull will not sink, and when bottomside-

up, it may serve as a crude life raft for the surviving crew. Righting most large multihulls, especially catamarans, without outside assistance might be extremely difficult and in some cases impossible (see Chapter 4), thus every means must be taken to minimize the risk of a capsize. These means include early sail reduction, sheet releases, mast floats, sponsons, and, in many cases, keeping end-on (rather than beam-on) to the wind and seas. Ballast keels increase stability, but they could hurt performance and make a multihull sinkable.

Sheets may be released automatically by the simple means of a hinged cam-action jam cleat held down with a length of shock cord. Tension on the elastic chord can be adjusted so that when wind pressure on a sail becomes dangerous, the hinged cleat will flip up in the direction from which the sheet leads to make it release. A more exact method is the Hepplewhite sheet release. This device, made in England, can be set to free a sheet automatically at any chosen angle of heel. An electronic control unit consisting of two mercury switches, one for port heel and one for starboard, sets the angle of heel at which the cleat flips up to free the sheet. Of course, in heavy weather one has to be wary of electrical devices that may be subject to short circuiting from wet wiring; thus sail should be reduced or removed early.

Although many fast trimarans are designed to sail with the windward ama out of water to reduce wetted surface, in my opinion, offshore catamarans should never be sailed with their windward hulls emersed, nor should trimarans be allowed to lift their main hulls clear of the water even momentarily. When hulls begin to lift out or leeward amas start to bury, corrective measures should be taken immediately. These measures might be to release the sheets and then reduce sail, and/or to luff up, or bear off before the wind. When a strong puff is taken on the beam or abaft the beam, most multihulls will gain stability more quickly by bearing off to a dead run. Heeling above moderate angles can be dangerous for several reasons: with any further heeling, stability will quickly deteriorate, wave action under the windward hull may create a capsizing moment, and the wind pressure under a wing deck (the platform connecting the hulls) and in some cases even the aerodynamic lift of wind passing over the deck may lessen stability.

Permanent or built-in anticapsizing measures, such as ballast keels, sponsons, and fixed masthead floats were mentioned in Chapter 2. A less practical but nevertheless possible emergency means of lessening the risk of turning turtle is the use of a temporary masthead float. This might be some kind of streamlined air bag (perhaps even a small rubber raft if its windage were not too great) that could be shackled to a masthead halyard and hauled aloft before the bad weather commenced. A better solution would be a small, folded and deflated bag, permanently installed aloft, that could be inflated by $CO_2$ either manually with a lanyard leading to the deck (see Figure 12) or automatically when the mast strikes the water during an extreme knockdown. If such an arrangement could be made reliable, it might be of great value even to many single-hulled craft.

When a multihull has a greater than normal stability range and resistance to capsizing, due to large size, ballast, specially placed sponsons, or having her hulls very far apart, she might lie a-hull in weather that is quite heavy. Indeed Dr. David Lewis weathered an Atlantic gale in 1964 in his heavily ballasted catamaran, *Rehu Moana,* by lying a-hull. Likewise, the unballasted catamaran *Golden Cockerel,* lay a-hull in the 1968 Single-hander's Transatlantic Race during a lengthy gale. Her skipper, Bill Howell, retracted her dagger boards to avoid tripping, and he reported that one sea lifted the catamaran and threw her 50-yards to leeward. Despite these and other successful hulling experiences, however, it seems the safest policy to keep a capsizable and non-self-righting multihull end-on to the wind and seas in extremely bad weather. Indeed, the 25-foot trimaran, *Clipper One,* turned turtle while lying a-hull, stripped of all sail, not far from the Cape of Good Hope during a gale in 1968. Her skipper, singlehander Tom Corkill, survived the accident after extricating himself from the cabin and clinging to the upturned boat for 18-hours before he was rescued. Despite the facts that the *Clipper One* had tremendous initial stability as a result of above-normal beam and she had no sail set, she was capsized by a sea breaking on her beam. It seems likely that she would have had a better chance lying end-on to such seas.

Some multihull enthusiasts advocate running off at high speed in bad weather. A champion of the tactic was Arthur Piver who claimed that a light displacement trimaran can surf down the face of storm waves and stay ahead of their breaking crests. Although it is true that a well-designed, directionally stable multihull can surf for hours in heavy winds and large seas with very careful and attentive handling of the helm, many authorities are opposed to the high-speed running technique in extremely bad weather with confused seas. Piver was eventually lost at sea in March, 1968, while singlehanding a trimaran of his design, and although no one knows how he disappeared, it does not seem inconceivable that he might have been overwhelmed while testing his high speed theory. As with single-hulled craft scudding at fast speeds, multihulls are subject to broaching-to and rolling over or pitch-poling in the very worst conditions. Travelling at high speeds in heavy weather some cats and some tris especially are also subject to capsizing diagonally, that is capsizing and pitch-poling simultaneously. This can happen when the bow of the leeward hull or ama roots while the stern of the windward ama is lifted. Risk of diagonal capsizing can be

*Dr. David Lewis'* Rehu Moana, *a heavily ballasted catamaran intended for 'round-the-world cruising. Her heavy displacement detracted greatly from her sailing performance. (Eileen Ramsay)*

minimized by keeping the mast and center of effort of the sail plan reasonably far aft and, according to trimaran designer, James Brown, by having amas of sufficient length forward with adequate buoyancy in their bows. On the other hand, trimaran designer, Lock Crowther, warns that excessively buoyant bows with a lot of flare can encourage a tendency to broach-to. When the lee bow begins to bury, it certainly seems prudent to reduce sail, slow down, and in extreme conditions to keep the sterns square to the waves.

The catamaran designer, Rudy Choy, has suggested running a cat dead before it under bare poles in the heaviest weather. He advocates towing all possible warps, lines, and drags astern to slow her speed. If she still tends to surf, he suggests plugging the self-bailing cockpit and filling it or letting it fill with water in order to weight her down and further reduce speed. Designer, James Wharram, who is a V-hulled catamaran enthusiast, advocates running off in bad weather, and he suggest slowing speed by towing automobile tires from each stern. However, he recommends a speed sufficient for good steering control in order that the stern can be held square to the seas.

If caught in a very heavy blow during a coastal passage, a shoal-draft multihull might have a dubious advantage over a deep-keeled monohull in that the former can more easily be run ashore and beached. However, such a tactic is usually one of final desperation. Obviously, every attempt should be made to claw off a lee shore before the vessel is deliberately grounded, regardless of her draft. On the subject of beaching in heavy seas, my feelings are similar to those of Captain A. J. Kenealy's on the subject of prayers in heavy weather. In an early (1905) manual on seamanship, *Boat Sailing in Fair Weather and Foul,* the Captain wrote: "Now praying on shipboard is not to be scoffed at, but it should be delayed until man has exhausted every possible means of saving the ship."

# 8 / POWERBOAT MANAGEMENT IN HEAVY SEAS

*Powerboats Offshore*

A powerboat designed for going offshore, of considerable displacement and moderate speed, should have many characteristics in common with the offshore sailboat. Boat designers and knowledgeable seamen nearly always agree that a proper offshore sailboat is far safer to take to sea than are most power craft; in fact it may perhaps safely be said that a sound approach to the designing of a seaworthy powerboat would be to incorporate into her hull and superstructure as many as possible of the desirable design features of able sailing craft. At any rate, motorboats that have nearly opposite characteristics to sound sailboats, such as many high-speed, planing boats and especially houseboats, with their flat bottoms, low freeboard, and lofty deckhouses, should not venture into unprotected waters. As said in Chapter 2, displacement offshore motorboats of the MFV type must be completely watertight, should have a low center of gravity to assure reasonable stability, modest-sized windows, sufficient draft to assure good propeller and rudder depth, and a reasonably balanced hull (in the fore-and-aft distribution of buoyancy). It is also advisable that such a vessel have some means to damp rolling, preferably some small sail that can also be used for emergency locomotion in the event of engine failure. Naval architect William Garden has suggested that when a steadying sail is to serve as occasional propulsion, it should be located far forward so that the powerboat can be made to run off before the wind satisfactorily. It is also advisable to have a means of setting a small riding sail aft when and if it becomes desirable to hold the vessel's bow up towards the seas.

Some permanent or built-in means of preventing severe rolling were mentioned in Chapter 2. A temporary or removable roll preventer is the paravane or fisherman stabilizer, illustrated in Figure 47. This device, sometimes called a "flopper-stopper," has been publicized and perfected for yacht use by the noted powerboat seaman, Robert Beebe. As can be seen in the illustration, this anti-rolling system consists of two heavy metal plates shaped like delta wings, suspended well below the water on wire or rope pendants from the ends of two booms rigged one on each side of the boat. Although the paravanes are intended for use in rough water, they could be dangerous in the most extreme weather offshore, because of the possibility of a boom or guy breaking or the heavy plates being thrown against the hull. Nevertheless, Beebe claims that he has carried his flopper-stoppers in gale-force winds and that they contribute to safety when it is desirable to run off with the seas on the quarter. A similar roll-damper called the "Roll Control" is also shown in Figure 47. This device has a valve flap which opens to let the plate sink but closes to resist rolling when the plate is lifted, but unlike the flopper-stopper, the Roll Control is not designed to be towed when the boat is moving with any speed. It is merely intended for boats at anchor or possibly when drifting slowly.

As for high-speed boats at sea, there is not any great risk in a fast, decked and buoyant motorboat making a short run offshore in fair weather, or a careful passage along a coast with numerous accessible inlets when she has some means of emergency propulsion, such as an auxiliary outboard motor, in case of engine failure. In my opinion, however, few if any planing motor craft, especially those with large open cockpits, should ever make extended passages a great distance offshore. Such boats are vulnerable to swamping or capsizing and turning turtle if caught in extremely heavy weather. So long as the high-speed boat stays reasonably close to shore, however, she has one outstanding virtue in that she can make a dash for port when bad weather threatens, but of course, this requires a reliable engine and a vigilant weather eye and frequent checks on radio weather reports. Some fast boats, usually those with fairly deep V-bottoms having the V carried well aft, are quite well designed to withstand pounding into rough head seas. This type of hull is often used for offshore powerboat racing. Nevertheless, it should be kept in mind that such a boat is by no means intended to cope with a bad storm at sea.

Should a small planing motor boat be so unfortunate as to be caught offshore in heavy weather, it is generally essential to keep her end-on, preferably bow to the seas. Of course, she should proceed towards shelter if possible, but her course might be a zig-zag one in the interest of avoiding or minimizing the dangers of heavy breaking seas. A wave breaking on the beam could easily capsize or swamp the normal high-speed boat. Thus a course that runs parallel to the crests of the waves (normally at right angles to the wind) might be negotiated in an alternating, weaving manner

## FIGURE 47: REMOVABLE ROLL STABILIZERS

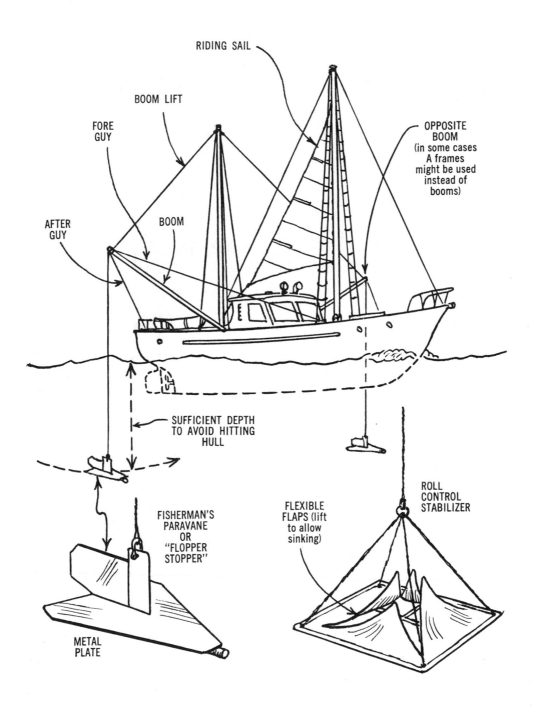

RIDING SAIL

BOOM LIFT

FORE GUY

OPPOSITE BOOM
(in some cases A frames might be used instead of booms)

AFTER GUY

BOOM

SUFFICIENT DEPTH TO AVOID HITTING HULL

FISHERMAN'S PARAVANE OR "FLOPPER STOPPER"

FLEXIBLE FLAPS (lift to allow sinking)

ROLL CONTROL STABILIZER

METAL PLATE

*A large MFV type cruiser. Note her "flopper-stopper" booms and roller furling headsails.* (National Fisherman)

that first brings the crests broad on the bow and then on the quarter. Generally, the speed should be quite slow but fast enough for good steerageway. In extremely heavy weather, even a skillfully steered zig-zag course might very well be too dangerous, and so most motorboats should be held end to the seas: by powering slowly into the seas (a tactic sometimes termed "dodging"), lying to a sea anchor, or possibly running off.

When the course lies dead to windward, the fast motorboat should power slowly into the seas with just enough speed to prevent her bow from being blown off. Too much speed can damage the hull through pounding or can cause the seas to break into the cockpit and swamp an undecked boat. It is well to remember that even a self draining cockpit usually drains very slowly. Even when the boat has ample flotation, the shifting of water in a large, filled cockpit during a roll can seriously affect the boat's stability. Also, driving with speed into a head sea puts a greater strain on the hull than many people realize. Many years ago, I was aboard an 85-foot air-sea rescue crash-boat which cracked six frames while driving towards port at a moderate speed into a head sea raised by a nearby tropical storm in the Gulf of Mexico. After discovering the damage, we were forced to run off, which we did successfully at moderately low speed until the weather improved somewhat.

*This Maine lobster boat type is quite seaworthy for coastal work, and her high speed allows her to reach shelter quickly in the event of heavy weather. Her large cockpit and low freeboard aft, however, make her unsuitable for coping with a bad storm at sea.* (National Fisherman)

Some motorboats, usually the heavy, sea-going types, will run off fairly well in heavy weather, but many small, high speed types with sharp bows and little deadrise aft can be extremely difficult in following seas. This latter type that is designed to plane easily in smooth water, has far more buoyancy aft than forward, and this tends to make the bow root when scudding in heavy weather, which could lead to broaching or even pitch-poling. There is one school of thought that advocates running off at high speed in order that the boat can keep her bow high and keep ahead of the wave crests. According to this theory, the boat would ride on the back of a wave and travel at the exact speed of the wave in order to keep ahead of the next following crest. This can work when running through a short stretch of regular breakers, but, in my opinion, such a practice could be very dangerous in heavy weather at sea. In the first place, storm waves at sea can run at 25 to 35 knots or faster, and it would be exceedingly difficult to keep ahead of them for hour after hour even in a high-speed boat. Secondly, fuel consumption is very great at high speeds, and thirdly, waves at sea are frequently very confused with wave trains mixing and seas crossing other seas or swells from several different directions. In such a case, the boat could easily poke her bow into a hollow and her high speed momentum could cause her to broach to and capsize or even pitch-pole. As said before, tank tests have shown that a boat running off at nearly the same speed as the waves is in a position of great instability when she is overtaken by a crest. Furthermore, with many shoal-draft powerboats there is the very real danger that the rudder and propeller will break water and cause a temporary loss of steering control. When overtaken by a crest it is usually far better to slow down and let the wave pass by in the quickest possible time.

Scudding under power might be a very effective tactic for a heavy, sea-going motor craft, but I would suggest slow to moderate speed, just enough for steering control. With a fast, planing, shoal-draft boat having sharply V'd sections forward, very flat sections aft, and a large open cockpit, even slow speed scudding could be dangerous. In such a case, it might be advisable, when progress cannot be made safely against the seas or the course lies downwind, to cut power and stream a sea anchor. Some shallow hulls with low windage forward and a small propeller may ride to a sea anchor over the bow if weight is kept forward, but if this will not work, the anchor might have to be put over the stern. The heavy MFV or even the decked-over express cruiser or offshore sport fisherman might have success with the Hanks method (described earlier) of towing the bight of a warp astern to help slow speed and smooth the seas with minimal hampering of steering control. With any powerboat, of course, great care must be taken, when towing drags, not to let lines foul the propeller.

Some prominent seamen, such as Thomas Fleming Day and Humphrey Barton, have suggested hulling in seagoing motor craft, but this tactic requires that the boat have many characteristics similar to an offshore sailer. For instance, the powerboat should have a reasonable stability range and have some means to damp rolling. A small riding sail can alleviate rolling, but this requires ample reserve stability, otherwise the sail could contribute to a capsizing in very heavy weather. One definite drawback to powerboats lying a-hull is that such craft often have very vulnerable deckhouses with large glass windows. Only if such windows are of heavy safety glass or are fitted with storm shutters would it be sensible to come broadside to heavy seas. As said in Chapter 2, a fine-mesh screen erected in front of the pilot house windows can be very helpful when hulling or powering into the seas. The success of hulling will not only depend on the suitability of the boat to the tactic but also on the nature of the seas. Long, fairly regular, deep-water waves might allow safe and reasonably comfortable hulling, but short, steep, shallow-water waves with frequently breaking crests of the plunging variety taken beam-on could be very dangerous.

*Running Inlets*

On coastal passages when bad weather threatens, harbors are often available, but sometimes they can only be reached by passing through a treacherous inlet. These inlets usually consist of narrow, sometimes twisting

*Two fishing boats entering an inlet. Notice the bar opposite the entrance and the offset channel that leads in from the right-hand side. (Edward D. Hipple)*

channels that pass through shoals over which surf is breaking continually. In most cases with a seaworthy sailboat having an able crew, it is probably better to head her offshore into deep water and get all the sea room possible to weather the blow rather than attempt running a dangerous inlet. With a maneuverable powerboat, however, that is not specifically designed for heavy weather offshore, it is usually more prudent to run the inlet and reach shelter provided certain precautions are taken. For a potentially dangerous inlet, these precautions include: carefully studying the approaches on the chart and reading about the inlet in the Coast Pilot, a visual study of the inlet itself to determine the state of sea and the location of breakers, a study of tables and especially observation of channel markers to determine the state of tide and current, preparation of the boat and crew (donning life jackets) for heavy seas, and perhaps contacting the Coast Guard when the boat is equipped with a radio telephone for a report on the condition of the inlet. It is generally agreed that treacherous inlets should be entered on slack water or preferably a flood tide, but only under the most urgent circumstances when the current is flowing against the seas. The entrance to the inlet (where the worst seas are usually located) should be crossed during a lull or smooth in the seas. This might occur after the seventh or eleventh wave or some other numerical spacing that seems to produce an especially high wave due to the mixing of wave trains. Obviously, every attempt should be made to avoid breaking crests. The boat should be held end-on (usually stern) to the seas. She must be carefully steered and handled to prevent her broaching-to or turning sideways to breakers. Of course, the passage should be through the deepest part of the channel, in the smoothest water. Preparations for running the inlet would include: making the boat watertight (closing hatches, ports, vents, seacocks except those on scuppers, etc.), checking to see that the engine is running smoothly, that the life raft is available, that all crew members have donned life jackets, and that all equipment that might be needed is ready for use. Such equipment would include an anchor with neatly coiled line, a bucket, a loud horn, and of course, a strong searchlight and flares if the inlet is approached at night.

There might be considered three methods of entering an inlet through breaking seas: (1) running before the seas at high speed, (2) running at low speed (with or without a drogue), and (3) entering backwards, bow to the seas. The first method is dangerous, but it can be successful when the boat is reasonably fast, of light displacement, and is directionally stable with highly controllable steering. She should pass through the breakers at the exact speed of the waves, perhaps about fifteen knots, in order that she can remain in the trough or on the back of a sea (never on its face). Too little speed will allow the crest to overtake the boat which will adversely affect her stability and subject her to the possibilities of broaching-to or of being pooped by the break, while too much speed will cause her to overrun the crest, slide down the wave face and perhaps root her bow and broach to or even pitch-pole. Another danger of being on a wave's crest is that in such a position a shoal-draft boat's propeller and rudder are very apt to emerge, which of course will deprive her of steering control. In my opinion, it is seldom advisable for a heavy displacement craft to run at a high speed before steep seas, because she will usually not have sufficient speed to keep up with the waves, and her own wave system may disturb the following seas and encourage them to break over the stern. As said earlier, I think it is dangerous even for light planing craft to run before steep seas for any length of time especially offshore, because sooner or later she is very apt to lose her position in the trough or on the back of the particular sea she is riding. However, the high-speed technique is sometimes justified, in passing through very short stretches of breakers.

Method two, which is sometimes referred to as "washing in," is generally a wetter but safer method of running through breakers. Boat speed should be just fast enough for good steerageway, but the engine should be throttled down to idling speed when a crest overtakes the boat. When this is done, the chance of the bow rooting is minimized, and the sea passes in the quickest possible time. However, a good deal of water may come over the stern; thus, the boat should have a self bailing cockpit with large drains. After the crest has passed, it may be necessary to speed up momentarily, throwing propeller wash against the rudder to turn the boat so that she has her stern square to the seas. Of course, motor craft with twin screws should be highly controllable when handled by skillful operators. Some authorities advocate towing a sea anchor astern to help hold the stern to the seas, but in my opinion, this suggestion is not very practical for the average boatman. Use of a sea anchor towed astern in surf requires that a seaman experienced in drogue handling tends the contraption and its lines. The drogue must be allowed to fill and thus cause a drag at precisely the right moment, when the boat speeds up as the crest overtakes her. At this time there is a tremendous strain on the rode, and after the crest passes, it is necessary to spill the drogue with a special tripping line, the handling of which, together with the rode, requires skill and practice. Also, it should be pointed out that the average modern motorboat is not fitted with proper bitts and fairleads for use of a drogue over the stern. Improperly handled, the device can spin and twist its lines, pull off a cleat or break its lines, dive and dredge up mud, porpoise (jump out of water), hamper steering, or even foul the propeller. Of course, a seaman who is experienced with this kind of drogue handling can often make good use of it in surf, but for the average boatman without experience, the sea anchor's use should probably be limited mostly to drift prevention to avoid lee shores as discussed in Chapter 7. On the other hand, a simple drag (or drags) towed astern, such as the bight of a heavy line towed in the manner suggested by Hanks (see Chapter 7), may be easy to handle, and could be of some help in controlling the boat's speed.

Method three, entering the inlet stern first, is the one used least, and this is not surprising, as it requires a strong flooding current and a boat that can be easily maneuvered in reverse. The boat is backed when she is in the trough, but she is given slow speed ahead in the crests to hold her bow up to the seas. In the meanwhile, she is being swept into the inlet by the current. The principle danger of the method is in losing steering control of the boat while she is being backed. Needless to say, skillful engine operation and helmsmanship is required to keep the boat on her proper heading with her bow square to the waves.

If it becomes necessary to take an auxiliary sailboat through breakers to enter an inlet, it is usually wise to carry reduced sail when the wind is favorable, because most boats of this type do not handle well in adverse conditions under power alone. Care must be taken, however, to see that the vessel does not knockdown, as a roll out (described earlier) could reduce the rudder's effectiveness. If the wind is fair, a headsail sheeted flat might help hold her stern up to the seas. Towing lines or drags astern might also help provided this had no harmful affect on steering control (see Scudding in Chapter 7). Should the rudder or propeller emerge at a crest, the drags may help hold the stern towards the wave. If the boat's

*A Coast Guard 44-foot lifeboat negotiating a breaker at the entrance to the Umpqua River, Oregon. She is self-righting and has been rolled over twice by the seas at this entrance. On each occasion she lost a man overboard and recovered him. On the second occasion, she also rescued all four occupants of a 16-foot outboard boat that had been broken into three pieces by the wave that capsized the lifeboat. (U.S. Coast Guard)*

propeller is abaft her rudder, as is the case on a few of the newer auxiliaries, then consideration should be given to using method three (with sail down), because the boat will be most maneuverable when propeller wash is thrown directly against the rudder. Remember, however, that the backwards approach should almost never be attempted unless the current is flooding with considerable strength.

Along some coasts with sand bars off their beaches and onshore winds there are concentrated current pathways called rip currents that flow towards the sea approximately at right angles to the shore. These might be considered escape routes for high water piled up by the wind and seas behind the bars which run parallel to the beach. A boat moving towards shore should generally avoid these rips, because small, choppy, spilling type breakers may develop; but if it becomes necessary to land on the beach or pass through the bars, there will be fewer large breakers in the rip current channels due to the fact that water in the channels will be deeper than over the bars. Of course, there is the additional danger of grounding when crossing a bar. Should it be necessary to pass through a very short stretch of surf, consideration might be given to dropping an anchor over the stern (or bow if the boat is backing) in order that the rode can be hauled on as each sea passes to help keep the boat end-on to the seas. Naturally this technique requires considerable anchor rode even when the surf runs over a very narrow shoal.

When crossing a bar or entering a rough inlet, oil might possibly be used to help calm the seas, but a considerable quantity would be needed to have any effect at all on shallow water breakers. Oil might be spread by pumping it through forward outlets, such as the head discharge, or it could be poured through a hose leading over the bow (when the boat is moving ahead). Very slow boat speed will be needed for maximum benefit. As said in the last chapter the most effective storm oils are those from vegetables, animals, and fish especially, but petroleum may be used when it is the only oil available.

Although contrary to my intentions, the last two chapters may have been a little frightening to anyone without blue water experience who is contemplating a passage offshore. However, it is my personal contention that a seaworthy, well found, and properly handled boat can live through the most extremely bad conditions at sea. Although boats are occasionally lost, the reason for this nearly always lies in some deficiency of the vessel's design and construction, or a very serious mistake in seamanship, or a grave error in judgment by her master. One hears talk of gigantic "freak" waves at sea which no vessel can possibly negotiate in the upright position, and it is true that such waves exist, but they are extremely rare. Monstrous freaks are nearly always born in regions where high, steady winds have the opportunity to combine with almost limitless fetch and perhaps where there are uncharted (or charted) shoals such as in the high latitudes north of the Antarctic continent. The sailor, who carefully charts his passages over the safest routes when favorable weather is expected, could spend several lifetimes at sea without meeting a really non-negotiable wave. Indeed, I think it is entirely accurate to say that a well-planned offshore passage in a suitable boat is far safer than a lengthy automobile trip on today's land highways.

# APPENDIXES

# A / UNITED STATES COAST GUARD AUXILIARY COURTESY EXAMINATION

January 1, 1972

Courtesy Motorboat Examination cannot be performed while the boat is underway. Boats longer than 26 feet must be observed safely waterborne and moored. Boats of less than 26 feet in length and of known stock design can be examined out of the water, provided they are built of materials which are not subject to warping or shrinkage. All through hull fittings on boats so examined must be properly installed in order for a decal to be awarded.

Use the following paragraphs as a check-off list to help you determine if your boat meets the requirements of Federal law, and the additional safety standards recommended by the Auxiliary. Legal requirements are based upon the class of the motorboat, which is in turn determined by its length. The length is measured in a straight line along the centerline from the foremost part of the boat to the aftermost part of the boat. Bowsprits, outboard motor brackets and similar attachments are not included in this measurement.

Class A — less than 16' in length
Class 1 — 16' or over in length and less than 26'
Class 2 — 26' or over in length and less than 40'
Class 3 — 40' or over in length and not more than 65'

## Numbering

Motorboats powered by engines of more than 10 horsepower are required to be numbered by the Coast Guard or by the State. In some States, boats not in this category must also be numbered. Check your State for its requirements.

The number must be properly displayed and the registration must be available for examination.

## Ventilation

All motorboats using gasoline or other fuel with a flash point less than 110° F., configured so that explosive or flammable vapors could be entrapped, must have at least two ventilator ducts fitted with cowls or the equivalent leading to each engine compartment or fuel tank compartment for the efficient removal of explosive gases. The exhaust ducts shall lead from the lower portion of the bilge, and the intake ducts shall lead at least midway to the bilge below the carburetor air intake. Cowls shall be located and trimmed for maximum effectiveness and to prevent displaced fumes from being re-circulated.

Classes A, 1, 2 and 3 — required on all motorboats using fuel with a flash point less than 110° F. the construction or decking over of which was commenced after April 25, 1940.

## Backfire Flame Control

Efficient means of backfire flame control is required for each carburetor on every inboard engine installed after April 25, 1940. Acceptable means of backfire flame control are:

A Coast Guard approved backfire flame arrestor secured to the air intake of each carburetor; or

Engine and fuel intake system which provides equivalent protection and is labeled to indicate Coast Guard acceptance; or

Any attachment firmly secured to the carburetor or arrangement of the air intake by means of which flames caused by backfire will be dispersed to the atmosphere in such a way as not to endanger the vessel or persons on board.

## Fire Extinguishers

Fire extinguishers are classed according to their size and type. Extinguishers must bear Coast Guard and/or Underwriters Laboratory "Marine Type" approved labels. Type B fire extinguishers, designed for extinguishing flammable liquids, are required on motorboats. Equivalent sizes and extinguishing agent are shown on this table:

| Classification (type size) | Foam (minimum gallons) | Carbon Dioxide (minimum pounds) | Dry Chemical (minimum pounds) | Freon (minimum pounds) |
|---|---|---|---|---|
| B-I | 1¼ | 4 | 2 | 2½ |
| B-II | 2½ | 15 | 10 | None |

Note: Carbon tetrachloride extinguishers and others of the toxic vaporizing-liquid type such as chlorobromomethane are no longer approved and are not accepted as required fire extinguishers.

The number of approved extinguishers required depends upon the class of the motorboat. One B-II extinguisher may be substituted for two B-I extinguishers. When the engine compartment of the motorboat is equipped with a fixed (built-in) extinguisher system, one less hand portable B-I extinguisher is required.

Classes A & 1 *outboard motorboats* so constructed that entrapment of flammable vapors *cannot occur* are not required to carry fire extinguishers.

Classes A & 1 motorboats which do not meet the above exception, and all Classes 2 & 3 motorboats must be equipped with fire extinguishers according to this table:

### Minimum Number of
### Hand Portable Fire Extinguishers Required

|  | No fixed system in machinery space | Fixed fire extinguishing system in machinery space |
| --- | --- | --- |
| Class A | 1 B-I | None |
| Class 1 | 1 B-I | None |
| Class 2 | 2 B-I or 1 B-II | 1 B-I |
| Class 3 | 3 B-I or 1 B-II and 1 B-I | 2 B-I or 1 B-II |

*Bell, Whistle or Horn*

The requirement to carry a bell depends upon the class of boat. All bells must emit a clear bell-like tone when struck. The type of whistle or horn required differs with the class of boat. All horns or whistles must be capable of producing a blast of 2 seconds or more duration. The requirements for bell, whistle or horn are shown in this table:

|  | Bell | Whistle or Horn |
| --- | --- | --- |
| Class A | none required | none required |
| Class 1 | none required | mouth, hand or power operated, audible at least ½ mile |
| Class 2 | required | hand or power operated, audible at least 1 mile |
| Class 3 | required | power operated, audible at least 1 mile |

Note: While it is not required that all classes of boat carry the bell, whistle or horn, Rules of the Road require all vessels to give proper signals if a signaling situation develops.

### Navigation Lights

All motorboats are required to display navigation lights prescribed for the class when operated between the hours of sunset and sunrise. The International configuration may be displayed on the high seas and on all United States waters. Motorboat Act of 1940 configuration *cannot* be displayed on the high seas.

### Lifesaving Devices

Every motorboat must have one approved lifesaving device in acceptable condition for each person on board or in tow (water skier, surf boats, etc.) Lifesaving devices must be readily accessible. Kapok and fiberglass lifesaving devices which do not have plastic covered buoyant pads are not acceptable.

CLASSES A, 1 and 2 motorboats must carry one approved life preserver, ring life buoy, buoyant vest, buoyant cushion, or special purpose water safety buoyant device for each person on board or in tow. CLASS 3 motorboats must carry an approved life preserver or ring life buoy for each person on board or in tow.

### Auxiliary Standards for Award of Decal

Before a boat can be awarded the Courtesy Motorboat Examination decal, it must meet all the foregoing requirements of the Federal law, and in addition it must meet the following standards considered necessary for safe operation:

*Lifesaving Devices* — There must be at least as many approved lifesaving devices, of the type required for the class of boat, as there are berths. A boat with less than two bunks must have at least two approved lifesaving devices aboard. Lifesaving devices must be readily accessible.

*Fire Extinguishers* — All Class A and Class 1 motorboats, whether or not they are equipped with a fixed fire extinguishing system, must carry one hand portable fire extinguisher of approved type.

*Navigation Lights* must be of a configuration specified for the class of boat and must be operative and fully visible through the required arc.

*Distress Flare* — All Class A, 1, 2, and 3 motorboats must carry a distress flare for emergency signaling.

*Galley Stove* — If carried, the galley stove must be securely mounted so that it cannot shift position. Stoves must be installed so that·no flammable materials in the vicinity can be ignited. Any of the common types of fuel may be used *except* gasoline.

*Permanently Installed Fuel Tanks* must be securely mounted so that they cannot shift position.

*Fuel Tank Vent* — A vent terminating outboard of the hull and compartments must lead to each permanently installed fuel tank.

*Fuel Tank Fill Pipe* leading to permanently installed fuel tanks must fit into a filling plate located on deck outside the cockpit to insure that spilled fuel flows overboard.

*Portable Fuel Tanks and Spare Fuel Containers* — Tanks and containers which exceed 7 gallons are not classed as portable tanks, and must meet all requirements for permanently installed tanks. Tanks and spare fuel containers of less than 7 gallons must be tight and sufficiently sturdy to withstand ordinary usage. Glass or other breakable materials may not be used for portable fuel tanks or containers.

*Carburetor Drip Pan* — A drip pan must be installed under all side draft or up draft carburetors not provided with an effective sump.

*Backfire Flame Control* — All inboard motorboats, regardless of date of construction or engine installation, must meet current Federal requirements for backfire flame control.

*Whistle or Sound Producing Device* — All Class A boats must carry a whistle or sound-producing device capable of producing a blast of 2 seconds or more duration and audible at least ½ mile.

*Ventilation* — All motorboats regardless of class or date of construction must meet the current Federal requirements for ventilation.

*Electrical Installation* — Wiring must be in good condition and properly installed. There should be no open knife switches located in the bilge.

*Anchor and Anchor Line* — The boat must be equipped with an adequate anchor and line of suitable size and length for the locality.

*General Condition* — The vessel must be in good overall condition, the hull sound, fuel lines intact and properly installed. The decal will not be awarded to a vessel which is not generally shipshape and in seaworthy condition.

Class A motorboats must carry the following additional equipment.

    Pump or Bailer       Paddle or Oar       Distress Flare

### Recommended Condition and Equipment Standards

While not cause for withholding the decal, the Auxiliary recommends the following standards of condition and equipment. Your boating pleasure depends upon the condition of your craft and how you outfit and maintain her.

Through hull fittings should have shut-off valves or wooden plugs accessible for use.

Fuel lines should lead from the top of the tank and be equipped with shut-off valves at the tank and engine.

Auxiliary generators should have separate fuel tanks.

All switches located in the bilges should be designed for submerged use.

Distress signaling equipment should be carried on every boat.

A manual bilge pump should be carried on every boat irrespective of any mechanical pumping devices.

Handrails should be secured with through bolts.

Spare cannisters should be carried for horns or whistles which operate from compressed gas.

Spare batteries and spare bulbs should be carried for battery operated lights.

A fully equipped first aid kit should be carried in every boat.

Have tools and spare parts on board in usable condition.

The safe loading plate affixed at the time of manufacture should be legible and the load capacities indicated thereon should not be exceeded.

# B / NORTH AMERICAN YACHT RACING UNION OFFSHORE EQUIPMENT LISTS, 1971

## Introduction

The purpose of these lists is to establish uniform minimum equipment and accommodations standards for offshore racing events throughout North America. The lists are intended to provide uniform racing. Their use does not limit or reduce the complete and unlimited responsibility of the owner or master for the seaworthiness and safety of the yacht.

These lists are not intended to replace, but merely to supplement requirements established by governmental bodies, the Racing Rules, and the Measurement Rules. Owners' attention is called to restrictions on location or movement of equipment contained in Measurement and Racing Rules.

All equipment must function properly, be readily accessible and be of a type, size and capacity suitable and appropriate for the intended use and the size of the yacht. It is expected that all equipment and accommodations will meet modern standards of safety and good seamanship and current practice.

As a convenience, Race Committees may avail themselves of these lists to establish minimum equipment and accommodations by reference to the appropriate list in race circulars.

## Definition of Offshore Racing Class Yacht

Offshore Racing yachts shall be self-righting hulls strongly built, properly rigged and ballasted, fully seaworthy and meeting the standards set forth herein.

## Classification of Offshore Events

The detailed equipment and accommodations standards have been arranged in groups to conform to four categories of offshore events as follows:

1. Long distance offshore races in open ocean where the vessel must be completely self-sufficient — perhaps for extended periods — and capable of withstanding heavy storms.
2. Distance races of extended duration along shoreline or in large, relatively unprotected bays or lakes which require a high degree of self-sufficiency of crew and yacht.
3. Medium distance races which extend across open water which is relatively protected.
4. Short day or overnight races close to shore and in relatively warm protected waters.

## Recommended Minimum Equipment and Accommodations Standards

|  | Race Category 1 | 2 | 3 | 4 |
|---|---|---|---|---|
| **Group A — Hull and Cabin** | | | | |
| 1. Completely strong and watertight hull capable of withstanding solid water and knockdowns without significant leakage. | x | x | x | |
| 2. Hatches, companionways and ports essentially watertight and capable of being closed securely with strong hardware. | x | x | x | |
| 3. Structurally strong, essentially watertight, self-bailing cockpit permanently incorporated as a structural part of the hull. | x | x | x | x |
| 4. Cockpit companionways, if below main deck level, capable of being blocked off to deck level by solid, essentially leak proof and rigidly secured, if not permanent means. | x | x | x | |
| 5. Maximum cockpit volume over lowest coamings not to exceed 6% x LOA x Max Beam x Freeboard Aft. Cockpit floor at least 0.02 x LWL above LWL. | x | x | | |
| 6. Cockpit drains adequate to drain cockpit quickly and not less in combined area than the equivalent of two ¾″ diameter drains. Yachts built after 1-1-71 must have combined area of drains not less than the equivalent of four ¾″ drains. | x | x | x | |

|  | 1 | 2 | 3 | 4 |
|---|---|---|---|---|
| 7. Rigid and strong coverings available for all windows more than two square feet in area. | x | x | x | |
| 8. Sea cocks or valves on all underwater openings except for integral deck scuppers. This does not apply to openings in the hull to accommodate the shaft, speed indicator, depth finder, etc. However, a satisfactory means of closing these openings shall be provided when it becomes necessary to do so. | x | x | | |
| 9. Life lines and pulpits: | | | | |
| a) Fixed bow pulpits (forward of headstay) and stern pulpit (unless life lines are arranged in such a way as to adequately substitute for a stern pulpit). Pulpits and stanchions must be thru bolted or welded. Taut double life lines with upper life line of wire to be secured to pulpits and stanchions. Pulpits and upper life line must not be less than 24″ above the deck at any point. Stanchions shall not be spaced more than 7 feet apart, except in the way of shrouds when life lines are permanently attached to shrouds. Lower life lines need not be extended through pulpits. Life lines need not be affixed to the bow pulpit if they terminate at or pass through adequately braced stanchions 24″ high set inside of and overlapping the bow pulpit. | x | x | | |
| b) Bow pulpit at least 18″ above the deck. | | | x | x |
| c) Taut single wire life line securely attached with a minimum height of not less than 18″. | | | x | |
| 10. Approved running lights which will remain unobstructed by sails and when the yacht is heeled in heavy weather. | x | x | x | x |

Group B — Accommodations

|  | 1 | 2 | 3 | 4 |
|---|---|---|---|---|
| 1. Permanently installed toilet. | x | x | | |
| 2. Permanently installed bunks. | x | x | x | x |
| 3. Permanently installed stove having safely accessible remote fuel shutoff control. | x | x | | |
| 4. Stove. | | | x | x |
| 5. Galley facilities including sink. | x | x | x | x |

| | 1 | 2 | 3 | 4 |
|---|---|---|---|---|
| 6. Permanently installed water tanks which must be capable of dividing water supply into at least two separate containers. | x | | | |
| 7. Permanently installed water tank plus at least one additional container capable of holding 5 gallons. | | x | | |
| 8. Water in suitable containers. | | | x | x |

## Group C — General Equipment

| | 1 | 2 | 3 | 4 |
|---|---|---|---|---|
| 1. Country of Registry approved fire extinguishers as required by Country of Registry, readily accessible in different parts of the yacht, but not fewer than 3. | x | x | | |
| 2. Country of Registry approved fire extinguishers as required by Country of Registry, readily accessible, but at least 1. | | | x | x |
| 3. Two manually operated bilge pumps, one of which must be operable with all cockpit seats and hatches and all cabin hatches and companionways closed. | x | x | | |
| 4. One manual bilge pump operable with all cockpit seats and hatches closed. | | | x | x |
| 5. Two suitable anchors and cables. | x | x | x | |
| 6. One suitable anchor and cable. | | | | x |
| 7. Water resistant flashlights and signaling light. | x | x | x | x |
| 8. First aid kit and manual. | x | x | x | x |
| 9. Foghorn. | x | x | x | x |
| 10. Radar reflector. | x | x | x | |
| 11. Set of international code flags and code book. | x | x | | |
| 12. Shut off valves at all fuel tanks. | x | x | x | x |
| 13. Mainboom topping lift permanently rigged. | x | x | | |

## Group D — Navigation Equipment

| | 1 | 2 | 3 | 4 |
|---|---|---|---|---|
| 1. Properly installed, adjusted marine compass. | x | x | x | x |
| 2. Spare compass. | x | x | x | |
| 3. Suitable charts, light lists and equipment for piloting. | x | x | x | x |
| 4. Sextant, tables, and accurate time piece. | x | | | |
| 5. Radio direction finder. | x | x | | |
| 6. Lead line. | x | x | x | |
| 7. Speedometer, log or other device for measuring speed or distance. | x | x | x | |

|  | 1 | 2 | 3 | 4 |
|---|---|---|---|---|

Group E — Emergency Equipment

| | 1 | 2 | 3 | 4 |
|---|---|---|---|---|
| 1. Spare running lights and power source. | x | x | | |
| 2. Storm trysail and storm jib. | x | x | | |
| 3. Heavy weather jib and reefing equipment for mainsail. | | | x | x |
| 4. Emergency steering equipment. | x | x | | |
| 5. Bolt or rigging cutters. | x | x | x | x |
| 6. Suitable tools and spare parts. | x | x | x | x |
| 7. Yacht's name on miscellaneous buoyant equipment such as life jackets, oars, cushions, etc. | x | x | | |
| 8. Marine radio transmitter and receiver suitable for the area of the race and equipped with a properly coupled emergency antenna system if the regular antenna depends upon the mast. Transmitter should have a minimum power of 25 watts. | x | x | | |

Group F — Safety Equipment

| | 1 | 2 | 3 | 4 |
|---|---|---|---|---|
| 1. Country of Registry approved life jackets for each member of the crew. | x | x | x | x |
| 2. Whistles (referee type) on life jackets. | x | x | x | |
| 3. Safety belts (harness type) for each member of crew. | x | x | x | x |
| 4. Covered life boat(s) or raft(s) rated to accommodate the entire crew and equipped with emergency provisions. Inflatable rafts must have automatic inflating devices, at least two separate air chambers and must have been inspected, tested and approved within three years by the manufacturer or other competent authority. | x | | | |
| 5. Life boat(s) or raft(s) rated to accommodate the entire crew. Inflatable rafts must have automatic inflating device, at least two separate air chambers and must have been inspected, tested and approved within three years by the manufacturer or other competent authority. | | | x | x |
| 6. Horseshoe type life rings equipped with whistles—(referee), dye markers and drogues as follows: | | | | |
|    a) 2 horseshoe life rings each equipped with high intensity automatic water light and attached with 25' of floating line to a pole with a flag: the pole to be of a length and so ballasted that the flag will fly at least 8 feet off the water. | x | | | |

|  | 1 | 2 | 3 | 4 |
|---|---|---|---|---|
| b) 2 horseshoe life rings, one equipped as in 6(a). |  | x |  |  |
| c) 1 horseshoe life ring with high intensity water light. |  |  | x | x |
| 7. Flare gun (Very pistol or equivalent) and flares, stowed in a waterproof container. | x | x | x |  |
| a) 12 red parachute flares. | x |  |  |  |
| b) 6 red parachute flares. |  | x | x | x |
| 8. Heaving line (50 foot minimum and floating type) readily accessible to cockpit. | x | x | x |  |

# C / DISTRESS SIGNALS

*International Rules of the Road*

Rule 31. (a) When a vessel or seaplane on the water is in distress and requires assistance from other vessels or from the shore, the following shall be the signals to be used or displayed by her, either together or separately, namely:

(i) A gun or other explosive signal fired at intervals of about a minute.

(ii) A continuous sounding with any fog-signal apparatus.

(iii) Rockets or shells, throwing red stars fired one at a time at short intervals.

(iv) A signal made by radiotelegraphy or by any other signaling method consisting of the group ...---... in the Morse Code.

(v) A signal sent by radiotelephony consisting of the spoken word "Mayday."

(vi) The International Code Signal of distress indicated by N. C.

(vii) A signal consisting of a square flag having above or below it a ball or anything resembling a ball.

(viii) Flames on the vessel (as from a burning tar barrel, oil barrel, etc.).

(ix) A rocket parachute flare or a hand flare showing a red light.

(x) A smoke signal giving off a volume of orange-coloured smoke.

(xi) Slowly and repeatedly raising and lowering arms outstretched to each side.

Note: Vessels in distress may use the radiotelegraph alarm signal or the radiotelephone alarm signal to secure attention to distress calls and messages. The radiotelegraph alarm signal, which is designed to actuate the radiotelegraph auto alarms of vessels so fitted, consists of a series of twelve dashes, sent in 1 minute, the duration of each dash being 4 seconds, and the duration of the interval between 2 consecutive dashes being 1 second. The radiotelephone alarm consists of 2 tones transmitted alternately over periods of from 30 seconds to 1 minute.

(b) The use of any of the foregoing signals, except for the purpose of indicating that a vessel or a seaplane is in distress, and the use of any signals which may be confused with any of the above signals, is prohibited.

## Inland Rules of the Road

Art. 31. When a vessel is in distress and requires assistance from other vessels or from the shore the following shall be the signal to be used or displayed by her, either together or separately, namely:

In the daytime —

A continuous sounding with any fog-signal apparatus, or firing a gun.

At night —

First. Flames on the vessel as from a burning tar barrel, oil barrel, and so forth.

Second. A continuous sounding with any fog-signal apparatus, or firing a gun.

# D / STORM WARNING SIGNALS

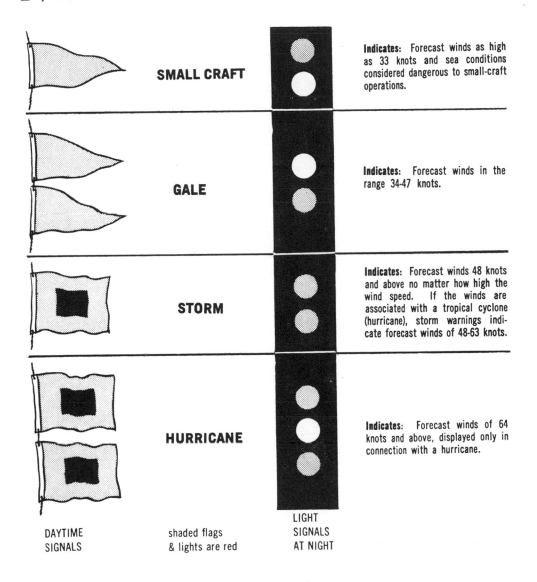

**SMALL CRAFT**

**Indicates:** Forecast winds as high as 33 knots and sea conditions considered dangerous to small-craft operations.

**GALE**

**Indicates:** Forecast winds in the range 34-47 knots.

**STORM**

**Indicates:** Forecast winds 48 knots and above no matter how high the wind speed. If the winds are associated with a tropical cyclone (hurricane), storm warnings indicate forecast winds of 48-63 knots.

**HURRICANE**

**Indicates:** Forecast winds of 64 knots and above, displayed only in connection with a hurricane.

DAYTIME
SIGNALS

shaded flags
& lights are red

LIGHT
SIGNALS
AT NIGHT

## E / BEAUFORT SCALE

| Beau-fort Number | Wind speed | | Seaman's Terms | Estimating wind speed | |
|---|---|---|---|---|---|
| | Knots | mph | | Observations at sea | Observations on land |
| 0 | under 1 | under 1 | Calm | Sea like mirror. | Calm; smoke rises vertically. |
| 1 | 1–3 | 1–3 | Light air | Ripples with appearance of scales; no foam crests. | Smoke drift indicates wind direction; vanes do not move. |
| 2 | 4–6 | 4–7 | Light breeze | Small wavelets; crests of glassy appearance, not breaking. | Wind felt on face; leaves rustle; vanes begin to move. |
| 3 | 7–10 | 8–12 | Gentle breeze | Large wavelets; crests begin to break; scattered whitecaps. | Leaves, small twigs in constant motion; light flags extended. |
| 4 | 11–16 | 13–18 | Moderate breeze | Small waves, becoming longer; numerous whitecaps. | Dust, leaves, and loose paper raised up; small branches move. |
| 5 | 17–21 | 19–24 | Fresh breeze | Moderate waves, taking longer form; many whitecaps; some spray. | Small trees in leaf begin to sway. |
| 6 | 22–27 | 25–31 | Strong breeze | Larger waves forming; whitecaps everywhere; more spray. | Larger branches of trees in motion; whistling heard in wires |
| 7 | 28–33 | 32–38 | Moderate gale | Sea heaps up; white foam from breaking waves begins to be blown in streaks. | Whole trees in motion; resistance felt in walking against wind. |
| 8 | 34–40 | 39–46 | Fresh gale | Moderately high waves of greater length; edges of crests begin to break into spindrift; foam is blown in well-marked streaks. | Twigs and small branches broken off trees; progress generally impeded. |
| 9 | 41–47 | 47–54 | Strong gale | High waves; sea begins to roll; dense streaks of foam; spray may reduce visibility. | Slight structural damage occurs; slate blown from roofs. |
| 10 | 48–55 | 55–63 | Whole gale | Very high waves with overhanging crests; sea takes white appearance as foam is blown in very dense streaks; rolling is heavy and visibility reduced. | Seldom experienced on land; trees broken or uprooted; considerable structural damage occurs. |
| 11 | 56–63 | 64–72 | Storm | Exceptionally high waves; sea covered with white foam patches; visibility still more reduced. | Very rarely experienced on land; usually accompanied by widespread damage. |
| 12 | 64–71 | 73–82 | Hurricane | Air filled with foam; sea completely white with driving spray; visibility greatly reduced. | Very rarely experienced on land; usually accompanied by widespread damage. |
| 13 | 72–80 | 83–92 | Hurricane | Air filled with foam; sea completely white with driving spray; visibility greatly reduced. | |
| 14 | 81–89 | 93–103 | Hurricane | Air filled with foam; sea completely white with driving spray; visibility greatly reduced. | |
| 15 | 90–99 | 104–114 | Hurricane | Air filled with foam; sea completely white with driving spray; visibility greatly reduced. | |
| 16 | 100–108 | 115–125 | Hurricane | Air filled with foam; sea completely white with driving spray; visibility greatly reduced. | |
| 17 | 109–118 | 126–136 | Hurricane | Air filled with foam; sea completely white with driving spray; visibility greatly reduced. | |

(U. S. Naval Institute)

# F / SEA STATE TABLE

| Hydrographic Office | | International | |
|---|---|---|---|
| Term and height of waves, in feet | Code | Term and height of waves, in feet | Code |
| Calm, 0 | 0 | Calm, glassy, 0 | 0 |
| Smooth, less than 1 | 1 | | |
| Slight, 1–3 | 2 | Rippled, 0–1 | 1 |
| Moderate, 3–5 | 3 | Smooth, 1–2 | 2 |
| Rough, 5–8 | 4 | Slight, 2–4 | 3 |
| | | Moderate, 4–8 | 4 |
| | | Rough, 8–13 | 5 |
| Very rough, 8–12 | 5 | Very rough, 13–20 | 6 |
| High, 12–20 | 6 | | |
| Very high, 20–40 | 7 | High, 20–30 | 7 |
| Mountainous, 40 and higher | 8 | Very high, 30–45 | 8 |
| Confused | 9 | Phenomenal, over 45 | 9 |

*(U. S. Naval Institute)*

# G / WAVE CHARACTERISTICS AS A FUNCTION OF WIND SPEED, FETCH, AND DURATION

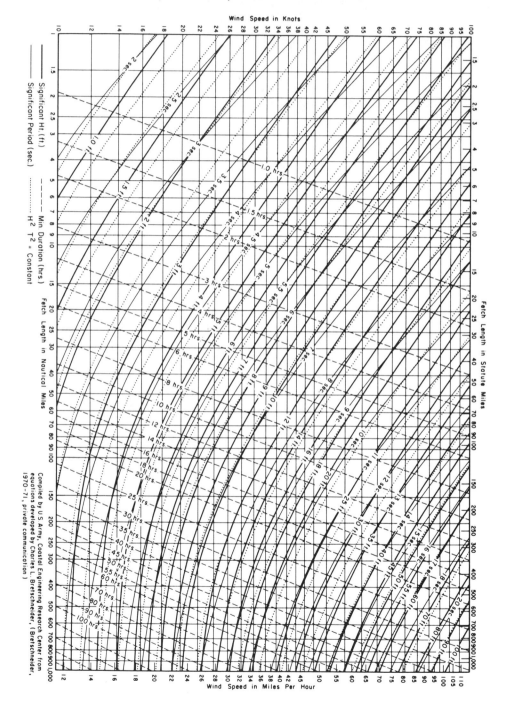

# INDEX

## (Italic page numbers indicate illustrations.)